For Rose and Fred

with best wishes

John White

1 December 2005

OLIANA

NELSON
THE ADMIRAL

FOREWORD BY THE FIRST SEA LORD
ADMIRAL SIR ALAN WEST GCB DSC ADC

COLIN WHITE

ROYAL NAVY

Royal Naval
MUSEUM
PUBLICATIONS

SUTTON PUBLISHING

This book was first published in 2005 by
Sutton Publishing Limited · Phoenix Mill
Thrupp · Stroud · Gloucestershire · GL5 2BU

Reprinted 2005

In association with the Royal Navy and the Royal Naval Museum

British Library Cataloguing in Publication Data
A catalogue record for this book is available from the British Library.

ISBN 0 7509 3713 0

By the same author

The End of the Sailing Navy
The Heyday of Steam
The Nelson Companion
1797: Nelson's Year of Destiny
The Nelson Encyclopaedia
Nelson – The New Letters
The Trafalgar Captains

Dedicated, with gratitude,
to the memories of
Captain Jimmy Pack and Captain Kenneth Douglas-Morris,
Naval Officers, Gentlemen and Mentors

Typeset in 10/13pt Sabon.
Typesetting and origination by
Sutton Publishing Limited.
Printed and bound in Great Britain by
J.H. Haynes & Co. Ltd, Sparkford.

Contents

List of Illustrations

PLANS

Campaign and battle plans will all be found in Appendix I (pp. 195–210)

SOURCES

RNM = Royal Naval Museum
NMM = National Maritime Museum
CSW = Author's collection

Foreword

The history of the Royal Navy is studded with famous battles, glittering occasions and a wealth of courageous heroes who fought and died in the service of their country. A succession of extremely capable and successful admirals harried, hounded and overcame some of the mightiest maritime nations of their generations: Edward Hawke chased the French Fleet to destruction at Quiberon Bay in 1759 ('to add something new to this wonderful year'); John Jervis defeated the Spanish at St Vincent in February 1797, and in October that year Adam Duncan captured eleven Dutch ships in the hard-fought battle off Camperdown. The history books of a more recent era recount the stories of John Jellicoe and how he drove the German High Seas Fleet from the North Sea after Jutland in 1916; and of Andrew Cunningham who in 1943 reported to the King that the Italian Fleet lay under the guns of the fortress of Malta.

Admiral Lord Horatio Nelson stands alone in the fascination he engenders both as an inspired naval tactician and a man of singular humanity, loyalty to The Crown and courage in the face of battle and severe hardship. Nothing in our maritime history is, perhaps, quite as potent a symbol of tactical brilliance as the Battle of Trafalgar, the benchmark by which victory at sea ever since has been judged. He was slight in stature, physically scarred by his hard-fought battles and possessed many of the frailties and weaknesses which we all share. And yet, two centuries after his climactic death in the moment of total victory, the leadership and commitment, the humanity and the concern for his people for which Admiral Lord Nelson was renowned, remain the standard by which modern naval commanders are often measured. Decisive and unfaltering in battle, his courage and selfless ambition are qualities that provide a beacon to which all aspire today. Much has changed since the Battle of Trafalgar, the world and warfare alike, but there is little doubt that Nelson would recognise in those serving in the navies of today the same strength of character and respect for the sea that he enjoyed with those who served alongside him.

Fifty years ago, Her Majesty The Queen paid tribute to Lord Nelson in her address at the Sesquicentennial Trafalgar Night Dinner, held in the Painted Hall of the Royal Naval College, Greenwich: 'He was not only a superb tactician and a dauntless fighter, he was also a man who loved his fellow creatures and strove always for the betterment of those he led. It is because the inspiration of Nelson is still a potent and living force, and because of his humanity, that we do him honour.' The spirit of Admiral Lord Nelson pervades the modern fighting force that is the Royal Navy today. He would be proud of today's Senior Service and in this book, Colin White reveals to us exactly why Nelson's name remains revered, two hundred years after his death.

Admiral Sir Alan West GCB DSC ADC, First Sea Lord

Introduction

T his is not another Nelson biography. His life and loves are being extensively covered in this bicentenary year by a veritable fleet of excellent books, each of them offering new material and fresh insights. This book seeks not to rival, but to complement and to support, these studies by focusing on one particular aspect of Nelson's life – his career as an admiral. It was commissioned by the Royal Naval Museum and has been supported throughout by the Royal Navy and so, right at the start of these introductory remarks, I would like to extend my warmest thanks to the First Sea Lord, Admiral Sir Alan West, and to the Museum Director, Dr Campbell McMurray, for their support and encouragement.

The book has its origins in the ground-breaking series of Nelson Decade Conferences, marking the bicentenaries of Nelson battles, that have been staged in Portsmouth since 1997. At each event, historians from the former opposition have been invited to contribute the results of their research and, as a result, our understanding of each battle has been considerably enhanced and new narratives have emerged.

At the same time, much new material on Nelson's own naval career has been located, largely as a result of my own Nelson Letters Project, commissioned by the National Maritime and Royal Naval Museums, during the course of which over 1,400 hitherto unpublished letters have been located in 35 archives, all over the world, private as well as public. A significant amount of this new material relates to Nelson's career as an admiral. Three of his 'Public Order Books' have been discovered, containing his working orders for the campaigns of the Nile (1798), Copenhagen and the Baltic (January–June 1801), and the Channel (July–October 1801). Additionally, over 400 letters and orders dating from his time in command of the Mediterranean in 1803–5 have been found in the hitherto untapped 'pressed-copy' letter books in the British Library. Moreover, examination of the originals of letters already printed in the great collections of Nelson's letters published in the nineteenth century has revealed that a number of these letters were edited and large amounts of material suppressed. Restoration of the excised passages has given us yet more interesting material relating to Nelson's naval career and, above all, his own private reflections on some of the key events in which he participated.

Additionally, over the last ten years, it has been my good fortune in the course of my work, to visit the sites of all the main events of Nelson's naval career and to speak with people who have researched them and know them well. I have also met with, and been educated by, those who are exploring new ways of bringing Nelson and his battles alive – through computer technology, war gaming, and re-enactments.

The products of all this scholarship, and all these new ways of looking at the subject, are dispersed in many different media and in numerous publications, and online sites, and each usually deals with only a small part of the story. So it was felt by the commissioning bodies that an overview is needed – a re-examination of the familiar narrative, and a re-telling of the story in the light of the new material, that will be accessible to the general reader. This challenging – but also very pleasant – task has fallen to me.

Early on in the project, I decided to focus on Nelson's eight years as an admiral – 1797–1805 – mainly because that is where most of the new material is concentrated. Moreover, since I have already covered his exploits in 1796–7 in my earlier book, *1797: Nelson's Year of Destiny*, I have not repeated myself here. So, while the battles of Cape St Vincent and Tenerife are covered briefly in this volume, the main narrative starts where *1797* ends – at the Grand Naval Thanksgiving Service in St Paul's Cathedral on 19 December 1797. The two books should therefore be read in conjunction, since this one flows naturally from its predecessor.

I have also consciously avoided any direct comparisons with modern tactical and strategic thought. Others, more able and experienced in these fields than I, have already shown how aspects of Nelson's leadership style can be given a modern slant but he, of course, never thought in terms of 'doctrine' as we understand it today. So I have concentrated on telling the story and am content to let my readers make for themselves any links that may be helpful to them.

One last preliminary thought. When I started work on this book, I subscribed to the common view that Nelson was fortunate in the timing and manner of his death and that he died with his work complete. I no longer believe this. The more I have studied his naval career, and especially the last two years when he was commander-in-chief in the Mediterranean, the more I have come to believe that, on 21 October 1805, Britain lost a leader of unique ability who had not yet reached his full potential. The story of his career as an admiral, in my view, is not one of a genius who sprang ready-made into his role, as many of his biographers have sought to suggest. Rather, it is a gradual progression by a very gifted, but also flawed, man who made some serious mistakes early on, but who also learned from those mistakes and thus matured by degrees into a finely rounded leader – not just a great fighting admiral, but a diplomat, administrator and intelligence officer as well. If he had been simply a great fighter, then his death at Trafalgar might indeed be seen as an appropriate culmination. But now we have a clearer idea, thanks to all the newly discovered material, of how much promise he was showing in other key areas of his profession, such a comfortable point of view no longer seems tenable. Most of his contemporaries viewed his death as a grievous loss to his country – and so do I.

Colin White
The Anchorage, Portsmouth
30 March 2005

A NOTE ABOUT THE LAYOUT

Like *1797: Nelson's Year of Destiny*, this book is a combination of new material that has emerged from recent research and a re-evaluation of 'old' material. Naturally, readers will wish to know what evidence I am using when I challenge the traditional story.

Often, it has been possible to include this sort of explanation in the main text. However, when such digressions would interrupt the narrative flow, I have used a method that was first developed in *1797*, and which was generally well received by both readers and critics. The material has been placed in special boxes, thus leaving the main narrative free of lengthy diversions.

Full references for all the material quoted in the text will be found in the endnotes, pages 216 to 228.

A short Glossary of some of the key maritime terms used in the text will be found on pages 214–15.

Full transcripts of Nelson's most important Battle Orders have been prepared and included, so that they can be easily referred to without having to search for them in other books. These will be found in Appendix I, pages 195 to 210.

Finally, maps of the main campaigning areas, and plans of the Battle of the Nile, Copenhagen and Trafalgar, will be found alongside Nelson's Battle Plans in Appendix I, pages 195 to 210.

Acknowledgements

The debts I have incurred during the preparation of this book are many and wide-ranging. As always, the bedrock of my support has been my professional colleagues – currently at two museums. At the Royal Naval Museum: Matthew Sheldon, Stephen Courtney and Allison Wareham. At the National Maritime Museum: Roy Clare, John Graves, Jill Davies, Daphne Knott, Andrew Davies, Brian Lavery, Pieter van der Merwe and David Taylor. I am also particularly grateful to Dewar McAdam, who has designed the campaign maps, and Michael O'Callaghan, who designed the battle plans.

Then, there are all the people whose archives I have visited and who have helped me to find the exciting new material featured in this book. In Britain, the chief of these have been: Chris Wright and all the staff at the British Museum; Andrew Helme at the Nelson Museum, Monmouth; John Curtis, and latterly Laura Shears, at Lloyd's of London; Robert Brown at the National Archive of Scotland, John Draisey at the Devon Records Office and, in Denmark, Nils Bartholdy of the Danish State Archive. In America my chief helpers have been: Mary Robertson and her staff at the Huntington Library; John Dann and his colleagues at the William Clements Library, Michigan; Jim Cheevers at the US Naval Academy Museum and Leslie Morris at the Houghton Library, Harvard. Additionally, there are the private individuals who have given me access to their personal collections of letters, especially Clive Richards.

There are also my fellow scholars and companions in Nelson research, all of whom are illuminating new aspects of Nelson's story and who have been extraordinarily generous in sharing their insights and discoveries. These include: Roger and Jane Knight, Joe Callo, Andrew Lambert, Tom Pocock, John Sugden, Marianne Czisnik, Tim Clayton, Michael Duffy, John Gwyther, Felix Pryor, Michael Nash, Peter Hore, John Hattendorf, Janet Macdonald, Roger Morriss, Nicholas Rodger, Nick Slope, Peter Warwick and Nick Tracy. I would also mention here my good friends of the Inshore Squadron, whose revolutionary computer programmes have helped me to understand, much more clearly than before, the detailed, minute-by-minute development of each of Nelson's battles. I am also grateful to the owners of the stunning square-rigged cruise ship, *Sea Cloud II*, and to the travel company Noble Caledonia, for inviting me to take part in their wonderful cruise of Nelsonian sites in the Caribbean in February 2005. I wrote most of the 'Trafalgar Campaign' under sail in the very waters where Nelson learned his trade and through which he chased the Combined Fleet in June 1805.

There are also my overseas friends and fellow scholars who have done so much to help me understand the point of view of 'the other side': Agustín Guimerá, with whom I first visited the battle site at Tenerife and, later, paid my respects at Cape Trafalgar and at the splendid Spanish Naval Pantheon; Ole Feldbæk, who escorted me around the Copenhagen battle site and introduced me to the treasures in the State Archive; Frank Goddio, who took me to the site of the wreck of *L'Orient* in Aboukir Bay, and Michelle Battesti and Remi Monarque, who have shared their Nile and Trafalgar research with me.

I must also pay tribute to my friends at Sutton Publishing: especially my commissioning editor Jonathan Falconer and Nick Reynolds, to Alison Miles the copy editor, to Martin Latham who has produced such a very handsome design for the whole book and to Michael Forder for the index.

Finally, there are my family and friends who have always had to share me with Nelson and the Royal Navy – but most especially this last year. As always, I owe a huge debt to my friend and PA, Anne Wallis, who has helped me to keep my head above water at an exciting, but frantic, time. To my dear mother, Margaret White, who has contributed to this book, as she has to every one I have written, by typing out in a few hours great tranches of text that would have taken me long days to do. And to my partner Peter Wadsworth, whose support and patient encouragement I value more than words can express.

LIST OF ABBREVIATIONS USED IN THE TEXT AND NOTES

BL	British Library
CRC	Clive Richards Collection
DRO	Devon Records Office
HL	Huntington Library, California, USA
Houghton	Houghton Library, Harvard, Cambridge, USA
Monmouth	The Nelson Museum, Monmouth
NA	National Archive (Public Records Office)
NAS	National Archive of Scotland
NLS	National Library of Scotland
NMM	National Maritime Museum
PML	Pierpont Morgan Library, New York, USA
RNM	Royal Naval Museum
SAD	State Archive of Denmark, Copenhagen
WCL	William Clements Library, Michigan, USA

St Paul's Cathedral: 19 December 1797

At about 11.45 a.m. on 19 December 1797, the newly appointed organist of St Paul's Cathedral, Thomas Attwood, began playing the elaborate introduction to Henry Purcell's celebratory anthem, 'I will give thanks unto thee, O Lord, with my whole heart'. King George III, the royal family and the entire British establishment had come to St Paul's to give thanks for Britain's victories at sea, and now the climax of the elaborate ceremonial had been reached.

As the soloists high in the organ loft came in with the first choral section of the anthem, a line of naval officers processed into the choir. They were carrying a remarkable collection of captured enemy colours: each flag was displayed on a pole, to the top of which was attached a sign bearing the name of the battle at which it had been taken. First came a brace of French tricolours: some captured at the Glorious First of June three years before, others taken at smaller-scale actions in 1795. Bringing up the rear were Dutch ensigns captured at the Battle of Camperdown in October 1797. But, before them, the flow of red, white and blue was broken by the vivid red and gold of Spain. These flags had been captured at the Battle of Cape St Vincent in February 1797, when a British fleet under Admiral Sir John Jervis had defeated a superior Spanish force. As each flag reached the high altar, the escorting officers handed them over to the Dean and Chapter, who arranged them in the chancel. The officers then returned to their places, and the service continued with the singing of the *Te Deum*.

The escorting officers had all served at the various battles that were being celebrated and included such famous names as Lord Duncan, the victor of Camperdown, and Lord Bridport, who had beaten the French off Groix in 1795. But there was one notable absentee: Sir John Jervis, now Lord St Vincent, was still on patrol with the Mediterranean fleet off Cádiz, where the Spanish fleet had taken refuge following February's battle. So, since he was unable to be there, the honour of presenting the captured flags had been given to some of his immediate

The Grand Naval Procession, 19 December 1797. The procession of naval officers and sailors escorting the captured enemy colours nears St Paul's Cathedral.

subordinates – among them, a slight man with an unruly shock of sandy-grey hair and a missing arm. Rear Admiral Sir Horatio Nelson was making his first appearance on the national stage.

In fact Nelson, then still only 39, was at a pivotal moment in his life. Only five months before, he had believed his naval career was at an end – cut away by the surgeon's knife and saw that had removed most of his right arm, after the upper part of it had been shattered by a Spanish musket ball during his abortive attack on the island of Tenerife. Now the stump of his arm had healed, his health was fully restored, and he had heard that he had been appointed to serve at sea once again, with his friend and patron Lord St Vincent. Indeed, just the day before the St Paul's ceremony, he had been in Chatham Dockyard watching his flagship, the fine 74-gun HMS *Vanguard*, being floated out of dock following a major refit. He was about to embark on the path of glory that would eventually bring him back, almost exactly eight years later, to the same spot in front of the altar of St Paul's where he had just stood to present the Spanish flags.

Next time, however, he would arrive in a coffin.

Captain Horatio Nelson, c. 1784. Cuthbert Collingwood captures the petulant look of his friend in a stubborn mood during his difficult period of service in the West Indies.

CHAPTER I

The Making of an Admiral: 1771–97

'I WILL BE A HERO': NELSON'S VISION

In early 1776, 17-year-old Midshipman Horatio Nelson, then serving in the frigate HMS *Seahorse* in the East Indies, fell ill with malaria. It was a very severe attack, which reduced him to a skeleton, and for a while he lost the use of his limbs. The local commander-in-chief, Commodore Edward Hughes, who obviously admired the youngster, arranged for him to go to England in the frigate HMS *Dolphin* to recuperate, and so, on 23 March, he began the long voyage home. During the course of it, he began slowly to recover, but he suffered periods of deep depression when he worried about his naval career and even, at one stage, 'almost wished myself overboard'. But then he suddenly experienced a catharsis – as he later put it: 'a sudden glow of patriotism was kindled within me and presented my king and country as my patron. "Well then" I exclaimed, "I will be a hero and confiding in Providence, I will brave every danger."'[1]

Nelson told that story to an acquaintance long afterwards, in 1802, and so, like all our stories of childhood experiences, especially ones we see as significant in retrospect, it had no doubt been embellished and refined over the years. Whatever the exact details may have been, it is clear that he saw the moment on board the *Dolphin* as an important stage in his own personal development – he apparently told close friends, such as Captain Thomas Hardy, that from then on he had in his mind's eye 'a radiant orb' that beckoned him onwards.

This intensely emotional, even spiritual, approach to his profession and to his own destiny is one of the characteristics that sets Nelson apart from the other naval officers who were with him in St Paul's on 19 December 1797. It is quite impossible to imagine men like Adam Duncan or Alexander Hood – let alone John Jervis – expressing themselves in this way. But it is clear that, for Nelson, service in the Royal Navy – and, in particular, service of his 'King and Country' (two nouns which often appear together in his letters and reported speech) – was much more

HMS Agamemnon *and the French frigates, 22 October 1793. Nicholas Pocock shows the* Agamemnon *after the sharp encounter that led Nelson to reflect on the 'time and manner' of his death.*

than a job. He viewed it as a vocation in a way that a priest or a nun would use that now rather devalued word.

Indeed, in Nelson's case, the religious analogy is particularly apt – for he was a devout Christian, who practised his religion daily, and it is clear that it was a source of great inner strength for him. In October 1794, after a sharp battle with a French squadron, in which he had come close to defeat and capture, he copied into his sea journal a passage from the *Spectator* which he believed expressed his feelings:

> When I lay me down to sleep I recommend myself to the care of Almighty God, when I awake I give myself to his direction, amidst all the evils that threaten me, I will look up to Him for help, and question not but that he will either avert them, or turn them to my advantage, though I know neither the time nor the manner of my death I am not at all solicitous about it, because I am aware that he knows them both, and that he will not fail to support and comfort me under them.[2]

He shared this faith with his men – but not in a proselytising sort of way, like some of his more evangelical colleagues. Characteristically, his ministry was practical – he made sure that public worship was regularly performed and had a standing arrangement with the SPCK (Society for the Propagation of Christian Knowledge) for the provision of Bibles and prayer books for the men in the ships he commanded. He told the Revd George Gaskin, Secretary of the SPCK, 'I am sure that a ship where divine service is regularly performed is by far more regular and decent in their conduct than where it is not.'[3]

His faith and his consciousness of his vocation as a naval officer gave him a deep-rooted sense of personal authority – although he had to learn, by gradual experience, how best to exercise it. In his early career he had a tendency to cocksureness that could be engaging but that must also, at times, have been intensely irritating. Perhaps his most famous such clash was with Sir Richard Hughes in the West Indies in the mid-1780s, when Nelson's strong sense of duty and moral rectitude brought him into conflict with a generally easy-going admiral, who for the sake of a quiet life was prepared to turn a blind eye to infringements of the Navigation Acts by American merchant ships. It has, however, recently been discovered that they had locked horns two years before while both serving in the Channel, when Nelson's letters to Hughes were little short of insolent.[4]

Nelson's behaviour in the West Indies, when he stood out almost alone against both his own commander and the vested interests ashore, also demonstrates another important aspect of his character – his moral courage. This, again, was a source of strength and authority for him. He was also physically brave. Stories abound in his early career of the way he always led from the front – and, by the time he appeared at St Paul's in 1797, he bore the signs in his own battered body. Most obviously, his right coat sleeve was now empty and folded across his chest. He had also lost almost all of the sight in his right eye following a wound sustained fighting ashore in the siege of the French-held town of Calvi in Corsica, and a sharp blow to the stomach during the Battle of Cape St Vincent had left him with an abdominal weakness, similar to a hernia, that regularly caused him pain. He once defined his leadership style succinctly in a letter to General Sir Robert Wilson. Speaking of General Sir Ralph Abercrombie, who was killed at the land battle of Aboukir in March 1801, he said: 'Your gallant and ever to be lamented Chief proved in the manner he fell what an old French general, when ask'd what made a good or bad general, replied in two words <u>Allons</u> – <u>Allez</u>. Your Chief & myself have taken the first and Victory followed.'[5]

He was a 'performance leader' – one who led by personal example and who also appreciated the value of distinctive appearance and behaviour, even to the extent of making a virtue of his missing arm. He gave his stump a nautical nickname, calling it his 'fin', and he used it to identify with his men. Visiting a young sailor in hospital who had just lost his arm, he said, looking ruefully at his own empty sleeve, 'Well Jack, you and I are spoiled for fishermen.' The fact that he was genuinely able to say 'you and I' in a difficult situation like that, clearly bound him closer to those who served with him and who, like him, had paid dearly for their service. It probably also helped that, as a teenager, he had spent a year serving 'before the mast' in the merchantman *Mary Anne* on a voyage to the West Indies and so had experienced at first hand the life and the hardships of the lower deck.

Once he became an admiral, his leadership 'style' was essentially consultative, as we shall see, and he signalled this characteristic before he actually flew his flag.

While in command of a small squadron off Genoa and Leghorn (Livorno) in 1795–6, he corresponded warmly with his senior subordinate, Captain George Cockburn of HMS *Meleager*, keeping him informed of developments ashore (Napoleon Bonaparte's first Italian campaign was then under way) and telling him, when leaving him in temporary command of the squadron, that he was 'perfectly assured that His Majestys Service in this Gulf will be most punctually attended to'.[6] He was a naturally affectionate man, with a pronounced gift for making, and nurturing, friends and this characteristic influenced his professional relationships as well. His later reputation as the enthusiastically passionate lover of Emma Hamilton has obscured the fact that, emotionally, he was actually most happy in the male environment of the Navy. Throughout his life he had close, and sometimes quite intense, friendships with men – for example, with Thomas Troubridge, whom he first met when they served together as midshipmen in the *Seahorse* in 1773. He often looked up to older men and spoke of them as father figures, notably Lord Hood, Sir John Jervis and Sir William Hamilton. He later surrounded himself with bright young officers who became surrogate sons. It is also clear that most of those who served with him found him fascinating, even lovable, and the sense of comradeship that he inspired and encouraged was a very important ingredient in his particular leadership style.

He also knew the value of personal one-to-one contact – and not only with his officers, but with the men as well. A little-known incident in late 1796 illustrates this. The frigate HMS *Blanche* had just taken part in a sharp action with two Spanish frigates, along with the frigate *La Minerve*, in which Nelson was temporarily flying his commodore's pendant. Although the appearance of a superior Spanish squadron had forced the British to break off the engagement, Nelson was pleased with the way that both ships had been fought and wished to thank the ship's company of the *Blanche*. Most officers would have assembled the men on the quarterdeck and made a stirring speech – but not Nelson. Instead, he ordered that the men should be sent to their action stations and then, as one of them remembered: 'as we ware [*sic*] in a line before our guns, he came round the decks and shook hands with us as he went along and telling us he was rejoic'd to find we had escaped.'[7] That way, they saw him close to and actually spoke to him – and, even more important, he saw them as individuals, and not as a sea of anonymous faces. As a result, later in his career, when he was famous and when crowds gathered to see him wherever he went, he was often able to pick out men who had served with him and call them forward to speak with them.

'CONFIDENT OF MYSELF': PRACTICAL SKILLS

One reason Nelson had such a distinctive personal style is that his own training and early career had been markedly different from those of many of his contemporaries.[8] He first went to sea, aged 12, in March 1771 under the patronage of his maternal uncle, Captain Maurice Suckling. Suckling did not keep his protégé close by his side, as was usual: instead he seems deliberately to have arranged for his nephew to have as wide a range of experience as possible. The voyage to the West Indies, which taught him the minutiae of working a ship, was under the command of one of Suckling's former junior officers, John Rathbone. On his return to his uncle's ship, HMS *Triumph*, Nelson spent much of his time operating small boats in the Thames and, as he later remembered, this made him 'confident of myself among rocks and sands, which has many times been of very great comfort to me'.[9] Then, still only aged 14, he took part in an expedition to the Arctic, during which he was given command of one of the boats of HMS *Carcass* by his captain, Skeffington Lutwidge, who became another mentor and a lifelong friend. No sooner was he back from the north than Suckling secured for his nephew a berth in the crack frigate HMS *Seahorse*, and it would appear one of his reasons for choosing that ship was that her Master, Thomas Surridge, was known to be a particularly good navigator: a note arranging an introduction for Nelson says, 'The Master is a necessary man for a young lad to be introduced to.'[10] The interest in, and aptitude for, navigation that Surridge instilled in his pupil remained with him for the rest of his life. Even when he became an admiral, Nelson still filled his journal with notes of navigational marks for places he was visiting for the first time. He also had superb recall. 'I scrawl this from recollection,' he wrote to an un-named officer in April 1804: and then followed with detailed directions for entering Leghorn Roads, obviously based on his own service there throughout the 1790s, remembering the name of 'the Guard House called Mezzo Spiago (*sic*)' and 'the church of Monte Nero which is difficult for a stranger as it has no steeple and looks like a long Barn in a clump of trees'.[11] Additionally, he was a very good weatherman – he kept a daily weather log and was adept at reading the signs and predicting changes in the wind and weather.

So, by the time he had his 'golden orb' vision, Nelson had already enjoyed a wide range of experience in different types of ship and different environments, which had not only given him an excellent grounding in the practical aspects of his profession but which had also helped to nurture his natural independence and energy.

As well as being a skilled navigator, Nelson was also a fine ship-handler. Once again, his distinctive early career contributed to this. Having recovered from his illness in 1776 and made up his necessary seatime in the battleship HMS *Worcester*, he passed his lieutenant's examination on 5 April 1777, and – again thanks to Suckling's influence – was immediately appointed second lieutenant of the frigate HMS *Lowestoffe*. After only a year in her in the West Indies he had so impressed her captain, William Locker, that he gave him command of a small schooner acting as the frigate's tender, the *Little Lucy*. So, still aged only 19, he already had his first independent command. He had also learned an important lesson from his new mentor. Years later, he told him, 'It is you who always told me, "Lay a Frenchman close and you will beat him."' Locker had himself been a pupil of the great mid-eighteenth-century admiral, Edward Hawke, the victor of the Battle of Quiberon Bay in November 1759, and this had been one of his precepts. Nelson made it the foundation of his own tactical plans,

Early influences: Admiral Sir Peter Parker, C-in-C West Indies (left), who gave Nelson some of his key early promotions and (right) Captain William Locker of HMS Lowestoffe, *a follower of Hawke, who taught Nelson the importance of close action.*

even to the extent of flying the signal 'Engage the Enemy More Closely' in all his battles – almost as if it was a personal slogan.

After a brief period of service in the station flagship, the 50-gun battleship HMS *Bristol*, under the aegis of Commander-in-Chief Sir Peter Parker – who quickly became another mentor and friend – he was promoted to commander and given the brig HMS *Badger*. Six months later, still three months short of his twenty-first birthday, he received the key promotion to post captain. His swift rise meant he had served as lieutenant for less than three years and so had spent very little time in the strict hierarchy of the wardroom – which perhaps accounts for his continuing independent spirit, and for his almost total lack of any pride of rank, even when an admiral and peer of the realm. Most importantly, however, he had spent most of his time in small ships, usually in command, and had learned, while still young, how to handle them in all weathers.

He now went on to command frigates almost continuously for the next eight years: first the *Hinchinbrooke*, then the *Albemarle* and finally the most handy of them all, the 28-gun sixth rate, *Boreas*.[12] By 1787, when at the age of 29 he finally went home to Britain on extended leave, taking with him his wife Frances, whom he had met and married on the island of Nevis, he had served no more than a few months in battleships.

NELSON'S MARRIAGE

In the past, Frances Nelson has been often portrayed by Nelson's biographers – most of whom of course are men! – as a cold and rather colourless woman. Certainly, she suffers from comparison with the earthy and glamorous Emma Hamilton and the high drama of Nelson's relationship with Emma makes his marriage to Frances appear very ordinary. But in fact they were happily married for over ten years and Lady Spencer, the wife of the First Lord of the Admiralty, later remembered Nelson telling her in 1797, apparently with all the eagerness of a newly-married husband, '. . . that he was convinced I must like her. That she was beautiful, accomplished; but above all that her angelic tenderness towards him was beyond imagination.'

Almost everyone who knew Fanny Nelson loved and respected her. Lord St Vincent remained in touch with her to the end of his life and Nelson's truest friends – for example Thomas Hardy – also refused to drop her. She has been unfairly blamed in the past for the breakup of the marriage and has been particularly criticised for failing to give Nelson the adulation and encouragement he craved. But such judgements tended to be based on a few brief and heavily edited extracts from her letters to him published by Sir Nicholas Harris Nicolas as footnotes in his *Dispatches and Letters*. When, in 1958, those letters were finally published in full by the Navy Records Society, it became clear that Fanny had been much more supportive than had hitherto been supposed. This impression of a warm, and loving, woman was confirmed by the discovery, in 2001, of a remarkable series of letters written by her to Nelson's friend and agent, Alexander Davison, at the time of the breakup of the marriage. They are full of poignant expressions of affection.

As a result, she is now, increasingly, seen as the innocent victim of a love affair that was extremely destructive as well as highly romantic.

(See White, *The Wife's Tale*)

Captain and Mrs Nelson. These two delightful portraits, painted within a few years of each other, capture the Nelson marriage perfectly: Frances serenely pretty, Horatio eager and boyish. The miniature of him was her favourite likeness, and she kept it in a special casket long after he had abandoned her.

As a result, to the end of his life he remained at heart a frigate captain: an insight which offers an important key to the way that he later handled the larger ships he commanded, and even whole fleets. So, for example, in 1793, he assumed command of the 64-gun battleship HMS *Agamemnon* and took her on a shake-down cruise through the Channel. When off Cape Barfleur, he spotted a small French squadron consisting of two frigates and two brigs and gave chase. The French ran for shelter among the shoals of St Marcou but soon found that the British battleship was coming in after them. Nelson reported to his Commander-in-Chief, Lord Hood:

> I stood close in with the Islands of St Marcou and when on the other tack nearly fetched the Sternmost frigate, they immediately tack'd but we soon got into their wake & stood after them . . . It blew Strong Gale, we were close in with the rocks to windward and sand breaking under our lee, had the ship touched the ground she must have been inevitably lost and without the destruction of their vessels which I own I had much at heart. But the Risk was too much and I was under the Mortification of ordering the Ship to be wore.[13]

That vivid account has only recently been discovered, and the image of the *Agamemnon* tacking in the frigate's wake, almost like a yacht in the Fastnet race, is a striking new addition to our fund of Nelson stories.

'AN ASSISTANT MORE THAN A SUBORDINATE': NELSON IN THE MEDITERRANEAN, 1793–6

Shortly after the chase at Cape Barfleur, Nelson and the *Agamemnon* sailed for the Mediterranean under Lord Hood's command, and so began the last, and in some ways the most important, stage of his apprenticeship. This was the first time Nelson had served for any appreciable period with a battlefleet – indeed, he had never taken part in any fleet action. Now, first under Hood and later under Sir John Jervis, he was able to observe at close quarters the way in which two of the finest British admirals of the late eighteenth century handled and organised their fleets. With both, he established close working relationships, and both employed him on special detached duties. In September 1793, Hood sent him on a diplomatic mission to Naples to persuade King Ferdinand IV to send troops to help the British defend the naval port of Toulon (some 30 miles east of Marseilles), which had been handed over to them by French royalists. This led to his first encounter with the British ambassador, Sir William Hamilton, and his beautiful second wife, Emma. Then, the following year, Hood placed him in command of naval forces ashore in the capture of the island of Corsica. He took part in the sieges of the fortified towns of Bastia and Calvi, landing guns, men and supplies from his ships and manhandling them over rough terrain to assist the Army. It was at Calvi that he lost the sight of his eye, when he was hit in the face by gravel and stones thrown up from a parapet by a French cannon ball.

The key mentors. Two admirals who helped to shape Nelson's later career: Samuel Lord Hood (left) and John Jervis, Lord St Vincent (right). Abbot's portrait of Jervis captures his strong, commanding presence – but also the genial twinkle in his eye that was sometimes there.

Nelson was impatient with the Army's carefully planned and methodical way of running sieges, based on long practice and sound mathematical principles. He wanted impetuous action: at the very start of the siege of Bastia, he harried the outlying French earthworks with long-range fire from the *Agamemnon*, forcing their defenders back behind their town walls. He then took his ship close in to the town itself, telling a friend later:

> no sooner did we get within reach, than they begun at us, with Shot & Shells, I back'd our Main topsail that we might be as long as possible in passing & return'd their fire for one hour & half when we were drawing to too great a distance for our shot to do execution, the fire from the Ships was well kept up, & I am sure that not ten shot where (*sic*) fired which did not do Service. On one battery a vast explosion of gun powder took place & the fascines which they have lined the Sea Wall with, took fire, and it was some time before they could extinguish it. The Enemy's fire was very badly directed, each Ship had a few shot struck her, but not a Man killed or wounded.[14]

He added, 'if I had force to have landed, I am sure the town might have been carried without any great trouble'. It was not the last time in his career that he would underestimate the force required to capture – and above all, to hold on to – a fortified land position.

Nelson's relationship with Jervis was even closer: in February 1796, he told his wife, Frances, in one of his affectionate monthly letters that the Admiral 'seems at present to consider me as an assistant more than a subordinate for I am acting without orders'.[15] By now commodore of a squadron operating off the Italian

Porto Agro, Corsica. Nelson and his men landed their guns and equipment in this small inlet for the attack on Calvi.

coast, Nelson had come to an important stage in his career, for he had begun to take important command decisions for himself – such as in September 1796 when, on his own initiative, he organised the efficient and bloodless capture of the island of Capraia in a model of combined operations. As he reported to Jervis: 'It would be doing injustice were a distinction to be made between the two services: all had full employment and I am confident that but one opinion prevailed, that of expediting the surrender of the Island by every means in their power.'[16]

By now he was getting noticed. Jervis's reports to the Admiralty were full of praise for him, and the First Lord, Lord Spencer, encouraged him to write directly, saying, 'It is very satisfactory to hear from you.'[17] He was also in regular correspondence with British diplomats ashore – notably John Trevor, the British Minister at Turin, and Francis Drake, the Minister at Genoa, as well as Sir William Hamilton in Naples. He quickly established good working relationships with them all and impressed them with his ability. A number of his letters to Drake have recently been discovered, and they show him dealing confidently with a wide variety of tasks and problems, and also working easily with the more experienced diplomat. 'You will Sir put my ideas into such language as you may judge proper,' he wrote at the height of a dispute with the authorities in Genoa about the nature of neutrality.[18]

He was also able to learn from negative experiences – as when he finally took part in his first full-scale fleet actions in 1795, under the uninspiring and hesitant command of Admiral William Hotham, who had temporarily replaced Hood when he went home on leave.[19] At the Battle of Genoa, on 13 and 14 March, in shifting and uncertain winds, and with the French avoiding action, Hotham ordered a general chase, allowing his faster ships to draw clear of their consorts and attack the rear of the French line. In the confusion of retreat, the 80-gun *Ça Ira* collided with one of her consorts, losing her fore and main topmasts. Dropping astern, she was harried by the frigate HMS *Inconstant*, commanded by Captain Thomas Fremantle. This gave Nelson in the *Agamemnon* time to catch up, and for three hours he skilfully tacked his ship to and fro across the Frenchman's stern, pouring in a series of well-aimed broadsides, while receiving scarcely any return fire. Some of the French ships, including the massive 120-gun three-decker *Sans Culottes*, turned to assist their comrade, upon which Hotham, still too far off with the rest of the fleet, was forced to order Nelson to break off the action. The following day, the battle was rejoined, and this time the *Ça Ira* was captured, along with the *Censeur*, which tried to help her. Content with this modest success, Hotham ended the engagement.

Nelson, however, was thoroughly dissatisfied with the result, believing that Hotham should have followed up their initial success much more aggressively. A letter has recently been discovered that he wrote two weeks later to the Revd Dixon Hoste, a Norfolk neighbour and a friend of his father. It contains a passage that reveals so much about the direction in which Nelson's ideas about fleet actions were already heading that it is worth quoting in full:

> We have done well & perhaps it is hardly fair to say we might have done better. Hotham is my very Old Friend [and] is as good a Man as ever lived & as Gallant an Officer but his head is not so long as Lord Hood. Had his Lordship been here I have no doubt in my mind but perhaps the whole French fleet would have graced our Triumph, such an opportunity seldom offers and much risque must be run to achieve great & Brilliant actions. But Hotham adheres to the old Adage <u>A bird in the hand is better far than two that in the bushes are.</u> I thought so differently that I proposed to the Admiral so soon as the Ça Ira Struck & Censeur – to stand after the Enemy & leave our Prizes & Crippled Ships with 4 Frigates to take care of themselves. We had 20 Ships in perfect order & it so might have gone if the Admiral had proposed, 'Let those who are in a state to pursue a flying Enemy hold up their hands,' he would not I am sure have found himself alone. But Hothams answer to Me was, 'We have suffered a good deal, we have a decided Victory & we must be contented.' My Mind is of a different nature for had we taken 20 Sail & could have had a fair chance for taking 21 I could never hold the business well done.[20]

So, already, he was dreaming of annihilation, and all his tactical planning and thought in the years ahead would be directed to this end.

The second battle that year, on 13 July off the island of Hyères, just outside Toulon, was even more disappointing. This time, Nelson delivered the French fleet right into Hotham's arms by a superb piece of scouting in which, once again, he handled the *Agamemnon* almost like a frigate, only to see his commander throw away the splendid opportunity he had been given. Having finally caught up with the fleeing French, Hotham spent over four hours in a favourable wind adjusting his line of battle. He then sent ahead some of his fastest ships, and a partial action ensued in which one French ship was set on fire and blew up. By now the van of the British fleet was catching up, but then, just as a decisive battle seemed imminent, Hotham, still 8 miles astern with the slower ships, hoisted the signal of recall. Once again, Nelson was furious. 'Had Lord Hood been here,' he told Frances Nelson, 'he would never have called us out of battle, but Hotham leaves nothing to chance.'[21] He was also very critical of the time Hotham had wasted in forming his line, and in this frustration we can see the origins of his later search for ways to get his fleet speedily into action without wasting time in forming a rigid line of battle. Moreover, he came away from these two encounters with a very poor opinion of the capabilities of the French fleet. He wrote to the Duke of Clarence, a regular correspondent, with whom he had made friends in the West Indies in the 1780s, 'I don't believe they can ever beat us in their present undisciplined state.'[22] This insight, too, was to colour the development of his tactical thought.

Despite these partial successes, and the more aggressive strategy that was pursued once Sir John Jervis became commander-in-chief in late 1795, the British position in the Mediterranean became steadily more difficult, especially when it became clear that Spain was going to enter the war on the French side. So, eventually, on 25 September 1796, Jervis received orders to withdraw his fleet outside the Mediterranean and to evacuate the British-held islands of Corsica and Elba. Nelson strongly disagreed with this retreat – indeed, we now know that he was so concerned that he briefly contemplated staying behind and offering his services to the King of Naples. In a recently discovered letter to Sir William Hamilton he wrote:

> To say I am grieved and distressed but ill describes my feelings on receipt of the positive order for the evacuation of the Mediterranean. 'Till this time it has been usual for the allies of England to fall from her, but till now she was never known to desert her friends whilst she had the power of supporting them . . . I yet hope the Cabinet may on more mature information change their opinion, it is not all we may gain elsewhere which can compensate for our loss of honor . . . I wish any mode could be adopted that Individually as an Officer (I may I hope without vanity say of some Merit) I could serve the King of Naples.[23]

In the end, however, he stayed with Jervis, who put him in charge of the evacuation of Corsica. This he carried off with consummate skill, keeping his nerve when all others were despairing, and succeeded in taking off every British serviceman and civilian, together with all their equipment, just hours before the invading French army arrived.[24] Among the evacuees was the British Viceroy of Corsica, Sir Gilbert Elliot, who became a close friend and supporter in later years.

'Zeal and ability': 1797 – Cape St Vincent and Tenerife

So, by the end of 1796, Nelson had won for himself a reputation among his peers as a thoroughly dependable and professional naval officer. But despite this widespread approval, he was not a wholly happy man. He felt that his devoted service and considerable achievements were not appreciated at home, and his letters to Frances at this time are full of complaints that his contribution to the war had not been publicly recognised or rewarded. All that was about to change dramatically early in 1797. The Spanish did indeed enter the war, as expected, and immediately began to plan an invasion of Ireland in conjunction with their French allies. In preparation for this, they began to move their fleets out of the Mediterranean, intending to join with the main French fleet at Brest. But they were thwarted right at the outset by Jervis, who intercepted and beat the main Spanish fleet in the remarkable Battle of Cape St Vincent, fought on 14 February 1797. It was Nelson's first experience of a major fleet victory, and he played a key role in bringing it about, flying his commodore's pendant in HMS *Captain*.

Past accounts of the battle have tended to portray Nelson as a lone genius who saved the day for the British by his unconventional approach – even to the extent of directly disobeying Jervis's orders at one point. Modern research into the logbooks of the ships involved and other contemporary accounts, including material from Spanish sources, has revealed a much more complex picture.[25] It is now apparent that Jervis himself handled the battle unconventionally right from the start. First, he hurried his ships into a loose line of battle, without any waste of time in forming them up, and then drove, like an arrow, for a gap in the Spanish formation. Then, having split the enemy fleet into two unequal halves, he divided his own fleet into attack groups, intending to concentrate his attention on the larger Spanish force. Nelson played a decisive role in this second phase with an act of inspired initiative. Seeing that his divisional flagship, HMS *Britannia*, was not complying with Jervis's signals, he took the *Captain* out of the line and sailed directly to assist the British van, which had begun to catch up with the rearmost Spaniards. Far from being an act of disobedience, it is now clear that he was acting in accordance with Jervis's intentions.

A fierce melée ensued, in which a number of Spanish ships suffered from the fast and accurate British broadsides. Two of them, the *San Nicolas* and the *San José*, collided while trying desperately to get out of range and became entangled. Seeing this, Nelson ordered the *Captain* to be placed alongside the *San Nicolas* and then personally led a boarding party to capture her. The *San José*, which had already been badly mauled by gunfire from other British ships, began firing on Nelson and his party in an attempt to help their comrades. So he led his men up her sides and captured her as well. He thus was personally responsible for capturing two of the four prizes that were taken on that day.

It was a remarkable feat, unprecedented in naval history, and Nelson was deservedly the hero of the hour. But his earlier lack of recognition still rankled,

Boarders away! William Bromley captures the ferocity of the close-quarters, hand-to-hand fighting at Cape St Vincent.

and so he made sure he was not overlooked on this occasion by sending a personal account of his exploits to his former captain, William Locker, with a request that he would have it published in the newspapers. This account overemphasised his own role in the battle and even suggested that the *Captain* and the *Culloden*, commanded by his friend Thomas Troubridge, had fought alone 'for near an hour'.[26] He obviously believed this sincerely, but it was demonstrably not true, and the claim made him unpopular in the triumphant fleet, where the general opinion was that everyone had contributed to the great victory.

All the same, Jervis now obviously valued Nelson very highly and regarded him as one of his most effective subordinates. Following the battle, the Spanish fleet took refuge in Cádiz and were blockaded by the British. Jervis formed a special inshore squadron of battleships which he placed under the command of Nelson, who had just learned of his promotion to rear admiral. Jervis also recognised his gift for inspiring men. When HMS *Theseus* joined the fleet in May with a half-mutinous crew, Jervis responded by asking Nelson and his flag captain, Ralph Miller, to transfer to her. It is clear that he placed the blame squarely on the shoulders of the ship's officers. Writing to his friend, the Duke of Clarence, on 26 May, Nelson explained that 'Sir John for certain reasons has wished Me to Join this Ship which has hitherto not been commanded to his liking.' Indeed, we now know that he agreed with Jervis, for he wrote, when the first news of the Spithead mutiny arrived, 'to us who see the whole at once we must think that for a <u>Mutiny</u> which I fear I must call it having no other name, that it has been the most Manly thing I ever heard of, and does the British Sailor infinite honor, it is extraordinary that there never was a regulation by authority for short Weights & Measures and it reflects on all of us, to have suffer'd it so long.'[27]

That passage was suppressed when Nelson's correspondence with Clarence was published later – clearly the editors did not think it was appropriate to publicise the fact that the Hero of Trafalgar had sympathised with mutineers! However, his sympathetic approach worked, for, not long afterwards, a note was dropped on the *Theseus*'s quarterdeck:

> Long live Sir Rob Calder
> Success attend Adl: Nelson
> God Bless Capt Miller
> We thank the Admiral for the Officers he has placed over us
> We are happy & Comfortable and will shed the last drop of our
> Blood in fighting the Enemies of our Country & in supporting the
> Admiral
> The Ships Company[28]

The reference to 'the officers he has placed over us' is significant. As was customary, Nelson had taken with him a number of his young 'followers', including his two particular favourites, Lieutenant John Weatherhead and Midshipman William Hoste, both of them the sons of Norfolk friends, and they had obviously been instrumental in establishing good order – helped by some old *Agamemnons* who had accompanied their commander. The transformation of the *Theseus* was certainly a tribute to Nelson's leadership skills, as his biographers have often pointed out. But it was also a striking demonstration of how important it was for an eighteenth-century officer to surround himself with high-quality followers – and on the lower deck as much as in the wardroom.

Shortly after arriving off Cádiz, Nelson learned that his exploits had at last received the official recognition that he longed for – he had been made a Knight of the Bath, with the right to wear the distinctive star of the order on the breast of his uniform coat. In fact, he had worked hard to get it: knowing that the usual reward for a junior flag officer was a baronetcy, which brought with it a title but no insignia, he dropped broad hints that he was not wealthy enough to support a hereditary award. His lobbying bore fruit on this occasion but, as we shall see, the ploy was to return to haunt him the next time he was considered for an honour.

The Spanish fleet remained behind the defences of Cádiz, despite all that Nelson and his comrades could do to dislodge them. So, instead, Jervis sought ways of bringing pressure to bear elsewhere, and in July 1797, remembering Nelson's previous success against Capraia, he sent him with a small squadron to attack the Spanish island of Tenerife. This was Nelson's first major operation as an admiral, and he tackled it with great thoroughness, consulting with his captains regularly, ordering special equipment and insisting on daily training for the men who would be landed.[29] In the end, all his careful preparations were frustrated by the one factor for which he could not plan – the weather. His landing force was prevented from reaching their objective by contrary winds and currents, and by the time they did manage to get ashore, the well-organised Spanish had taken up strong defensive positions from which they could not be dislodged. At this point, Nelson could quite legitimately have abandoned the operation, but he received intelligence from the shore that the Spanish had very few professional soldiers, and that they were in a state of disarray and confusion. At a council of war with all his captains, Nelson was urged to attack again, and he needed little persuasion. It was the decision of an inexperienced commander who had not fully weighed the risks against the likely gains.

The new attack was a bloody disaster that lost Nelson almost a quarter of his force in killed or wounded. The first part of the intelligence report had been correct – the Spanish defenders were indeed very thin on the ground. But the second part had been completely wrong – carefully organised by their governor, Antonio Gutiérrez, an experienced professional soldier, the small Spanish defending force was in fact alert and ready. As the British sailors and Royal Marines stormed the town mole and citadel, they were mown down by concentrated fire – including Nelson himself, whose upper right arm was shattered by a musket ball. A few small parties managed to struggle ashore and barricaded themselves in a monastery. But, surrounded and cut off from their comrades, they eventually agreed to surrender.

Luckily for Nelson, his stepson, Josiah Nisbet,[30] was at his side in the boat, and he saved his life. First, he staunched the flow of blood from the dangerous wound and then managed to get Nelson back to his flagship, where the arm was amputated. At this point, it seemed that the attack was succeeding, and so within moments of the operation, Nelson was using his left hand to apply a wavering signature to an ultimatum addressed to the Spanish governor. But, shortly afterwards, more accurate news came from the shore, and so his second and slightly more legible attempt at a signature was at the bottom of a letter to General Gutiérrez, thanking him for the very humane way in which he had treated his British prisoners, offering them food and drink and taking the wounded into the town's hospital. With the letter went a cask of beer and some cheese, to which Gutiérrez responded by sending Nelson some Malmsey wine.

It was a very severe setback, the worst Nelson had so far suffered in his career, and it showed that his preferred tactics of shock and surprise could be countered by a determined and experienced opponent. Not unnaturally, he was very depressed – both by the large number of casualties and by the blow to his own future prospects. As he wrote in a letter to Jervis, 'a left handed admiral will never again be considered as useful therefore the sooner I get to a very humble cottage the better and make room for a better man to serve the state'.[31] To make matters worse, the casualties included Lieutenant John Weatherhead, who died of his wounds a few days later. Greatly affected by the loss of his protégé, Nelson wrote to the young man's clergyman father, 'when I reflect on that fatal night I cannot but bring sorrow and his fall before my eyes. Dear friend he fought as he had always done by my side.'[32]

Jervis, who had by then been created Earl St Vincent as a reward for his great victory, was sympathetic and sent Nelson home to Britain to recover. After a depressing voyage in which he again talked of finding 'a hut to put my mutilated carcase in', Nelson arrived to find himself the hero of the hour. The disaster at Tenerife was ignored and the hero of St Vincent acclaimed – first by the crowds at

*Nelson wounded at Tenerife. Nelson,
his shattered arm tightly bandaged, is
helped into the boat by his stepson,
Josiah Nisbet.*

Portsmouth where he landed, and then in Bath where he went to join his wife and father. Newspaper articles sang his praises, and letters began to arrive inviting him to accept the freedoms of various cities, including the City of London. The first popular prints of him began to appear. This public adulation, the first he had ever received, restored his flagging spirits, and within a month he was talking of returning to sea, writing to St Vincent, 'if you continue to hold your opinion of me I shall press to return with all the zeal, although not with all the personal ability, I formerly had.'[33]

First, however, he had to recover from the loss of his arm; but this was still causing him such pain that he had to take opium in order to sleep. As he told Thomas Fellowes, who had been his purser in the *Boreas*: 'My Arm from the unlucky circumstance of a Nerve being taken up with the Artery is not yet healed nor do I see any prospect of the ligatures coming away.'[34] None of the doctors in Bath was able to help, and so he and Frances travelled to London, where they consulted a number of specialists. The consensus was that the arm was best left to heal by itself, and in the end that is exactly what happened. One morning Nelson woke after an unusually sound sleep to find that the pain had suddenly disappeared. Characteristically, one of his first acts was to send a note to the nearest church, St George's Hanover Square, asking for special prayers of thanks to be said the following Sunday.

This then was the man who attended the service at St Paul's on 19 December 1797. Although still under 40, he had already seen twenty years' active service in the Royal Navy. His careful early training and wide experience, encompassing both heady success and depressing failure, had worked upon his natural ability and his strong personal dedication to produce an admiral of unique promise. Now all he needed was an opportunity to prove himself.

'The Band of Brothers'. Nelson (halfway up the tree trunk) and the captains who served with him at the Nile.

VICTORS OF THE NILE

CHAPTER II

The Battle of the Nile and the Mediterranean: 1798–1800

Following the thanksgiving service in St Paul's, Nelson travelled to Bath to join his wife, Frances, and his father, who were wintering there. As an admiral, he no longer had to concern himself with the wearisome business of fitting out and manning his ship. That task was now performed by his flag captain, Edward Berry, who had been his first lieutenant in the *Captain* and had served with him as a volunteer at Cape St Vincent. It was not until the end of March 1798 that the *Vanguard* was ready to receive him and by then his desk work as an admiral had already begun. Much of it concerned patronage, which was to form a major component in his correspondence from now on. Lady Collier, widow of Vice Admiral Sir George Collier, was assured 'I shall have much pleasure in having so fine a lad [her son Francis] under my wing and indeed it is our duty to be useful to the children of our brethren.' He would also be expected to entertain his officers regularly, and letters to his secretary, John Campbell, outlined the stores he would require: '20 sheep dry fed of the best but not largest kind & plenty of good hay to be well prepared on board for those we cannot get in Portugal, Corn, Fowls, Ducks, Geese, &c: &c: . . . 4 hampers Bristol Water 1 cask of Loaf Sugar 10 Kegs of tripe 2 boxes Oyster 1 box Essence Spruce.'[1]

Nelson reached Portsmouth on 29 March and joined the *Vanguard* the following day. As she was only a two-decker, she did not have a separate suite of rooms for an admiral, and so he occupied the captain's cabin, immediately under the poop and opening directly on to the quarterdeck. Letters from Berry to him during the fitting-out tell us that some of the cabin's furnishings were standard dockyard issue – the painted cloth covering the floor, for example – with a few personal items, such as carpets, curtains and a looking-glass, to add a more homely touch.[2] The cabin also had an open stern gallery – then an increasingly unusual feature, but one that Nelson clearly appreciated, since he asked for it to be enlarged slightly during the ship's refit, by moving the bulkhead separating it from the cabin. On 1 April, they set sail with a convoy under escort, but were forced to put back into the St Helen's anchorage, at the extreme eastern point of the Isle of Wight, when the wind turned westerly. They were pinned there for a week – during which Nelson discovered that a number of items were missing from his luggage, and he worked off his frustration at the inactivity by sending irritable notes to Frances – 'I can do very well without these things but it is a satisfaction to mention them,' he wrote.[3] However, his strong affection for her also shone through – 'you are always uppermost in my thoughts,' he assured her, and she replied warmly: 'Indeed I have always felt your sincere attachment and at no one period could I feel it more strongly than I do at the moment and I hope as some few years are past, time enough to know our dispositions, we may flatter ourselves it may last.'[4] Finally, on 8 April, the wind came round the east, and he was off again. Having escorted the convoy to Lisbon, he joined Lord St Vincent's fleet off Cádiz on 30 April. 'The arrival of Sir Horatio Nelson has given me new life, you could not have gratified me more in sending him,' wrote the old admiral to Lord Spencer.[5]

While Nelson had been in England recovering from the loss of his arm, the war had moved into a new phase. Peace negotiations, which had been continuing spasmodically throughout 1797, finally broke down, and so Prime Minister William Pitt was now working to construct a new coalition of European nations against France. Another major British naval victory against the Dutch at Camperdown in October 1797, combined with the earlier defeat of the Spanish at Cape St Vincent, had ended, at least for the time being, the threat of invasion. So Pitt and his colleagues now felt able to turn their attention to the Mediterranean again. The Austrians, whom they wished to persuade into the coalition, demanded that Britain should make a show of strength in the area and, at the same time, intelligence was beginning to come in of a major French expeditionary force being prepared at Toulon and at nearby ports. In view of the continuing lack of any major bases, and the continuing difficulty of obtaining supplies, ministers still did not feel able to deploy a large fleet permanently in the area. But they were confident enough to consider sending a special detached squadron to find out what the French were up to and, if possible, to thwart their plans. It would be a highly responsible command, for which special qualities of leadership were required – and it would seem that everyone thought of Nelson. Later, after Nelson had won his stunning victory at the Battle of the Nile, the Duke of Clarence wrote to his friend to assure him that it had been the King's idea to appoint Nelson for the task. Sir Gilbert Elliot, now elevated to the peerage as Lord Minto, wrote reporting a conversation in which he had suggested the idea to Lord Spencer. Spencer did indeed write to St Vincent suggesting Nelson for the command, but by the time his letter reached Cádiz in early May 1798, the old admiral had already sent his protégé into the Mediterranean with a small squadron. It was not a popular decision: other admirals in the fleet, senior to

Nelson, felt that this decided 'plum' should have been given to them, and one, Sir John Orde, even went so far as to take the dangerous step of protesting formally St Vincent: 'I cannot conceal from your lordship how much I am hurt.' It was the start of an escalating feud between the two men, into which Nelson was eventually drawn as well. Although Orde maintained that his protest had not been intended to cast any doubt upon Nelson's abilities, Nelson nonetheless always thereafter regarded him as a rival, even an enemy.

St Vincent's initial orders to Nelson, issued on 2 May, envisaged a simple reconnaissance 'to endeavour to ascertain . . . the destination of that Expedition',[6] and, to begin with, Nelson was given only a small squadron of three battleships (*Vanguard*, *Orion* and *Alexander*) and five frigates. They called in first at Gibraltar for supplies, from where Nelson reported to St Vincent, on 8 May: 'We are under weigh but I shall not make sail to eastward till dark – indeed some of my squadron seem so slow in their movements that it will be late till we are clear of Europa.'[7] Clearly, some of the captains in the squadron had not yet got used to their new admiral's style.

However, they were not to remain in ignorance for long. For, on the same day that they sailed from Gibraltar, Nelson started his first Public Order Book – a system for communicating personally with his captains and ships' companies that he was to use in all his campaigns thereafter. Three of these books have survived: one for 1798–9, covering the whole of the Nile Campaign and subsequent operations in Naples; one for January–May 1801, covering the Copenhagen and Baltic Campaigns, and one for July–October 1801, covering Nelson's period in command of the anti-invasion forces in the Channel.[8] It is also clear from surviving fragments that he employed similar books during the Mediterranean Campaign of 1803–5 and the Trafalgar Campaign. These were not formal records kept by secretaries, but working books, used for the quick transmission of day-to-day matters. The contents are scribbled hurriedly, with many erasures and interlineations; there are no indexes, nor any numbering schemes. Minimal punctuation and frequent capitalisation combine to give them an urgency similar to modern e-mails and, with their urgent, almost breathless, style, they conjure up a vivid sense of Nelson's presence.

The orders would be copied into the book, and often were signed by Nelson – indeed, occasionally, he would alter the wording of an order himself, thus demonstrating the close personal interest he took in the content of the book. All the ships in company would then send an officer to the flagship to make a copy, and sign the book to show that they had done so (see illustration on p. 84). The copy would then be transferred into the daily order books of the individual ships' captains. Other admirals used a similar system to convey routine orders but, characteristically, Nelson also used the books to convey his own ethos and leadership style. So, the very first order, dated 8 May 1798 as the squadron left Gibraltar, reads: 'In order that every Ship of the Squadron may be ready at day break to make a sudden attack upon the Enemy, or to retreat should it be deemed expedient, the decks and sides are to be washed in the Middle watch, the Reefs let out of the Topsails whenever the weather is moderate, topgallant yards got up and everything clear for making all possible sail before the dawn of day.'[9] In other words, there would be no excuse for anyone to be 'slow in their movements' again!

From Gibraltar, Nelson took his squadron towards Toulon and, on the 17th, they captured a small French warship whose crew, under interrogation, confirmed that the French were preparing a major expedition involving at least fifteen battleships and large numbers of troops. Although they also claimed that 'no one knows to what place the armament is destined',[10] which meant that the most vital piece of information was still missing, all the senior officers of the squadron, Nelson included, felt that it was an auspicious start to their campaign – as the second in command, James Saumarez, recorded, 'we began to make exulting reflections on the advantages of our situation.'[11] Nelson took the squadron to a position some 75 miles to the south of Toulon, where he hoped to be able to intercept more ships and build up his store of intelligence.

Then, during the night of the 20th, with very little warning, the weather suddenly worsened, until by 10 p.m. the wind had increased to 'heavy squalls' from the north-north-west. Both *Orion* and *Alexander* had struck their upper yards, but Berry kept his topgallant and royal yards up, as if expecting good weather. Gradually the force of the wind increased, compelling the ships to take in more and more sail – indeed both *Orion* and *Alexander* had their topsails blown out. In the *Vanguard* the upper yards were now putting severe additional strain on the masts and, at about 1.30 a.m. on the 21st, the maintopmast fell, followed about half an hour later by the foretopmast. Then, in a final blow, the foremast itself gave way and crashed over the side at about 3.30 a.m., taking part of the bowsprit with it. It was a very grave series of accidents indeed, and the ship was now in real danger.

When the first accident occurred, Nelson was in his cabin – the sailing of the ship was a matter for Berry, as her captain, and not for the admiral. But it is clear from his later report to Lord St Vincent that Nelson immediately went onto the quarterdeck and took personal command – all the references to ship-handling are in the first person. Berry was, after all, relatively inexperienced; he had only recently been promoted to captain and had never commanded a frigate, let alone a battleship. Now the highest order of seamanship was required, and all Nelson's long experience and training came to the fore. Daylight showed that the ship was heading straight towards the coast of Corsica, and the first priority was to get her out of danger by wearing. Without foresails this was a very difficult manoeuvre, but Nelson managed it, using a spritsail – an old-fashioned sail hung from a yard under the bowsprit. This gave his hard-pressed crew a lull in which they could cut free the wreckage of rigging and masts that was dragging in the water, still attached to the ship and further impeding her progress. Even when this had been done, the ship still rolled heavily.

By 4 a.m. on the 22nd the wind had moderated enough for Nelson to consider his next move, and he signalled the *Alexander* to take his ship in tow. This Ball did with consummate skill – even, at one point, directly refusing Nelson's order to cast off the tow when it looked as if both ships might be driven ashore. Eventually, on the morning of 23rd all three battleships came to anchor in the bay of San Pietro on the south-west coast of Sardinia. Of the five frigates, however, there was no sign. Having become separated from the squadron during the storm, they eventually regrouped at a pre-arranged rendezvous south of Toulon and waited for Nelson. When he did not reappear by 31 May, the senior officer, George Hope, decided that the admiral must have returned to Gibraltar for repairs and so he left the area – just days before Nelson, having repaired the *Vanguard* using his own resources at San Pietro, reached the rendezvous himself. It was the first of a number of 'near-misses' during the campaign and in many ways the most serious. For, if the frigates had still been with Nelson in the crucial weeks that followed, it is likely the other near-misses would not have happened.

Meanwhile, off Cádiz, St Vincent had received new orders from London. The Cabinet now wished to make a significant show of strength in the Mediterranean, and so the Admiralty had decided to redeploy its battlefleets. Instead of keeping most of its forces concentrated in the Western Approaches to meet the invasion threat, they now reinforced St Vincent, using a squadron from the Channel fleet under Sir Roger Curtis, which meant that St Vincent in turn could send a significant force into the Mediterranean to join Nelson. Accordingly, on 24 May, nine battleships left Cádiz under the command of the senior captain, Nelson's old comrade and friend, Thomas Troubridge of the *Culloden*.

As Troubridge entered the Mediterranean, Nelson's crews were completing repairs to his shattered flagship at San Pietro. It seems that it did not even occur to him to send the *Vanguard* back to Gibraltar for a full dockyard refit: instead, within 24 hours of anchoring on 23 May, a new mizzen topmast had been prepared by the carpenters of the *Orion*. Meanwhile, the *Alexander* sent over eighteen shipwrights and then, having lashed the *Alexander* alongside the *Vanguard*, they drew out the stump of the foremast, using blocks and tackles rigged on the *Alexander*'s yards, and then lowered their own spare foretopmast into place to act as a new, rather stumpy, foremast. By the morning of the 27th the work was complete – it had taken them just three days. As Nelson reported to Frances, 'The exertions of Sir James Saumarez and Captain Ball have been wonderful and if the ship had been in England months would have been taken to send her to sea.'[12] Putting to sea again, they returned north to Toulon, where they met the *Mutine*, commanded by Thomas Hardy, already one of Nelson's protégés.[13] He brought Nelson his new orders from St Vincent and news of the approaching reinforcement. Finally, on 7 June, Troubridge's force hove into sight.

'MY ANXIOUS MIND': THE CHASE

Nelson now had fourteen battleships under his command – and they were, for the period, an unusually homogeneous force. Six of them – *Vanguard* herself, *Audacious*, *Bellerophon*, *Defence*, *Goliath* and *Zealous* – were effectively sister ships, having been built from the same design by Surveyor to the Navy Sir Thomas

Slade (who also designed the *Victory*). The rest varied in some respects but really the only odd ones out were *Minotaur*, a design copied from a French prize, and the *Leander*, a 50-gun fourth rate, a type regarded as obsolete by 1798. The captains, too, were a well-matched group. On 11 May, writing to inform Nelson of the proposed reinforcement, St Vincent had promised, 'You shall also have some choice fellows of the in-shore squadron',[14] and he was as good as his word: the ships now under Nelson were all commanded by seasoned and experienced officers, most of whom were around his age and had worked with him before in the Mediterranean and again off Cádiz. They were a ready-made team, men who were already friends and who, for the most part, shared Nelson's ideas and ideals. The one exception, apparently, was Davidge Gould of the *Audacious*, who appears to have been rather out of sympathy with his colleagues. Years later in 1803, writing to Troubridge of the *esprit de corps* of his Mediterranean fleet, Nelson said, 'more Zeal and attention with good humour I never saw exceeded, it is like the Nile fleet without Davidge Gould.'[15]

It is important to emphasise at this stage that Nelson had not been appointed a commander-in-chief; nor was this a full-scale fleet. He had a single task: his orders from St Vincent said succinctly that he was to use his 'utmost endeavours to sink burn or destroy' the French armament. So he had none of the infrastructure of a fleet to support him – for example, there was no captain of the fleet to assist with the administration. Indeed, his original orders envisaged that he would stay in the Mediterranean only 'so long as the provisions of your Squadron will last', or until he found somewhere that he could obtain supplies. Everything about this operation, as originally planned, was temporary – in modern parlance this was a task force, with a specific objective, and it was expected that, once the objective had been achieved, it would return to base.

Nelson immediately proceeded to make the objective clear to all those serving with him. In the days immediately following the junction of the two divisions, he issued a number of memoranda, using the Public Order Book: all of them were concerned with bringing the enemy fleet to action. The ships were to keep in close formation to avoid the risk 'that an opportunity of bringing the Enemy to battle may be lost, which I am sure would grieve the whole Squadron'. They were to be ready to anchor by the stern, in case the enemy were discovered in an anchorage, and new signals were introduced to allow Nelson to direct his ships to concentrate on one section of the enemy's line.[16]

Most interesting is Nelson's detailed battle plan, issued on 18 June 1798 (see Appendix I, p. 195). The first of his plans for a fleet action, it foreshadows his later, and more famous, plans in a number of ways. At this stage he was expecting he would meet the French expeditionary force, made up of a large fleet of transports and a smaller force of warship escorts, at sea. So, first, instead of holding his own force together in a single rigid line, he divided the squadron into three divisions, each with a specific task. Second, he delegated to the commanders of those divisions responsibility for the direction of their forces, and made special signalling arrangements to enable them to do this. So, even this early in his career as an admiral, Nelson was prepared to decentralise control, and this was to be a key component of all his future battle plans. Third, the plan is shot through with Nelson's aggressive longing for annihilation: for a complete victory rather than the capture of a few ships, as in Hotham's two actions in 1795. In the Public Order Book the words 'The Destruction of the Enemys Armament is the Sole Object' are emphasised in large letters, inked in boldly. As a result, the words leap off the page, almost as if Nelson himself is standing beside the reader and saying them aloud in his enthusiastic manner.

The discovery of the Public Order Book, and appreciation of the use Nelson made of it to exercise personal command, enables us to settle a controversy that has emerged recently over Nelson's command methods. For years biographers and naval historians, citing the personal testimony of Edward Berry, have attributed the British success at the Battle of the Nile to the pains Nelson took to brief each of his captains about his plans in advance of the battle. In his *Narrative* of the campaign Berry wrote: 'It had been his practice during the whole of the cruize, whenever the weather and circumstances would permit, to have his captains on board the Vanguard, where he would fully develop to them his own ideas of the different and best modes of attack, and such plans as he proposed to execute upon falling in with the Enemy whatever their position or situation might be.'[17]

In subsequent accounts of the campaign this statement was taken to mean that Nelson held regular conferences with *all* his captains (although, in fact, Berry does not specifically say so). However, in 1998, while researching for his definitive book on the Nile Campaign, Brian Lavery noticed that the logs of the ships in Nelson's squadron revealed that some captains, such as Thomas Troubridge and James Saumarez, were sent for more frequently than others, and that some were not sent for at all. He therefore concluded 'the inference . . . that Nelson had regular general conferences during the run-up to the Battle of the Nile is clearly wrong'. This judgement was challenged in 2003 by Nelson biographer Edgar Vincent, who claimed 'it is inconceivable that Berry's recollections should be so wide of the mark', and suggested, rather implausibly, there must have been informal meetings that went unrecorded in the log books.[18]

We can now show how it was actually done. A pocket book belonging to Captain Henry Darby of HMS *Bellerophon*, and still in the hands of his descendants, has recently come to light. Comparison with the Public Order Book shows that Darby copied down all the key battle orders highlighted above – and yet Lavery's research shows that Darby only visited the *Vanguard* twice during the pre-battle voyage, compared with nine visits by Troubridge and five by Saumarez. It would seem, therefore, that Nelson first consulted with some of his closest colleagues in face-to-face meetings, and then communicated the key points that had been decided to the other captains by means of the Public Order Book. So the old image of Nelson meeting constantly with all his captains in plenary seminars – always an unlikely scenario, given the problems of gathering everyone together from ships that were almost constantly under way – can now be finally discarded. But the really important point – that he consulted with colleagues about his plans for fighting the enemy and then shared the results of the consultations with all his captains – can still stand.

However, before the enemy could be fought they had to be found, and that proved difficult. We now know of course that the French were planning a bold and imaginative stroke that they hoped might win the war for them: an invasion of Egypt, followed by an overland attack on the rich British possessions in India. A large expeditionary force had been gathered together in just ten weeks – 35,000 troops in 400 transports, escorted by 13 battleships – and placed under the command of the rising star General Napoleon Bonaparte, with Vice Admiral François-Paul Brueys d'Aigallieri in command of the naval forces. The warships varied widely in their quality and usefulness. At one end of the scale was the mighty 120-gun flagship and Nelson's old opponent at the Battle of Genoa in 1795, the *Sans Culottes*, now renamed for the second time in her career – this time *L'Orient*, in honour of the expedition. She was supported by three of the fine, powerful 80-gun third rates in which the French shipyards specialised and six modern 74s. But, to make up the numbers, the French had also brought out of reserve three very elderly ships: *Guerrier* and *Peuple Souverain*, which dated back to the mid-1750s, and the *Conquérant*, which had been launched as long before as 1746 and was able to carry only 18-pounders on her main gundeck. It was therefore a much less unified force than Nelson's, and this disparity was reflected in the captains who apparently did not get on well together – as one commented, 'You would have thought the ships were commanded by thirteen different nationalities.'[19]

So speedy was the assembly of this force, and so tight the security surrounding it, that no definite intelligence of its true destination reached the British. Various ideas as to the enemy's intentions were put forward: an invasion of Ireland, similar to that planned in conjunction with the Spanish the previous year, was the favourite. Other possible targets included Portugal, which would eliminate Lisbon, and thus rob St Vincent's fleet of its last remaining major base in the area. Some vague rumours that Egypt might be the French objective did circulate, but they were largely discarded as fanciful.[20]

By the time Nelson regained his station off Toulon, the harbour was empty. Sailing on 19 May, the French armada steered south down the east coasts of Corsica and Sardinia, collecting reinforcements from Genoa, Civitavecchia and Ajaccio as it went, and eventually arrived off Malta on 6 June, the day before Nelson rendezvoused with Troubridge and his reinforcements, hundreds of miles away to the north. The island fell without a shot being fired and, having introduced whirlwind reforms and pillaged the rich art collections and treasures of the Knights of Malta, Napoleon sailed again on 19 June, heading for his main objective.

Nelson, meanwhile, was desperately searching for news of his prey. He began by systematically searching all the possible anchorages where the French might have arranged to rendezvous, but without frigates to do the reconnaissance for him, it was a painfully slow process, and it was not until 14 June that he heard definite news that the French had been seen off the north of Sicily. By then he had renewed his contacts with Sir William Hamilton in Naples, sending Troubridge into the port in the *Mutine* to consult with the ambassador and find out what intelligence he could offer. 'If their Fleet is not moored in as strong a Port as Toulon, nothing shall hinder me from attacking them,' Nelson promised. Hamilton had in fact been told, over a fortnight before, of the true destination of the French but, believing that it was a piece of misinformation, he failed to pass it on to Nelson until later, and even then with a disclaimer: 'Bonaparte writes his word that he is gone to the Levant and for that reason I should think he may have taken quite another direction.'[21] On the other hand, news was now coming in of the French attack on Malta, and both Hamilton and Nelson guessed that this might be a prelude to a major attack on Sicily. So Nelson sailed immediately and, to save time, took the squadron through the hazardous Straits of Messina – the famous Scylla and Charybdis of classical mythology. The Revd Cooper Willyams, Chaplain of the *Swiftsure*, who wrote a memoir of the campaign, was disappointed to find that the straits did not live up to the poetic description of their tumultuous waves, like 'a voracious monster roaring for its prey'. Even so, he did note that the current was 'extremely rapid'.[22] Nelson, who had learned his trade among the shallows of the Thames, had shown that he was not afraid of braving navigational hazards with his entire fleet, and this was to be a recurring theme in his subsequent career as an admiral.

By 22 June, the squadron was off the south-east tip of Sicily, Cape Passaro, and early that morning Hardy, in the *Mutine*, encountered a Ragusan merchantman. From her master he learned that the French had taken Malta and that they had sailed on the 16th. No information was given as to their destination but now, by process of elimination, Nelson had become certain that it had to be Egypt. However, before he acted on this hunch, he decided to consult with his key colleagues, and so at 7 a.m. he summoned Saumarez, Troubridge, Darby and Ball to the flagship, and also invited Berry to the meeting. When they arrived, they were presented with a set of questions by Nelson designed to get their support for an immediate voyage to Egypt. His questions, and their replies, have survived, and they provide a striking vignette of his consultative style.[23] Berry was unequivocal in his support: 'I am clearly of the opinion that the French armament are steering for Alexandria and that it would be most advisable to pursue them immediately.' Saumarez was equally decisive, as was Troubridge, who pointed out that it would be best to try to overtake them before they reached Alexandria. Ball and Darby were a little more circumspect but both agreed that, as Darby wrote, 'it is most probable they are gone to the eastward'.

As the discussions continued, reports were coming in to the *Vanguard* of sightings of strange sails. At 6.46 a.m., just before the captains were summoned, the *Leander* had signalled 'Strange ships are frigates', but the only answer she received was a recall. Again, at 8.29, she signalled 'Ships seen are frigates' but, by now, Nelson and his colleagues had made their decision, and all their attention was focused on getting the squadron to Alexandria as fast as possible. It is easy to see how this happened: the information gathered by Hardy suggested that the French were days ahead of them to the east, and so it would have been a further waste of time to wait while the strange sails were investigated. In fact, however, the Ragusan's intelligence had been wrong in one important respect: the French had sailed from Malta on the 19th, not the 16th, and so the sails sighted by the *Leander* had been those of Brueys's frigate screen. If Nelson's frigates had still been with him, they would no doubt have found the French armada, and the fleet battle which Nelson had envisaged in his memorandum of 18 June would have been fought off Cape Passaro on 22 June. It is one of the great 'what-ifs' of history. If Napoleon had been captured or killed at that stage of the campaign, what different course might the war have taken?

Six days later, on 28 June, the British squadron came in sight of Alexandria to find the harbour full of ships – but none of them French. Hardy had been sent on in the *Mutine* to warn the Egyptians of the French approach, but he rejoined Nelson on the 29th with the news that there was no trace of the enemy. Nelson's reaction demonstrated both the strain that he was under – and his inexperience. First, he drafted a long and detailed letter to St Vincent defending his decision to go to Egypt. He showed it to Ball, who wisely advised him not to send it – 'I should recommend a friend never to begin a defence of his conduct before he is accused of error,'[24] – but Nelson sent it anyway. More important, he also gave orders to sail immediately for Turkey in a desperate search for the French. Little more than 24 hours after he had left, Bonaparte's armada came into sight and began preparations for a landing.

It was the third near-miss of the campaign, and for this one Nelson must bear full responsibility. Having made his decision to sail east, based on the best intelligence available to him, he should have taken time to think through more carefully what might have happened. It seems extraordinary that he does not appear to have considered that the French might be behind, rather than in front of, him. His natural impetuousness, which had served him so well at Cape St Vincent and elsewhere, had, on this occasion, led him into a serious error. Although he never discussed this particular mistake in any of his correspondence, it is clear that he did learn his lesson – as we shall see, when faced with a very similar situation in the great campaign of 1805, he was able to curb his impatience and wait until he had gathered all available information before making his decision.

For now, however, he was groping in the dark, checking every possibility. It is worth reminding ourselves that this was his first experience of independent command, and nothing seemed to be going his way. The few letters he wrote at this time show the incredible strain he was under: the long, rambling, self-justifying letter to St Vincent ended: 'However erroneous my judgement may be I feel conscious of my honest intentions which I hope will bear me up under the greatest misfortune that could happen to me as an Officer – that of Your Lordship's thinking me wrong.' To Hamilton he wrote, 'You will I am sure and so will our Country easily conceive what has passed in my anxious mind.'[25] That letter was written from Syracuse in Sicily, where he eventually took the squadron on 20 July to replenish their water and supplies. After four days' respite he was off again to Greece, and it was there, on 28 July, that he began, at long last, to get definite information: the Turkish authorities had learned of the French invasion of Egypt. Having made a very fast passage, the squadron arrived off Alexandria on the 31st to find the harbour crammed with shipping and the French tricolour flying.

'IT WAS ABSOLUTELY IRRESISTIBLE': THE BATTLE

Arriving off the port on 1 July, the French had begun their landings the following day: hearing that Nelson's squadron had been sighted, they were anxious to get their soldiers ashore as soon as possible. Although the operation was a shambles, it met with little resistance, and within 24 hours Alexandria was in French hands. Three weeks later, on 21 July, while Nelson was watering at Syracuse, Napoleon decisively defeated the Mamelukes at the Battle of the Pyramids and entered Cairo shortly afterwards. So, by the time Nelson finally returned to Egypt, the country was already effectively under French control.

Having covered the landings at Alexandria, Admiral Brueys began to consider where he should take his fleet.[26] Alexandria itself, with its narrow entrances, could only be entered by the larger warships, especially *L'Orient*, if they had first been lightened, and even then only in favourable weather conditions. Brueys favoured retiring to Corfu, from where he could cover the army from any British attack, but Bonaparte wanted to keep the fleet close to him and so in the end, really as a compromise, they agreed on the anchorage at Aboukir Bay, some 15 miles to the east of Alexandria. There, Brueys anchored his ships in a defensive line, with its head covered by the rocks and shoals surrounding a small island at the mouth of the bay. In January 1782, he had been a lieutenant in the French fleet under the Compte de Grasse at the Battle of St Kitts, when Nelson's mentor, Samuel Hood, had repulsed a determined French attack on his battleline, which he had anchored so that its van and rear could not be turned. It would seem that Brueys planned to copy this exploit, but Hood's success had been based on his careful placing of his ships, and in this Brueys was much less skilful than his model. To begin with, he placed his ships too far apart – some 120 yards. This meant that they could not assist each other with covering fire, and the gaps were big enough for enemy ships to slip through. The ends of his line were still exposed and, when a member of his staff, Captain Alexandre-Henri Lachadenède, pointed out this weakness and suggested covering the head and tail of the line with troopships from the convoy, Brueys agreed but did nothing about it. He did take the step of arming the island – but only with two mortars and four 6-pounder cannon, which were scarcely an effective defence. He placed his three oldest and weakest ships – *Guerriere*, *Peuple Souverain* and *Conquérant* – at the head of the line, believing that the shoals and rocks would deter the British from attacking that end. In the centre, he placed his huge flagship, supported by the 80-gunners *Franklin* and *Tonnant*, but even this step weakened, rather than strengthened, his line. Because these ships drew more water than the standard 74s, the whole line had to be placed further out from the protecting shoals – thus leaving enough space inshore for the lighter-draft British battleships to manoeuvre.

Nor were Brueys' problems due only to his own faulty planning. His ships were short of men – most had been undermanned when they sailed from Toulon and Bonaparte had taken others as reinforcements for his army. Additionally, roaming bands of Egyptians were attacking any French party that went ashore – for example, for water – and so large armed parties had been landed on the nearby beaches, a long row away from the ships. Michelle Battesti has calculated that, as a result, some of the French crews that fought in the battle were at one-third strength.[27] Finally, the sailors were short of food and suffering from the heat and dysentery – indeed, Brueys himself was unwell. He wrote on 20 July, 'I am not enjoying good health . . . Colic, headaches and a form of dysentery have reduced me to extreme weakness.'[28]

None of these weaknesses were immediately apparent, however, to the British when they finally sighted their quarry in the early afternoon of 1 August. At first, the reports from the advance ships had been disappointing – although Alexandria was full of French ships it was clear that the battlefleet was not present. Then, at last, at about 2.45 p.m., the *Zealous*, scouting to the east, saw the masts and yards in Aboukir Bay and signalled 'Sixteen sail of the line at anchor.' At that moment, the squadron was scattered, *Alexander* and *Swiftsure* still reconnoitring Alexandria and Troubridge's *Culloden* some 7 miles astern, towing a prize ship captured some days before. Sunset was only about four hours away and the enemy were in an apparently strong position, within a bay for which Nelson himself had no accurate charts. The prudent course of action would have been to gather his forces, carry out a careful reconnaissance and then attack the following morning. Some admirals, no doubt, might even have contented themselves with establishing a close blockade of the Egyptian coast.

Clearly, neither of these options even entered Nelson's head. Within minutes of receiving the *Zealous*'s report, he had recalled his outlying ships while with the rest of his force he sailed headlong for Aboukir. As he did so, he made three operational signals: 'Prepare for anchoring with springs and sheet cable taken in at the stern port', 'Attack the enemy's van and centre' and 'Form line of battle as most convenient.' The order to prepare to anchor by the stern was particularly significant. As we have seen, he had already indicated as early as 8 June that he intended to do this if the enemy was discovered at anchor, and so his captains had been given time to prepare for such an eventuality. This is an important consideration: ships were not normally fitted for stern anchoring, and so special arrangements had to be made in advance – complicated work that could not have been done in the few hours remaining before the battle. Hence, it seems fair to assume that the ships had already made most of the necessary preparations. This emphasises the point that one of the reasons Nelson was able to attack at once was that he had anticipated the conditions in which such an attack would be made. The importance of this sort of detailed preparation is a recurring theme in Nelson's story.

As his leading ships passed the island at the mouth of the bay, still with all possible sail set, rather than under 'fighting sail' as was usual, Nelson ordered signal number 16 to be hoisted, 'Engage the Enemy More Closely.' In fact none of his ships was yet in range, but it was not just an operational order – he was also using it almost as a battle-cry, reminding his captains of the sort of action he wanted. It was of course the maxim he had been taught in the *Lowestoffe*, by William Locker, the pupil of Hawke – and so in that signal can be seen the long and brilliant inheritance on which Nelson and his comrades were building as they sailed headlong into Aboukir Bay.

Seeing the entrance beginning to open up to starboard of him, Nelson now began to issue verbal orders to adjust his rapidly forming battleline. Hailing Hood in the *Zealous*, he asked if he thought they had advanced far enough to the east to be clear of the shoals. Hood replied that if he might have the honour of leading the fleet he would keep the lead going and sound his way in. 'You have my leave and I wish you success!' shouted Nelson and took off his hat in salute. Hood tried to return the gesture but the wind caught his hat and blew it overboard. 'Never mind, Webley,' he told his first lieutenant. 'There it goes for luck! Put the helm up and make sail!'[29] As the *Zealous*, followed by Thomas Foley's *Goliath*, began to round the island, Ralph Miller tried to slip the *Theseus* into the line behind them but, as he passed the *Vanguard*, Berry hailed him and said that Nelson wished him to be his next ahead. So Miller had to let James Saumarez's *Orion* and Davidge Gould's *Audacious* pass him before taking his place. This ad hoc forming of the line of battle, ships jostling each other for a position in the lead like schoolboys in a tuck-shop queue, was far removed from the fussy precision of Hotham's over-cautious behaviour in the opening moves at Hyères.

Meanwhile, on board the *L'Orient*, Brueys was being given conflicting advice. Apparently, despite all his preparations, his first impulse when the British were sighted was to set sail and give battle under way, and in this he was supported by one of his most effective subordinates, Vice Amiral Armand-Simon-Marie Blanquet de Chayala. However, his more cautious chief of staff, Vice Amiral Honoré-Joseph-Antoine Ganteaume, pointed out that their crews were so weakened, because of disease and the large numbers ashore, that it was safer to stay where they were.[30] In effect, he did very little to prepare for the battle: the frigates were ordered to send men on board the battleships to reinforce their depleted crews, and the battleships themselves to fit springs on their anchor cables, so that they could be turned to direct their broadsides.

By 6 p.m., the *Zealous* and *Goliath* were almost within range of the French, still vying for the place of honour at the head of the line, until Hood told Webley to shorten sail and let Foley take the lead. As we have seen, Nelson had earlier ordered a concentration on the van and centre of the enemy and so, without realising it, his leading ships were aiming for the weakest links in Brueys' line. As they came within gunshot, Foley remarked to the Master of the *Goliath* that he wished he could get inside the leading French ship, since he expected she would be unprepared on that side.[31] Spotting the *Guerrier's* anchor buoy 240 yards ahead of her, they realised that there was indeed room for a very well-handled ship to get through and decided to risk it. Foley had intended to fetch up on his opponent's port side, but anchoring by the stern was a very difficult manoeuvre at the best of times and, in the heat of action, with his broadsides already sweeping the Frenchman's decks, Foley misjudged the moment for letting go and fetched up, instead, alongside the *Conquérant*. Seeing what had happened, Hood dropped his anchor at once and brought the *Zealous* alongside the *Guerrier*, pouring in another murderous broadside as he did so. Within 7 minutes, her foremast came tumbling down, just as the sun set, raising cheers from the approaching British ships. Right at the outset, therefore, the British had won a decided moral advantage. (See plan on p. 196.)

One by one, the British ships crashed into action, shortening sail as they approached, dropping their anchors and letting fly with their first, doubleshotted broadsides – a superb achievement of collective seamanship. It has been calculated that only 40 minutes elapsed between the moment the French opened fire and the arrival of the seventh British ship, and the last in the first 'wave', the *Minotaur*.[32] Subjected to these repeated hammer blows, the French van fought back with extraordinary courage – Hood later reported that he hailed the *Conquérant* twenty times before he could get her captain to surrender. But they were completely overwhelmed and outgunned, and by 9 p.m. most of them had surrendered or drifted out of the line. The hailstorm of fire which they had to endure was intensified by the fact that when Nelson arrived in the *Vanguard*, he decided that the waters inshore of the French line were becoming too crowded, and so he led the rest of his ships down the outside of the line, thus doubling on the van. Darkness had fallen and it is clear from a number of accounts that this doubling led to a number of instances of 'friendly fire'. It seems Nelson learned from this experience, for some years later, in February 1804, when another night action seemed likely, he issued this general order to his captains: 'Lord Nelson has no doubt but that great attention will be paid that none but the Ships of the Enemy will be fired into, for which purpose it is recommended not only to be careful that the Signal Lights for knowing each other are clear and well placed on the Signal staff, but also that the Ship should be hailed if there is the smallest doubt of her being a British Ship.'[33] It is arguable, therefore, that he might have done better to have started his attack at a point further down the French line. On the other hand, by taking the French van ships between two fires in this way, he ensured their early collapse.

By about 8 p.m. the only British ship missing was the *Culloden*: in his eagerness to get into battle, Troubridge sailed too close to the rocks surrounding the island and ran his ship aground. Despite repeated attempts, and the assistance of Hardy in the *Mutine*, he was unable to get her afloat until the following day. As the last ships came into action, the British attack began to reach down to the French centre, and here the battle was more evenly matched and thus more protracted. The *Bellerophon* found herself up against the mighty *L'Orient* and was driven out of the battle a dismasted wreck. But her place was taken by the late arrivals *Alexander* and *Swiftsure*, and another fierce gun battle ensued. Meanwhile, the *Peuple Souverain* had drifted out of the line, leaving a large gap into which Thomas Thompson neatly inserted the little *Leander* – right across the bows of the powerful 80-gunner *Franklin*. From there he could rake his much larger opponent

A relic of L'Orient. *Divers from Frank Goddio's team raise a carronade from the wreck of the great French flagship, August 1999.*

without receiving any serious fire in return. The French line was being gradually rolled up and, with the wind blowing straight down the line, there was little that they could do to assist each other. To add to their discomfiture, a raging fire broke out on board the *L'Orient*. Before long, it had taken such a hold that it was clear the flagship was doomed. A number of the French ships astern of her, the *Tonnant*, *Heureux* and *Mercure*, cut their anchor cables to get clear of the inevitable explosion, thus opening more gaps in the French line. Eventually, at about 10 p.m., her magazines detonated – first the smaller one amidships, which blew off her stern and drove her forwards in the water, and then the larger grand magazine, which threw shattered pieces of her hull, and even full-sized cannon, hundreds of yards through the air. Two hundred years later nautical archaeologist Frank Goddio and his team found her massive rudder and part of her midships section surrounded by a wide-flung debris field. They also found the discarded anchors of the ships that had scrambled to get out of the way of the devastation.[34]

Ships very rarely blew up in action in those days, and the horrific fire followed by the earth-shaking double explosion – so loud, we are told, that it was heard in Alexandria 15 miles away – profoundly shocked all those who witnessed it. So much so, that there was apparently a short lull in the battle, perhaps lasting as much as 10 minutes. Among the horrified onlookers was Nelson – by now wearing a bloody bandage around his head. Two hours earlier, he had been struck on the head by a piece of 'langridge' – a particularly nasty form of anti-personnel shot

Nelson wounded at the Nile. *The wounded Nelson comes on deck to view the burning of the French flagship,* L'Orient.

consisting of loose bolts, nails, and other pieces of scrap metal tied together in a bag and fired at close quarters from a cannon. It carved a slice of flesh from his forehead, baring his skull for more than an inch, and sent him reeling into Berry's arms. Blinded by the blood, and in intense pain, he thought for a while it was a death wound, sent his remembrances to Frances and, in a typical gesture, asked that Thomas Louis of the *Minotaur* should be sent for, so that he could thank him for the support his ship had given him in the early stages of the battle. When, eventually, Surgeon Michael Jefferson was able to inspect the wound more closely – Nelson insisted on waiting his turn in the line of wounded – it became clear that the wound was not life-threatening. So he sent for his secretary, John Campbell, intending to begin his victory dispatch, but Campbell, wounded himself and unnerved by the sight of his bleeding Admiral, was unable to write. The Chaplain, Stephen Comyn, was sent for but, in the end, Nelson began to pen the dispatch himself. The document now in the British Library is a duplicate in Nelson's own hand – as we shall see, the original was lost – and so we are not able to assess how much of it he was actually able to write. It is probable that he simply jotted down some notes that formed the basis of the final version. Even so, there can be few other times in history when a victory dispatch was started before the battle it celebrated was even over.

Despite the bravado of this gesture it is quite clear that the wound was both very painful and physically disabling. Having been fetched on deck briefly to watch *L'Orient* burn and explode, Nelson played little further part in the battle that night, which indicates that he was more prostrated by the blow than the traditional stories suggest. It is hard to imagine that he would have stayed below for so long unless he was seriously incapacitated. Indeed, some months later he told Lord Howe, 'Had I not been wounded and stone blind there cannot be a doubt but that every Ship would have been in our possession.' This assessment was independently supported by one of his opponents: commenting on the British failure to follow up their success with the same aggression as their initial attack, Captain Lachadenède wrote: 'I presume that Nelson, having been wounded and no longer in the role of commander, the English captains lacked that ensemble, that concert and that united view of command so necessary for seizing an opportunity rapidly.'[35]

Nonetheless, the scale of his victory was already impressive, and it was about to be made even more complete. When dawn broke at about 4 a.m. on the 2nd a second battle began at the southern end of the French line, involving some ships of the French rearguard, and others from the centre that had drifted in that direction to get out of the way of the danger zone surrounding *L'Orient*. However, both sides were exhausted, and the fighting was spasmodic and confused. Nelson, by now partially recovered, began to urge some of his ships to move on down the line and take on the French rear, and the *Zealous*, *Goliath* and *Theseus* followed his orders. As a result of this move, three more French ships were taken or destroyed, but only after heroic defences: *Tonnant*'s captain, Abel-Nicholas Dupetit-Thouars, appallingly wounded, eventually bled to death exhorting his crew, 'Ne vous rendez jamais!' The last ship to surrender was the *Mercure*, at 8 a.m.

Meanwhile, the commander of the French rear, Contre Amiral Pierre de Villeneuve, had watched the battle rolling inexorably towards him, pinned in position by the wind, which was still blowing straight down the French line. He was much criticised for his inaction at the time, and even the latest French historian of the battle, Michelle Battesti, believes that his behaviour was symptomatic of 'a persistent malaise that characterised the French navy over a long period'.[36] Eventually, however, he did manage to extricate his own ship, the *Guillaume Tell* and the *Généreux*, and to escape, together with two frigates. He left behind him a scene of utter destruction: eleven French battleships and two frigates captured or destroyed. The human cost was commensurate: there were over 3,000 French casualties and, because of the destruction of *L'Orient*, the division between killed and wounded was almost equal. Usually in a battle of that period, the wounded were three times the number of killed. Casualties among senior officers had been particularly high: one admiral and four captains killed; one admiral and seven captains wounded. The British, by contrast, had lost none of their ships, although a number were very badly damaged, and had suffered 218 killed and 617 wounded. It was the most complete and decisive victory in the age of sail.

Nelson had no doubts at all about how it had been achieved. In his victory dispatch to St Vincent, which he finally finished on 3 August, he wrote warmly: 'Nothing could withstand the Squadron Your Lordship did me the honour to place under my command. Their high state of discipline is well known to you and the judgement of the Captains together with their valour and that of the Officers and Men of every description, it was absolutely irresistible.'[37] And, in a private letter to Admiral Sir Roger Curtis, some weeks later, he used a phrase to describe his relationship with his colleagues that has become a metaphor for his particular style of leadership. He spoke of 'the honour of commanding the finest Squadron that ever graced the Ocean', and then went on: 'We were, and are, & I trust ever will be a band of Brothers, never do I believe, did every individual in a fleet before exert themselves to their Utmost, were I to praise one more than another I should reproach myself.'[38]

His victory dispatch also began with the resounding phrase, 'Almighty God has blessed his Majesty's Arms in the late Battle by a great Victory over the Fleet of the Enemy' – as always, Nelson knew how to catch the eye of the reading public. In an age when most battle reports were dry, formal documents full of facts and statistics, his bristle with excitement and colour. Nor was the opening evocation of God an empty sentiment: the day before he completed his dispatch, he used the same words in a short memorandum to his captains informing them that he intended 'returning Public Thanksgiving for the [victory] at two o'clock this day and he recommends every ship doing the same as soon as convenient'.[39]

The original dispatch was carried to Lord St Vincent by Berry, who took passage with Thompson in the *Leander*, but she was captured on 18 August by the *Généreux*, one of the French fugitives from the battle. As was customary, the dispatch was thrown overboard in a weighted bag to prevent it falling into enemy hands, and Berry had to wait to be exchanged before he could continue his journey to England to carry the news verbally. However, Nelson had sent his

---

'THE BAND OF BROTHERS'

Nelson used this phrase on a number of occasions to describe the remarkably close and friendly relationship that existed between him and the captains who served under his command at the Battle of the Nile on 1 August 1798. It is a quotation from the famous Agincourt speech in his favourite Shakespeare play, *Henry V*. By extension, it has come to encompass all those officers who were particularly close to Nelson or who served with him in his battles, and thus has become a metaphor for his distinctively 'collegiate' style of leadership – a style that set him apart from most other admirals of his time. It has also become part of the 'Nelson Legend' and so has tended to obscure the often quite subtle ways in which his professional relationships actually worked.

In fact, the phrase is most apt when applied to the original Nile captains. They were a particularly close-knit team even before they came under Nelson's command, and the trust and instinctive understanding that existed between them was therefore unique, and it was not repeated to quite the same degree in any other fleet that Nelson commanded.

Moreover, it is now clear that not all his captains were equally close to Nelson. During the Nile campaign, he tended to consult most often with Troubridge, Saumarez (his second-in-command) and Ball, and then transmitted his ideas to the rest of the captains through written orders. Similarly, on the eve of Copenhagen he dined with close friends such as Hardy, Foley and Fremantle and then stayed up for most of the night dictating his orders to the remainder of his subordinates.

Nor was the composition of the inner circle static. Of the original Nile 'band', only Hardy served with Nelson in all his battles. Some former close colleagues – such as Berry or Troubridge – became physically separated or estranged. New men – such as Keats or Blackwood – joined the group. So we can now see that, unsurprisingly, Nelson's pattern of relationships was rather more complex and fluid than the older accounts of his life have suggested.

---

former flag lieutenant, now newly promoted to commander, Thomas Bladen Capel, in the *Mutine* to Naples with a duplicate dispatch. Having reached Naples on 4 September, where he enjoyed a rapturous reception, Capel returned home overland, finally reaching London on 2 October.

'WE ARE OVERWHELMED WITH KINDNESS': THE AFTERMATH OF VICTORY

Berry's departure with the dispatch meant that Nelson had to find a new captain for the *Vanguard*. Throughout the long chase, Thomas Hardy's little *Mutine* had done all the work usually assigned to the frigates, and Hardy himself had performed a number of special missions – always with the utmost efficiency. So now he got the all-important step to post captain – and command of the flagship. Hardy was a much better seaman and ship administrator than Berry. He was also more phlegmatic and calm and, in him, Nelson found his perfect match. He once asked Hardy why they got on so well, and the big Dorsetman put it down to his own flexibility: when Nelson wished to play the captain, Hardy was content to be his first lieutenant; but

Captain Thomas Hardy. The portrait on which this miniature was based was painted c. 1800, and it gives an excellent impression of Hardy at the time he was serving with Nelson.

he was always ready to return to his role of captain when Nelson wished to be an admiral again. Hardy later recorded a most moving example of their closeness and compatibility. After Nelson's death, when he was pacing the quarterdeck alone, he noticed that, after years of walking the deck together, he had unconsciously shortened his long, six-footer's stride to match that of his shorter companion.

As Berry and Capel set off, Nelson returned to his desk work. Short notes went to his captains: on 3 August, Henry Darby of the shattered *Bellerophon* was told, 'I grieve for the loss of your brave fellows but look at our glorious Victory.' There was the matter of prize money to be arranged. Nelson told his eldest brother Maurice: 'The fleet has appointed Davison[40] <u>sole</u> agent for the Ships capt'd at the battle of the Nile, whatever assistance you may give Davison or whatever he may wish to serve you in, I beg that I may never be considered directly or indirectly As having anything to do with the agency.' As a Clerk in the Navy Office, Maurice had expected to be appointed the prize agent himself, and he complained. Nelson's characteristic reply has recently been discovered: 'I am truly sorry you should think I neglected you abt: the Agency but it was no more in my power to name an agent than an Emperor. All the Captains had Brothers, Cousins or friends, as all agreed this could not be done, they agreed for me to name a Man who I thought could serve them best.'

There was a letter to the Governor of Bombay announcing the victory. 'Bonaparte had never yet to contend with an English Officer and I shall endeavour to make him respect us,' he told him. And he was as conscious as ever of the value of the public gesture. The sword of Amiral Blanquet of the *Franklin* was sent to the Lord Mayor of London with the request that he would accept it 'as a remembrance that Britannia still rules the waves'.[41] London appreciated the gift, and the sword was proudly displayed in the Guildhall.[42]

Most of Nelson's letters at this time mention his health. Superficially his head wound was healing fast, but the after-effects were making him feel low and depressed. Hood was told on 11 August, 'I am so unwell that I can hardly get thro' the fatigue of refitting the Squadron & Prizes.' And writing to Sir William Hamilton to tell him of the victory, and to ask that the facilities of the naval dockyard at Naples be put at his disposal to repair his most heavily damaged ships, he said, 'my head is so indifferent that I can scarcely scrawl this letter'. Replying, on 8 September, Hamilton first told his friend of the ecstatic response to the news of the victory in Naples, adding: 'You may well conceive, my dear sir, how happy Emma and I are in the reflection that it is you, Nelson, our bosom friend that has done such wonderous good in having humbl'd these proud robbers and vain boasters.' He ended by warmly inviting Nelson to stay at his house when he came to Naples, to 'repose the few wearied limbs you have left', and promising that Emma would look after him. So it was that when he arrived at Naples on 22 September, Nelson went ashore to stay at the Palazzo Sessa.[43]

In view of what was to happen as a result of his involvement with Naples, it is worth emphasising at this point that, in the summer of 1798, the Kingdom of Naples and Sicily was Britain's only major ally in the Mediterranean. As well as providing a secure base for operations against the French in the Italian peninsula, it possessed the only naval dockyard then available to the British east of Gibraltar. Additionally, Sicily was a good source of supplies. So there were sound strategic reasons for going to Naples, as well as personal ones. When Nelson's ships arrived, they received a rapturous welcome and, for really the first time, he and his men were able to appreciate the wide-flung effects of their stunning victory. As he told Sir Roger Curtis, 'We are overwhelmed with kindness and an Artery of poetry is let loose.' A week later, his fortieth birthday was the occasion for a huge and lavish celebration, both of him and of the victory at the Nile. His first reaction to such extravagance was characteristic: 'Naples is a dangerous place,' he told Lord St Vincent.[44]

His arrival at Naples coincided with an abrupt change of gear, both in the Mediterranean and in the wider war. As we have noted, up to the Battle of the Nile the British had had a single objective: to seek out and destroy the French fleet. Now that Nelson had so completely achieved the objective, the strategic situation, and thus his own role, was transformed. The virtual elimination of the French fleet meant that the Mediterranean effectively became a British lake, and so a wide range of new opportunities presented themselves for Britain and her allies to go onto the offensive. First, there was the blockade of Egypt, to ensure that supplies and reinforcements did not reach Napoleon. Then news came that the Maltese had rebelled against their new French overlords, and so the opportunity arose to recapture the island. Additionally, plans were discussed for an attack on the Spanish island of Minorca, with its superb harbour and dockyard facilities at Port Mahon. And, in Naples, Nelson's newly acquired status as victor enabled him to persuade a hesitant King Ferdinand and his Ministers to contemplate an invasion of northern Italy.

At first, everything still seemed to be going Nelson's way. Having refitted his ships at Naples, he paid a brief visit to Malta in late October, where he found that the Maltese, armed and assisted by Saumarez on his way down the Mediterranean with the prizes captured at the Nile, had already driven the French within the massively defended citadel-capital of Valetta and had now settled down for a long siege. Nelson instituted a blockade by a small squadron under the command of Alexander Ball and then returned to Naples, where preparations were already under way for an attack on Leghorn (Livorno). A Neapolitan army of 5,000 men was escorted by some of Nelson's Nile veterans, augmented by ships of a Portuguese squadron under Admiral de Niza, and Leghorn surrendered on 29 November, without a shot fired, after the troops had been successfully landed (despite a gale) to take possession of the town gates and mole head battery. Nelson's main preoccupation was with the posturing Neapolitan General Naselli who, he reported, clearly considered him 'as a nothing, as a Master of Transport', and who refused to allow Nelson to be a joint signatory to the summons to the port until forced to do so by the civilian negotiators. He was also concerned about the terms of the capitulation, which spoke of Leghorn as being neutral. Nelson maintained this was impossible, since French privateers had been operating out of the port only 24 hours before the allied attack, and his view prevailed.[45]

Before he had set off from Naples, the news arrived of the first British reactions to the victory at the Nile, and Nelson learned that he had been created a peer – but only as a baron, the lowest rank possible. His family and friends were outraged, and he was bitterly disappointed. St Vincent had been made an earl for a much less decisive victory, and most people had expected that Nelson would be given a viscountcy, as Duncan had following the Battle of Camperdown. The official reason given was that Nelson was not a full commander-in-chief, but a subordinate admiral; but we now know that he was, at least in part, the author of his own misfortune. The first impulse of both Pitt and Spencer had indeed been to recommend him for a viscountcy; but when they raised the matter with the King, George III, they found he had remembered that following the Battle of Cape St Vincent Nelson had asked not to be given a baronetcy, on the grounds that he was not wealthy enough to support a title. 'This', wrote the King, 'puts his getting a peerage quite out of the question but it is a reason that he should have a handsome pension settled on him.'[46] Spencer was therefore forced to do some fancy footwork and ended up proposing a barony and a pension as a compromise, to which the King agreed. Unfortunately, however, rumours of a likely viscountcy had already begun to circulate and so, when the lesser award was announced, everyone – Nelson included – suspected a conspiracy. It soured what should have been a triumphant moment for him and added to a growing sense he was nursing that he was not properly appreciated back at home. The conspiracy theory continued to flourish in most Nelson biographies until the correspondence between Spencer and the King was discovered by Terry Coleman in 2003.[47]

The apparent meanness of the British response was thrown into sharp relief by the generosity of other countries. The Sultan of Turkey sent a rich package of gifts, including the famous 'chelengk', or plume of triumph, made from diamonds, which Nelson immediately started wearing in his uniform hat, to the amusement of some of his followers. The Tsar of Russia presented him with a jewelled miniature of himself, receiving in reply one of Nelson's characteristically warm-hearted letters, sprinkled liberally with enthusiastic capitals: 'The Invaluable Gift of Your Portrait shall I assure you be cherish'd as the dearest drop of my blood and my constant prayers shall never cease being offered to the Almighty for your Imperial Majestys health and success against the Common Enemy by Your Majestys Most Devoted & faithful Servant.'[48]

Meanwhile, the main Neapolitan army under the Austrian General Mack had taken Rome and, on the same day that Leghorn surrendered, King Ferdinand entered Rome in triumph. But this marked the high point of the allied success. The smaller, but much better-organised, French armies struck back, and within days Ferdinand was in ignominious retreat to Naples. Nor did he stop there: panic seized him and his court and, instead of making a stand, they decided to flee to their second capital of Palermo in Sicily. Luckily for them, Nelson had returned to Naples with his ships on 5 December, and he conducted a model evacuation, keeping his nerve and bolstering the shattered nerves of the Neapolitans with a series of hurriedly scribbled but reassuring notes, which have recently been discovered. 'Every part of the embarkation shall go on,' he told the Prime Minister of Naples, Sir John Acton, firmly, 'we must trust at all times in Gods providential care, all will be well I have no doubt and all caution shall be taken which my Judgement shall suggest.'[49] Despite fierce storms, the passage was made successfully – although one of the royal princes, a sickly lad, died during the voyage – and, on 26 December, the King and his family landed safely at Palermo, while, in Naples, the victorious French, and their Neapolitan supporters, triumphantly proclaimed the Parthenopean Republic.

'I HAVE HAD NOT ONE EASY MOMENT': NELSON FALTERS

Nelson's arrival at Palermo marked the beginning of a strange and strained period in his life when he often behaved oddly and out of character. It also marked the beginning of the most controversial period in his career: even in his lifetime he was criticised for the degree to which he allowed himself to become enmeshed in the internal politics of Naples in 1799, and the controversy has continued ever since – indeed, with the advent of the Trafalgar bicentenary, it has recently broken out afresh.

The controversy centres on two incidents that occurred in June 1799, when Nelson took his fleet to Naples in support of the closing stages of the very bloody and violent counter-revolution that ended with the reinstatement of King Ferdinand on his throne. First, there was the trial and summary execution of one of the key figures of the short-lived Parthenopean Republic, Commodore Francesco Carraciolo. The death sentence was not in itself wrong: Carraciolo, an officer of the former Neapolitan Royal Navy, had served against his sovereign in the civil war and so had clearly committed treason. But the speed, and apparent callousness with which his trial was conducted, under Nelson's aegis, and the sentence of death carried out, caused unease at the time and still casts a shadow over Nelson's reputation today. It shows the darker side of the ruthlessness that gained him some of his most notable successes.

Second, there was the question of the fate of a number of the key republicans who surrendered in the belief that they would be allowed passage to France. Instead, they found themselves imprisoned in ships guarded by Nelson's fleet and about a hundred of them were eventually handed over to the royalists for brutal execution. Here, the issues are much more complex. Nelson always maintained that he believed that their surrender was unconditional and their fate was therefore a matter for the King of Naples to decide. He and his men played no part in the ensuing bloodbath – indeed there is evidence that throughout the crisis, he kept his men firmly in check and punished any who used undue force. But his presence, along with his fleet, in support of King Ferdinand's savage revenge, left an unpleasant memory in Naples that has never been erased. A more experienced admiral would have remained detached from the internal affairs of a foreign state.

There is also continuing controversy over the way in which he dealt with the wider affairs of the Mediterranean theatre. For example, at one stage he disobeyed a direct order from the Commander-in-Chief, Admiral Lord Keith (who replaced the ailing St Vincent in June 1799), to concentrate his ships to assist in countering a threat to Minorca from the French Brest fleet, which entered the Mediterranean in the summer of 1799 in an attempt to win back the command of the sea lost at the Nile. For this he was censured by the Admiralty: 'their Lordships do not, therefore, from any information now before them, see sufficient reason to justify your having disobeyed the orders you had received from your commanding officer.' Eventually, in June 1800, he was recalled to Britain, effectively in disgrace.

From the professional point of view, the most notable change in Nelson's behaviour was that, between January 1799 and July 1800, when he finally returned home, he spent only eight months at sea – for the remaining eleven he remained fixed at Palermo and, most often, on shore: when there was no British warship in the port, his flag was flown in a transport ship.[50] During his first extended period ashore, between December 1798 and May 1799, at least three important campaigns were under way: in Malta, as we have already seen; in Syria, where Sir Sidney Smith was helping the defenders of Acre in Palestine to hold up the advance of Bonaparte's army; and in Naples. In each case, Nelson sent ships and supplies and expressions of support – but during the first half of 1799, he never once visited any of these important locations in person. Such a 'hands-off' approach is so utterly uncharacteristic that it is clear evidence that something was wrong.

Additionally, his pride in his own achievements, always a strong trait, became decidedly more marked, and sometimes even positively over the top. He has often been described as a vain man but, interestingly, most of the stories told of him to justify such a judgement date from this period – later in his career, as we shall see, he usually displayed a more becoming modesty. In 1799–1800, however, he often appeared at functions festooned in his awards and decorations and speaking

---

THE NAPLES CONTROVERSY

The Neapolitan civil war, and the restoration of the monarchy, falls outside the scope of this book and so the account given here is necessarily very brief. However, the intricate political debate has been well-rehearsed recently in a number of important works.

For a modern expression of the contrary view, see Terry Coleman, who devotes a significant portion of his biography *Nelson: the man and the legend* to the subject, including an appendix giving a most useful short summary of the literature and manuscript sources.

For a modern defence of Nelson, see Andrew Lambert's biography *Nelson: Britannia's God of War*.

The various accounts since 1799 have been listed and most ably analysed and assessed by Marianne Czisnik in her two articles in *The Trafalgar Chronicle* (see bibliography for details).

However, by far the best, and most balanced, analysis of the whole affair has just appeared as this book goes to press: Roger Knight's magisterial biography of Nelson, *The Pursuit of Victory*.

---

vaingloriously of his own achievements – it was at this time that General Sir John Moore famously described him as 'more like a Prince of the Opera than the conqueror of the Nile'.[51] Even in the brief periods when he was at sea, this parading continued. Miss Cornelia Knight noted the contents of his cabin in 1800: 'A carving in wood of an immense three-coloured plume of feathers which ornamented the cap of the figure of William Tell when that ship struck to the Foudroyant; four muskets taken on board the San Josef and the flagstaff of L'Orient saved from the flames

Rear Admiral Lord Nelson, c. 1799.
Grignion captures Nelson in a relaxed and
informal mood during one of his many
periods ashore in Palermo.

Sir William and Lady Hamilton. The cultured connoisseur-ambassador and his beautiful wife captured by Grignion (right) and Johann Schmidt (left). The portrait of Emma was Nelson's favourite – he called it his 'guardian angel' and it hung in all his flagships from 1801 to 1805.

when that ship was blown up.'[52] The great cabin of the *Victory* was never decorated in this self-aggrandising way – but by then Nelson had recovered from the mysterious malaise of insecurity that afflicted him in 1799 and 1800.

Third, there was his developing relationship with Sir William and Lady Hamilton, who had accompanied the Neapolitan Court to Palermo. Much ink has been spilt in analysing his relationship with Emma Hamilton, but it is worth highlighting that Sir William was also an important player in the relationship that developed during Nelson's initial five-month stay in Palermo. In the past he has been written off as a senile old cuckold, but recent studies have reinstated him as an experienced diplomat, cultured connoisseur and cool, enlightened man of the world.[53] The generally accepted assumption now is that he both knew what was going on and also silently acquiesced in it. His influence on Nelson may not have been as emotionally charged as that of his wife, but it was strong nonetheless, and the two men developed a close bond, resembling that of father and son, which shaped and defined their working relationship as ambassador and admiral. The three called themselves the 'Tria Juncta in Uno' – a joking reference to the motto of the Order of the Bath, to which both Nelson and Hamilton belonged. And in a real sense they actually were a threesome: not sexually of course, but certainly emotionally. It is no coincidence that, when Hamilton eventually died, in 1803, Emma was holding him in her arms and Nelson was holding his hand.

Finally, even Nelson's manner changed. Always a man with a low irritation threshold, there are signs that, at this time, he became positively bad-tempered. Even more significantly, instead of being prepared to listen to arguments from his colleagues and to debate with them, he started to insist dictatorially on having his own way. A recently discovered account of the incidents in Naples in late June 1799 by the British Vice Consul, Charles Lock, depicts him cutting short a heated debate with Captains Hallowell and Hood over the fate of the Neapolitan revolutionaries with the angry cry, 'I see you are all against me, I am determined to obey my orders <u>right</u> or wrong: it shall be done, I will be obeyed!' A far cry indeed from the easy collegiality of the days before the battle of the Nile.[54]

So what was going on? Explanations of Nelson's uncharacteristic behaviour in 1799 and 1800 abound. There is speculation that his head wound may have caused a temporary character change and, certainly, his letters at this time speak of constant headaches and depression. Indeed even his handwriting changed character in this period, becoming markedly flatter and more constricted than usual. There is also, of course, the fact that he was beginning to fall in love with Emma Hamilton, and once their relationship became sexual, probably in late 1799, his emotional life became very complicated, and even lurid, as his extraordinarily explicit letters to her show. There are even those who have gone so far as to suggest that his behaviour was not really uncharacteristic at all – in other words, that what we see in Naples is an aspect of the 'real' Nelson: the part of his character that Terry Coleman provocatively has called 'a natural born predator'.[55]

It is likely that all these factors contributed, in varying degrees, to his behaviour. There is, however, one other possible cause that has not been much explored before and that may well have been the catalyst that started the chain reaction. Close examination of Nelson's correspondence in the weeks immediately following the evacuation of Naples reveals that the sudden reverses of December 1798 came as a great shock to him – so much so, he seems to have actually lost his confidence for a while. After the stunning victory of the Nile, and the heady adulation following it, the initial campaign in northern Italy had seemed to be going equally well. But then, in less than a month, the situation had been completely reversed and, although he had managed to extricate the King and Queen and their immediate entourage – albeit by the skin of their teeth – there was no disguising the fact that he had suffered a humiliating defeat. It was arguably the most significant reverse in which he was involved in his entire career and one for which he was very largely responsible. So, as he arrived in Palermo in January 1799, he was having to confront the fact that his first attempt to plan a campaign on a major scale, with the fates of whole countries at stake, had ended in disaster.

It is clear that this weighed heavily on him and affected him deeply. His letters home in January and February 1799 contain constant mentions of depression and ill-health: 'God knows since the battle I have had not one easy moment and what has brought me here [i.e. the evacuation of the royal family] adds not to my comfort,' he told Sir Roger Curtis on 17 January. The same day, he wrote to Frances, 'my command here has no occasion to be envied and if I can with propriety get away I shall do it'. A few days later, in a most revealing letter to Lady Parker, who was effectively a mother-figure to him, he was even more explicit about the depth of his depression and the cause of it: 'I am worse than ever, my spirits have received such a shock that I think they cannot recover it. You who remember me always laughing and gay would hardly believe the change but who can see what I have and be in health? Kingdoms lost and a Royal Family in distress.'[56]

At the same time, it is also clear that he was simply overwhelmed by the flood of new responsibilities that had suddenly come his way, and the resulting correspondence. Up to this point, all his experience had been as a ship or squadron commander: now he was having to adjust to the totally different role of theatre commander and, moreover, he was being forced to learn 'on the job'. As he explained to Clarence in April 1799, he was by then conducting all the business of the Mediterranean: 'Besides the business of sixteen sail of the Line I have the constant correspondence of Petersburg, Constantinople, Vienna, Venice, Trieste, Smyrna, Florence, Leghorn, Earl St Vincent, Minorca and Lord Spencer.'[57]

It is worth emphasising again that he did not have the resources usually available to a commander-in-chief to help him with all this work; he had no captain of the fleet and only an ordinary admiral's secretarial staff. So, he was physically ill, emotionally drained and depressed, and faced with a rapidly changing situation for which none of his previous experience had prepared him, and for which he did not have the necessary resources. In these circumstances, it is perhaps scarcely surprising that some of his judgements were questionable.

On the other hand, there were still flashes of the old Nelson – usually when action at sea was imminent. So, for example, his first sojourn ashore at Palermo effectively ended on 12 May 1799 when news arrived there that the French Brest fleet had been seen off Oporto in Portugal, heading south. The assumption was that they were coming into the Mediterranean to join with their Spanish allies and attack Minorca or Sicily. Here was a situation that Nelson could easily understand, and he reacted with all his old energy. Letters went off to Troubridge, who was operating in the Bay of Naples, and to Ball off Malta ordering them to join Nelson off Marettimo, an island off the westernmost point of Sicily. 'No time must be lost,' he told Ball, with all his old verve, while Troubridge was urged, 'I am all impatience until you join me.' On 19 May he went back on board the *Vanguard* for the first time since the turn of the year: 'how dreary and uncomfortable the Vanguard appears,' he told Emma. 'I am now perfectly the <u>great man</u> not a creature with me.' He had left with her, as a parting gift, a little pocket prayer book that Captain William Locker had given him over twenty years before. 'God protect this great & Brave man,' Emma wrote on the flyleaf in her scrawling hand.[58]

Once at sea, Nelson forgot his loneliness in the anticipation of another fleet action. The day after he sailed, he issued an 'Order of Battle and Sailing', his first since the weeks before the Battle of the Nile. It shows that he expected to have twelve ships with him, including three Portuguese, considerably fewer than the French were reported to have, and he told Emma on 21 May: 'I have been fighting with the Marquis [de Niza], Troubridge, Louis and Hood, my new plan of attack.

Prayer book. Presented in May 1799 by Nelson to Emma. It had originally been given to him by his mentor, Captain William Locker, in 1777.

They all agree it must succeed.' This is the same pattern as in 1798 – a conference with his seconds (in this case, de Niza as well as Troubridge) and two other close associates, followed by communication of the plan to the rest of the fleet. The 'Order of Battle and Sailing' has survived, but sadly the plan itself has not. But we can get some idea of its main objective from a note that Nelson sent to St Vincent, whom he expected to be hot on the heels of the enemy: 'before we are destroyed I have no doubt but that the Enemy will have their wings completely clipped that they may be easily overtaken.'[59] This idea of sacrificing his own fleet in the hope of inflicting disabling damage on a superior opponent was a concept he would return to later in his career.

It was at this moment, when the fleet was assembled off Marettimo, that Captain Ben Hallowell presented Nelson with a bizarre, but significant, gift: a coffin made of wood taken from the wreck of *L'Orient*. The accompanying note explained that the gift was being made so that 'when you are tired of this life you may be buried in one of your trophies'. It is, surely, most significant that Hallowell waited until they were all together at sea, the Band of Brothers once more, instead of making the presentation ashore in Palermo. It would seem that Hallowell, an old friend and comrade, was worried about his Admiral's recent behaviour and that the present was loaded with meaning – a metaphorical, as well as a literal, *memento mori*. However, Nelson was delighted with the gift and displayed it prominently in his cabin until his servant, Thomas Allen, finally persuaded him to have it stored below. Even then he still kept it, and eventually he was indeed buried in it, as Hallowell had wished.

The French fleet did not, after all, come in his direction, and on 30 May Nelson returned to Palermo where, on 8 June, the coffin joined all the rest of his belongings on board his new flagship, the splendid new 80-gunner HMS *Foudroyant*, which had finally arrived from Britain. She had been intended for him all along, but she had only been finally completed a few months before.

Nelson also took with him into the *Foudroyant*, as was customary, a number of his 'followers', including two lieutenants, Edward Parker and William Layman. The record of the move, in the Public Order Book, is the first mention in Nelson's papers of these two young men, each of whom was to play a key role in Nelson's later life. Parker's earlier career is unknown, although there is a hint in some of Nelson's later letters that he may have been a protégé of Lord St Vincent. He also soon became a favourite with Emma Hamilton, and there is evidence that when she and Nelson became lovers he acted as a go-between, carrying their letters. Another transfer was Hardy – by now, Nelson had realised what an asset Hardy was and did not want to part with him. But even Hardy was unable to counter the growing influence of Emma. One can imagine the expression on his face when this note arrived: 'My Barges Crew & 10 more good quiet men are wanted here tomorrow at noon to attend & carry the dinner &c: and Lady Hamilton will be obliged to each captain if they will have the goodness to allow one or two of their best servants to come to her house to attend at table.'[60]

In August 1803, Nelson wrote to a Sicilian friend, recalling that the King of Naples had created him Duke of Bronte and granted him an estate as a reward for his services. He went on: 'I paid more attention to another Sovereign than my own . . . I repine [regret] not on those accounts. I did my duty to the Sicilifying my own conscience and I am easy.'[61] That passage suggests that he knew exactly what he was doing in 1799 and that he had sincerely believed that such repressive action was necessary. Certainly, once he left the Mediterranean in 1800, he never allowed his conscience to be 'Sicilified' again. With Nelson's own judgement before us, it is difficult to avoid the conclusion that his time in the Mediterranean during the twenty months following the Nile was one of the least satisfactory and productive periods in his career. When all the explanations for his uneven performance have been weighed

BRONTE

On 13 December 1799, King Ferdinand of Naples created Nelson Duke of Bronte, a region in the north-east of Sicily close to Mount Etna. Nelson was very proud of the title (which, appropriately, means 'thunder') and immediately started using it in his signature. To begin with he signed himself 'Bronte Nelson' but eventually, after much experimentation, settled on 'Nelson & Bronte'. He always used the ampersand and never used an accent on the last 'e'.

King Ferdinand of Naples. An unknown miniaturist captures the essential stupidity of this most unattractive monarch, for whose sake Nelson 'Sicilyfied' his conscience.

and debated, the simple truth remains that he was not yet experienced enough to command a theatre as complex as the Mediterranean, with its tangled diplomacy and many different political and strategic demands. Nor was he cut out to be a subordinate to an effective, but plodding, admiral like Keith. His performance as a task force leader in 1798 had been impressive – he had made mistakes, as we have seen, but he had achieved his objective in a striking and brilliant way. The sensible course would have been to have recalled him straightaway and found him another task, leaving older and more experienced heads to deal with the operational and diplomatic Pandora's box that his victory had opened. At least some of the responsibility for Nelson's failure must rest on the shoulders of those who continued him in an appointment for which he was not yet fitted.

On the other hand, it is also true to say that Nelson learned some important lessons during his two-year stint of service in the Mediterranean in 1798–1800. And, as a result, when he next held independent command, he performed very much better.

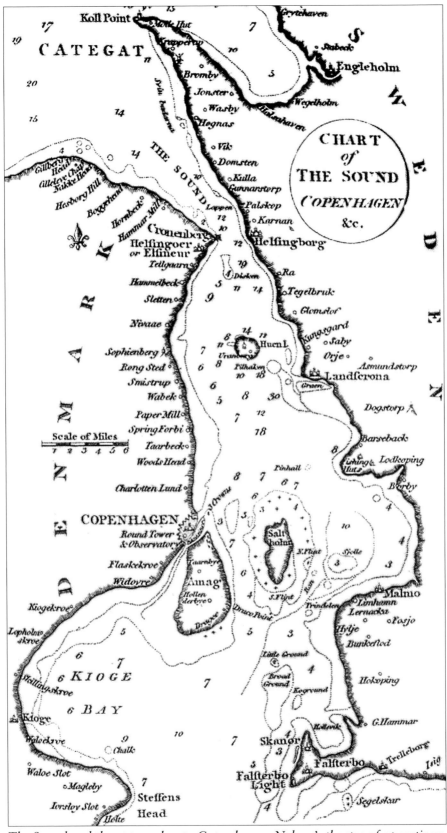

The Sound and the approaches to Copenhagen. Nelson's theatre of operations for most of the 1801 Baltic campaign. At the top is Elsinore, where the British entered the Baltic, centre left is Copenhagen and at the bottom is Køge Bay where the fleet was based after the battle.

CHAPTER III

The Battle of Copenhagen and the Baltic: January–July 1801

Following his recall from the Mediterranean in June 1800, Nelson returned home overland accompanied by Sir William Hamilton – and, of course, Emma, who was now carrying her first child by Nelson. Setting off from Leghorn in July, they embarked on what quickly became a triumphal progress through Austria and Prussia, during which Nelson was hailed as the victor of the Nile. The festivities slowed them down so much that they did not reach Britain until 7 November. Elsewhere, the war was still raging furiously and British forces were engaged in a number of vital operations. Against such a backdrop, Nelson's leisurely journey through Germany increased the impression his superiors already had of a man who had lost his taste for active service. St Vincent, in particular, was disappointed in his protégé and wrote to his secretary, Evan Nepean, the Secretary to the Admiralty, in characteristically robust terms: '[Nelson] cannot bear confinement to any object; he is a partisan; his ship always in the most dreadful disorder and [he] can never become an officer fit to be placed where I am.'[1] When he wrote those angry words, St Vincent was Commander-in-Chief of the Channel fleet, so he was effectively ruling Nelson out as a candidate for higher command.

It was therefore a considerable relief to the First Lord, Lord Spencer, when Nelson made it clear to him at their first interview that he wanted to serve again – and with Lord St Vincent. It is interesting that after his first, and very mixed, experience of independent command, his immediate instinct was to ask to be placed under the wing of the man who had most influenced his career and under whom he had been happiest. Perhaps he needed the reassurance of subordination to a man he admired, and with whom he felt safe, after the complexities and disappointments he had encountered in the Mediterranean. His appointment to the Channel fleet was announced in early January 1801, just after his promotion to Vice-Admiral had been gazetted. He busied himself with appointments: Hardy was to be his flag captain, of course, and the Revd Stephen Comyn, who had served with him in the *Vanguard* and *Foudroyant*, was to be his chaplain again.

Almost his last act before leaving London, on 13 January 1801, was to bid farewell to his wife, Frances. The brief weeks since his return had been strained and painful, and it is clear that, so far as he was concerned, their marriage was at an end. But, like so many absconding partners, he was unable to tell her so directly and, as a result, she went on trying to effect a reconciliation in the months ahead. However, Nelson had now decided to cast in his lot with Emma and, having made a generous financial settlement for Frances, he wished to be left alone. Indeed, they never met again.[2]

In Plymouth his new flagship awaited him, the *San Josef*, which he had helped to capture at the Battle of Cape St Vincent. Eighteen months before, in July 1799, he had written from the Mediterranean to Spencer: 'If under all the circumstances I am not removed from my situation, and the St: Joseph is not otherwise disposed of, it would flatter me very much to have her for the Ship destined to bear my Flag. I press it no further relying on your goodness.'[3]

That request can be read at one level as a particularly blatant example of his tendency to self-promotion. But it can also be cited as evidence of his instinctive appreciation of the importance in leadership of symbolic gestures: in this case, the victor of the Nile, flying his flag in the greatest of his trophies. Spencer was shrewd enough to understand the underlying purpose of Nelson's request and personally ordered the *San Josef* to be reserved for him. However, when he arrived, on 17 January, she was still not ready, despite Hardy's best efforts, and in particular Nelson's own quarters were still not finished, the officials in the Dockyard having assumed that he would not want to get to sea 'till the winter was more worn away'. They were quickly disabused of that notion and soon, as Nelson told St Vincent, 'all are bustle'.[4] Less than a week later, the *San Josef* was anchored in Cawsand Bay, riding out a gale, and eventually, on 2 February, she joined the rest of the Channel fleet in Torbay. Nelson went ashore to report to Lord St Vincent, who was at that time commanding from on shore, while living at Torre Abbey.

When Nelson returned to his ship he found waiting for him a letter that told him that he was now a father – Emma had given birth to a daughter a few days before. Delighted and excited to have a child of his own at last, his letters to her at this time are full of love and gratitude to the woman who had given him his heart's desire. And the arrival of Horatia, as the child was called, ended forever any chance that he might return to Frances. '[M]y own dear wife,' he told Emma, 'for such you are in my eyes, and in the face of heaven . . . I love I never did love anyone else. I never had a dear pledge of love till you gave me one.'[5] And when, a few days later, poor faithful Frances wrote offering to come and nurse him, having heard that his good eye was troubling him, she was told abruptly: 'I only wish people would never mention My Name to you, for weither I am blind or not it is nothing to any person. I want neither nursing or attention. And had you come here I should not have gone on Shore nor would you have come afloat. I fixed as I thought a proper allowance to enable you to remain quiet and not to be posting from one end of the Kingdom to the other.'[6] In private life, as in his professional career, having identified his objective, Nelson was utterly ruthless in pursuing it.

In the event, Nelson's spell with the Channel fleet was very short. By the time he arrived at Torbay, a situation was developing in the Baltic that required a sudden and vigorous response. At that time, the Baltic was a vital source of trade and maritime supplies for Britain, worth over £3 million in the prices of the day. So when, in late 1800, under the influence of a pro-French Russia, the Baltic states formed an 'Armed Neutrality of the North' and placed an embargo on British ships, the British government felt compelled to take action. As it happened, the crisis had come at a moment that favoured Britain: in February, the Baltic was still frozen and it would only become accessible gradually – the thaw beginning at the mouth of the sea and moving slowly until finally the Russian ports were freed from ice. It was therefore possible for Britain to take on her opponents one by one, starting with Denmark. But, to benefit from this advantage, swift and decisive action was required. St Vincent was consulted at all points in the preparations, and he wrote to Evan Nepean: 'If you are active our Fleet will be in the Baltic before any of the leagued Powers can get theirs to sea, and thereby cut off all possibility of junction between the Russ and the Dane.'[7]

He also advised that the command of the fleet should be given to Admiral Sir Hyde Parker who, although elderly and cautious, had considerable experience of the Baltic. Nelson was appointed as his second. This particular combination was presumably decided upon because it was felt that the talents of each would complement the other – but it was to prove a difficult and often strained

Vice Admiral Sir Hyde Parker, c. 1785. This engraving shows Parker as a younger and more vigorous man than the hesitant commander-in-chief of the 1801 Baltic expedition.

relationship. Nonetheless, the ensuing campaign was to offer Nelson the opportunity not only to remind his superiors of his fighting skills but also to demonstrate that he had learned some important lessons in higher command from his experiences in the Mediterranean.

Then, just when speed and a clear vision of the objective were vital, the administration of the country was plunged into confusion. Prime Minister William Pitt was determined to push through the emancipation of Roman Catholics, but the King was equally determined that such a move would be against his coronation oath. Eventually, after much uncertainty, Pitt resigned on 5 February and, on 8 February, it was announced that he would be replaced by the Speaker of the House of Commons, Henry Addington. A Government reshuffle began, as a result of which Lord Spencer left the Admiralty, and one of Addington's first steps, on 9 February, was to write to Lord St Vincent to invite him to become the First Lord. The King, with his customary sensitivity, remembered that 14 February was the anniversary of the Battle of Cape St Vincent, and so it was on that day that the old earl was invited to call at the Queen's House (now Buckingham Palace) to discuss his new office. The first meeting of the new Board of Admiralty, which included St Vincent's other favourite, Captain Thomas Troubridge, was held on 20 February. Then, with the handover only half-complete, the King suffered a recurrence of his old illness of porphyria and was unable to carry out his official duties, leaving Pitt still technically Prime Minister. However, the relapse lasted only a few weeks and soon the King was well enough again to accept the seals of office from Pitt and hand them to Addington.

Fortunately St Vincent was already in post when the King fell ill and so, amid all this political turmoil, the preparations for the Baltic expedition continued. As almost his last act in office, on 17 February, Spencer formally appointed Parker and Nelson – and, even before this, both had been advising on the composition of the force. On 14 January Parker had written to Spencer recommending, among other things, that six colliers should be converted to mount eighteen to twenty 24-pounders.[8] Nelson, meanwhile, was urging Spencer that '10,000 troops ought to be embarked to get at the Danish Arsenal.'[9] Now, with St Vincent at the helm, the pace of the campaign suddenly quickened. Nelson was ordered to transfer his flag to the shallower-drafted *St George*, and so, after less than a month in his new quarters on board the *San Josef*, he had to move all his belongings to another ship. There was also a general changeover of personnel, since Nelson took with him most of his 'followers', including all the *San Josef*'s lieutenants and, of course, Hardy. Even Chaplain Stephen Comyn exchanged with Andrew Lawrence of the *St George*.[10]

'GET RID OF US MY FRIEND!': THE FLEET ASSEMBLES

On the 18 February 1801 Nelson was ordered to sail round to Portsmouth to collect the ships that were being assembled there and to embark troops. Arriving on the 23rd, he first went up to London on three days' leave, during which he saw his daughter for the first time. He also took the opportunity to call on Parker, who was still in town and, as he told Troubridge, 'I have assured him that I have only to know his Wishes to execute them as punctually as the Strongest Orders'.[11] Then he returned to Portsmouth.

The officer commanding the troops, Lieutenant-Colonel Sir William Stewart, later wrote a detailed account of the campaign for Nelson's early biographers Clarke and M'Arthur, and he remembered vividly the change in tempo that Nelson's arrival, on the 27th, caused: 'He sent for me immediately on his arrival . . . . he said that "not a moment was to be lost in embarking the troops for he intended to sail the next tide." Orders were sent for all boats and the whole were on board before mid-day.'[12]

Similar urgency was conveyed to the ships – Captain Tyler of the *Warrior* was told to 'proceed without a Moments further loss of time', and the new Secretary to the Admiralty, Evan Nepean, was assured, 'All the Ships have their orders to proceed to Yarmouth Roads with all possible expedition.'[13] The *St George* was undergoing essential repairs but, rather than lose the wind, Nelson ordered the ship to be moved down to the St Helen's anchorage with the workmen still on board. The wind came fair on 2 March, and they were sent ashore as the *St George* got under way with seven other battleships in company, setting a course for the Downs, the anchorage of Deal. 'This day fortnight', Nelson had written to Davison, 'I hope from my heart to have the St George touching the Danish admiral.'

This was the first time that he had been entrusted with getting a new fleet to sea, and the sense of urgency and energy that he imparted was quite distinctive. It was a style of leadership that he was to repeat, and refine, over the ensuing years.

His achievement is the more remarkable, since it is clear that Emma was being unkind to him at this time. Although he destroyed all her letters, his anguished replies have survived: sometimes he wrote to her as often as three or four times each day. Joy at the birth of their child, and love for 'my own dear wife' as he was now calling her, mingled with frantic jealousy of other potential lovers – even including the notoriously licentious Prince of Wales. It would seem that, far from trying to allay his fears, Emma was quite deliberately stirring them.

Once at sea, his interest in ship-handling remained as strong as ever and, on the way up-Channel, he decided to put the *St George* through her paces. Under Stewart's amused gaze, he proceeded to give the orders to put the ship about – but the big three-decker griped and missed stays. 'Well now, see what you have done,' said Nelson peevishly to the Officer of the Watch. 'What do you mean to do now?' The Officer replied that he did not know, upon which Nelson said, 'Well I am sure if you do not know what to do with her no more do I either,' and stalked off to his cabin. Stewart decided that this incident was 'illustrative of much *nâiveté*' and, like the incident in the *Vanguard* off Sardinia in 1798, it has been used in some biographies to suggest that Nelson was not a particularly good seaman. But what Stewart did not know, and what the biographers have forgotten, is that, apart from his few weeks in the *San Josef*, this was the first time in his entire career Nelson had served in a three-decker – all his previous ships had been frigates or third rates. Clearly, he was still trying to handle the lumbering *St George* as if she was the *Boreas* or the *Agamemnon*.

At the Downs, Nelson went on shore briefly to call on the Commander-in-Chief, his former Captain, now Admiral, Skeffington Lutwidge. Meanwhile, the ships of his squadron were busy collecting flat-bottomed boats which were to be taken to the Baltic for landing the troops. They also took on board pilots to guide them into Yarmouth Roads but found them a mixed blessing. 'We have a damned stupid dog on board,' Nelson told Troubridge, 'as obstinate as the devil.'[14] It was a problem that was to recur during the ensuing campaign.

Nelson and his division, complete with all the extra equipment, arrived at Yarmouth Roads on 7 March, just over a fortnight after he had received his orders at Plymouth. He found waiting for him an approving letter from St Vincent: 'Many thanks for the spur you have given to the movement of the ships at Spithead.'[15] He also found almost total inertia. Parker had left London over a week before but, although his flag was flying temporarily in HMS *Ardent* until his flagship arrived, he was still living ashore with his young wife, whom he had married just a couple of months earlier. Worse, when Nelson called on him at 8 a.m. the next morning – which, as he told Stewart, he regarded as 'a very late hour for business' – Parker confined himself to formalities and cut the meeting short after only a few minutes.

Nelson was appalled. Not only was the fleet nowhere near ready to sail – and with no sign of any great urgency about the preparations either – but it was clear that Parker was not going to share the decision-making with him. He poured out his concern not only to Emma but also to Troubridge, who was of course now well-placed to pass Nelson's 'unofficial' comments on to St Vincent. 'Fame says we are to sail on the 20th,' he wrote, 'and I believe it unless you pack us off. I was in hopes that Sir Hyde would have had a degree of confidence, but no appearance of it . . . Get rid of us my friend and we shall not be tempted to lay abed until 11 o'clock.'[16] Troubridge took the hint and, about the same time, St Vincent heard rumours that the sailing date had been chosen to allow the new Lady Parker to hold a farewell ball on the 19th. On 11 March an Admiralty messenger arrived in Great Yarmouth bringing Parker a doubleshotted broadside from the First Lord: 'I have heard by a sidewind that you have intention of continuing at Yarmouth till Friday on account of some trifling circumstances . . . I have sent down a messenger purposely to convey to you my opinion, as a private friend, that any delay in your sailing would do you irreparable injury.'[17] Shortly after reading this, Parker went on board his flagship, the *London*, the signal was made to unmoor, and the following day, 12 March, the fleet sailed.

So Nelson had achieved his first aim, to hasten the sailing of the fleet; but he was still unable to break through Parker's reserve. Indeed, every action of the Admiral seemed designed to slight and distance his junior. For example, when, on 13 March – that is, the day *after* the fleet sailed – Nelson at last received his copy of the Order of Sailing and Battle, he found that Parker had placed some of the weakest ships in the van alongside the *St George*. 'You may make your comments,' he told

Troubridge, to whom he was now writing regular bulletins, 'I feel mine. It was never my desire to serve under this man.'[18] Nonetheless, he still sought ways of breaking the ice, and that same day an opportunity offered itself when Lieutenant William Layman managed to catch a fine turbot. Nelson sent it across to the flagship with his compliments, and the next day Parker responded, thanking him for his 'kind attention' and urging him not to make 'a Visit of ceremony'. He also, at last, told his second-in-command a little of his instructions: 'I am to allow forty eight hours for negotiations after the Delivery of the Dispatches of our Ministers . . . it will most probably Oblige [us] to anchor short of Cronenburg [Kronborg].'[19] This was not at all what Nelson wanted to hear. 'I hear we are likely to anchor outside Cronenburg Castle, instead of Copenhagen, which would give weight to our negotiation,' he told Alexander Davison. 'A Danish Minister would think twice before he put his name to a war with England when the next moment he would probably see his Masters fleet in flames and his capital in ruins.'[20] He demonstrated this aggressive spirit with one of his characteristic symbolic gestures: as soon as the fleet sailed, he ordered the *St George* to be cleared for action, telling Troubridge: 'It is not so much their [the ship's bulkheads] being in the way as to prepare people's minds that we are going at it and that they should have no other thought but how they may best annoy their enemies.'[21]

'OUR COUNTRY DEMANDS A MOST VIGOROUS EXERTION OF HER FORCE': PERSUADING PARKER TO ATTACK

There now ensued a frustrating and taxing fortnight, during which Nelson had to use all his powers of persuasion and considerable charisma to get the cautious Admiral, and his equally cautious advisors, to move on Copenhagen. The fleet made a leisurely voyage from Great Yarmouth, feeling its way slowly towards the opening of the Kattegat, which it finally reached on 19 March. By 21 March, it was anchored off the Swedish coast at Skälderviken. There, as he had told Nelson he would, Parker waited for the British negotiators, Nicholas Vansittart and William Drummond, to return from Copenhagen, which they duly did on 22 March. Vansittart told Parker that the negotiations were at an end and ordered him 'to execute such Instructions as you have received'. However, he also painted a very gloomy picture as to the strength of the Danish defences, which depressed Parker so much that he wrote to the Admiralty: 'it will be very difficult for us to dislodge them without vessels of force of a less draught than the ships of the line.'[22] Clearly, he was beginning to assemble reasons for not attacking Copenhagen.

On board the *St George*, Nelson was in a very different mood. He had spent the preceding days making detailed notes in his journal about the various landmarks, the depth of water and so on – as always, he was gathering as much local information as possible, both for present use and for storing away for any future operations. On 23 March, he was in the middle of writing to Troubridge 'I have only to regret our loss of time . . . Now we have only to fight and I trust we shall do honour to our country', when he broke off to say, 'The commander in chief has

just sent for me and shall have my firm support and honest opinion if he asks for
it.'[23] William Layman commanded the boat that transported his admiral to the
London and later heard what happened in the flagship's great cabin. His account
gives us a fascinating glimpse of Nelson in action.

Apparently the meeting began in great despondency, with Parker and the two
diplomats 'dismayed'. However, said Layman:

> Lord Nelson questioned those just arrived from Copenhagen not only to the
> force but as to the position of the enemy. Such interrogatories he called, 'bringing
> people to the post.' Having learned that the great strength of the enemy was at
> the head of the line, supported by the Crown Battery, his Lordship emphatically
> observed that to begin the attack there, would be like taking the bull by the
> horns and that he therefore suggested the attempt by the tail.[24]

So, the germ of a battle plan was even then forming in his mind. Realising that
Parker was beginning to contemplate staying where he was and waiting for the
fleets of the Armed Neutrality to come out to him, Nelson set about persuading
the Admiral to make a move. The safest approach appeared to be to enter the
Baltic by the Great Belt, thus bypassing Copenhagen altogether and, although
he would have preferred to go directly through the Sound, Nelson agreed to
this. Accordingly, on 24 March, the fleet weighed anchor and began sail
towards the Great Belt, led by Captain George Murray in the *Edgar*, who knew
the route well.

However, the movement had scarcely begun before Parker halted the fleet and
sent for Nelson for another conference. He wrote: 'I am to beg your pardon for
giving you so much trouble, but having most seriously reflected on our Plan of
going up the Belt, I find many reasons occur against the Idea.' It turned out that he
had been told of the dangers of the Belt by both his Captain of the Fleet, William
Domett, and the Captain of the *London*, Robert Otway, and was now
reconsidering the option of going via the Sound. Nelson's notes of what he said at
this second conference have survived, since he wrote them out in letter form and
sent them to Parker some time after the campaign.[25] They are a model of clear
exposition, assessing the various options and giving firm, unequivocal advice on
two alternative courses of action. They also give us an echo of the words he used
to fire up his hesitant superior: 'here you are with almost the safety, certainly with
the honour, of England more intrusted to you than ever yet fell to the lot of any
British Officer . . . I am of the opinion the boldest measures are the safest and our
Country demands a most vigorous exertion of her force directed with judgement.'
And there is the usual Nelsonian warmth in the *envoi*: 'In supporting you, my dear
Sir Hyde, through the arduous and important task you have undertaken, no
exertion of head or heart shall be wanting from your most obedient and faithful
servant.' Nelson recorded the result of his eloquence in his journal: 'Sir Hyde told
me he was uneasy about going round by the Belt in case of accidents and therefore
thought of going by Copenhagen to which I cordially assented and the fleet was

tacked.' He later added a note recording 'the satisfaction of altering a very erroneous opinion'.[26]

One other important decision was made as a result of the 24 March conference. Realising that an attack on the Danish defences outside Copenhagen was looking increasingly likely, Parker instructed Nelson, on 26 March, to take a force of ten battleships and most of the smaller ships of the fleet under his direct command 'to be employed on a particular Service', as Nelson noted in his journal.[27] He wrote exultantly to Emma: 'Sir Hyde Parker has by this time found out the worth of your Nelson and that he is a useful sort of man on a pinch, therefore if he has ever thought unkindly of me I freely forgive him.'[28]

Now, at last, Nelson could prepare his force for action, as he had clearly been longing to do ever since he arrived at Great Yarmouth. He at once began issuing a steady stream of orders. Although he had not yet seen the Danish line of defence for himself, he had already begun to consider how he would attack it – so much so, that he was ready at once to explain his ideas to his subordinates. 'All day employ'd in arrainging & explaining to the Different Officers the Intended Mode of Attack,' read his journal entry for 26 March.[29] He was envisaging an assault by the battleships on the line itself, followed by an assault by troops carried in ships' boats on the Danish forts, especially the Trekroner battery. The ships under his immediate command were now ordered to prepare to anchor by the stern. As already noted (see p. 30), eighteenth-century ships were not designed to do this, and so, based on his experiences at the Nile, he gave technical advice as to how it was to be done: 'I recommend the Stern Cable to be passed round the after bitts & the Crosspiece to be lashed & shored. As much Warping may be necessary it is also Strongly recommended that the Foremost Capstan be got up ready for Service.' Next, the battleships were to prepare their launches to receive the troops, and precise orders were given as to how they were to be manned and armed. Signals were added to the lists to enable Nelson to control the movements of the flat boats, and the boats themselves were to be numbered and listed, together with details of the troops they were to carry, so that he could give his orders with more precision.[30] As at Tenerife, his attention to the minutiae of the attack was impressive. Moreover, the fact that he was able to issue such very detailed orders within a few hours of being given the command by Parker shows that he had been thinking them through long before 26 March.

The *St George* drew too much water for safe navigation among the shoals off Copenhagen and so, as the men of his new force worked into the night to carry out his orders, Nelson moved to a smaller ship. He chose the 74-gun *Elephant* – most probably because she was commanded by his old friend and former Nile colleague, Thomas Foley. It is also possible that it was another of his symbolic gestures: the elephant was the symbol of the Danish royal family. With him went his immediate staff, including Layman, his Signal Lieutenant Frederick Langford, and Edward Parker, from whom he was by now inseparable. He also took with him his favourite portrait of Emma, his 'guardian angel' as he called it, telling her, 'as I cannot have the pleasure of looking at the original it makes me happy even looking at the picture of my very dearest friend I have in the world'.[31] The following morning, in another characteristic gesture, he ordered all those ships now under his direct command to hoist the blue ensign. Nelson's ships were to fly Nelson's flag.

While his second was energising his men, Parker still hesitated, insisting on finding out first from the Governor of the formidable Kronborg castle at the entrance to the Sound whether he had orders to open fire. The Governor craftily bought time for his countrymen to strengthen the Copenhagen defences still further by insisting that he had to send to the capital for instructions – meanwhile, the fair wind that had been blowing for days died away to a calm, causing yet more delay. Nelson used the pause to exercise his crews in hoisting the flat boats in and out and to position the bomb vessels, now under his direct orders, so that they could enfilade the Danish batteries while the fleet passed through the Sound. He told George Murray, who was in overall charge of them, 'I was glad to see you placed where you are for it is a post of great consequence'.[32] Finally, neither the Danes nor Parker could find any more excuse for delay, and at 5 a.m. on 30 March, the fleet weighed anchor and began approaching the entrance to the Sound. As the *Elephant* got under way, Nelson was writing the latest of his notes to Troubridge. Already he was beginning to sound like a commander-in-chief: 'The spirit of this fleet will make all difficulty from enemies appear as nothing. I do not think I ever saw more zeal and desire to distinguish themselves in my life.'[33]

The solid, battlemented and turreted castle of Kronborg, with its impressive, grass-covered skirts of heavily armed gun batteries, had an almost legendary

Kronborg, Elsinore. The towers of the old castle can be seen over the massive earth ramparts, protecting the powerful gun batteries which so worried the British.

reputation for strength and impregnability – and it certainly looked formidable. But, as the British quickly discovered, its guns could not cover the whole width of the Sound. There was a channel in the middle, about 800 yards wide, where no gun could reach. Moreover, the guns on the Swedish side, which had been expected to join in, remained silent, allowing the British to veer more to the eastern side of the channel. So the entire fleet remained well out of range throughout its stately, two-hour parade past what Nelson, writing to Emma Hamilton that evening, called: 'the fancied tremendous fortress of Kronborg'. He went on: 'More powder and shot I believe were never thrown away for not one shot struck the British fleet. Some of our ships fired but the *Elephant* did not return a single shot, I hope to reserve them for a better occasion.'[34]

Eventually, at about 10 a.m., the British fleet anchored in Copenhagen Roads, and Nelson could see for himself the task that lay before him. His first act on dropping anchor was to go out on a personal reconnaissance. 'I have just been reconnoitring the Danish line of defence,' he told Emma. 'It looks formidable to those who are children at war but to my judgement with ten sail of the line I think I can annihilate them, at all events I hope to be allowed to try.'[35]

'TO CLEAR THE WAY FOR A BOMBARDMENT': NELSON'S BATTLE PLAN

The city of Copenhagen, and the main Danish naval arsenal, lay close to the deepwater channel and so were vulnerable to bombardment from the sea. In an attempt to prevent such an attack, the Danes had moored a hurriedly assembled line of old warships and floating batteries in the main channel, manned with a mixture of professional sailors and hastily raised volunteers. At the northern end of the line, defending the entrance to the port and naval dockyard of Copenhagen, was the newly constructed Trekroner battery, built on wooden piles on the edge of the shoals, and the line was made the more formidable by the fact that the Danes had removed all the usual markers from the channels.[36]

On Tuesday 31 March, Nelson went for another look at the Danish defences and this time took with him the artillery experts from the British bomb vessels, recording in his journal their opinion 'that if those Defences were clear'd away there was a probability they might throw shells into the Arsenal'. Consequently, at a Council of War held later that day on board the flagship HMS *London*, the object of the operation was defined: 'to fight the Danish Defences of their Arsenal and endeavour to clear the way for a bombardment.'[37]

From the various reconnaissance reports, it appeared that the Danish line was stronger at its northern end, where it rested against the Trekroner battery and where the Danes appeared to have placed some of their largest and most powerful ships, such as the *Sjaelland*, a 74-gun battleship, and the 64-gunners *Infrødsten* and *Holsten*. In fact we now know that the southern end of the line was stronger than the British thought. The southernmost ship, the *Prøvestenen*, was a cut-down three-decker with stoutly constructed sides and armed on her lower gundeck with 36-pounders. Next to her was the *Wagrien*, a former two-decker armed with

24-pounders, and close by was another former battleship, the *Jylland*, also armed with 24-pounders.[38] On the basis of the information available to him, Nelson decided to attack from the southern end of the line and overwhelm it with concentrated gunfire before moving on to attack the northern end. It was a tactic that he had used before at the Nile.

However, at the Nile, Nelson's fleet had been able to take the French lines on two sides, and that did not appear to be an option in this case. Early in their reconnaissance, the British decided that the Danes had placed their ships on the shoreward edge of the shoals, and this crucial misconception was to influence all their planning, and indeed their manoeuvring, on the day of battle. In fact we now know from Danish sources that their line was well clear of the shoals and close to the centre of the navigable channel. Since outflanking did not appear to be an option, Nelson had to find another way of bringing an overwhelming concentration on the southern end of the line, and he solved the problem with an ingenious tactic that had first been devised by Lord Howe.[39]

In essence, he planned to 'leapfrog' his ships into action. His lead ship, the 74-gun *Edgar*, was ordered to pass down the Danish line, firing as she went, until she reached the *Jylland* (see battle plan on p. 200). Her next astern, the *Ardent*, was ordered to do likewise and then, passing the *Edgar* on her unengaged side, to attack *Svædfisken* and *Kronborg*. Similarly, the *Glatton* was to leapfrog ahead of *Ardent* to take on the *Dannebrog*. At this stage, two of the lighter British battleships, *Isis* and *Agamemnon*, were to take up positions abreast of *Prøvestenen* and *Wagrien*, which, Nelson hoped, would by then be half-beaten by the successive broadsides of three powerful ships. Once all these ships were in position, the rest of the fleet would leapfrog past them – again on their unengaged side – and take on the rest of the Danish line. Finally: '1, 2, 3 and 4 being subdued, which is expected to happen at an early period, the *Isis* and *Agamemnon* are to cut their cables and immediately make sail and take their station ahead of the *Polyphemus* in order to support that part of the Line.'[40]

By these means, the southern end was to be crushed and defeated, followed by the rest of the line in succession, in a rolling attack. Once the Danish ships had been knocked out, or forced to surrender, the troops would be sent in flat boats, which were ordered to accompany the attacking force, to take possession of the captured Danish ships and to storm the Trekroner battery. In this way, Copenhagen Roads would be cleared of its defences, and Nelson could then bring up his bomb vessels and threaten the city and arsenal with bombardment.

'EXPLAINING THE INTENDED MODE OF ATTACK': THE EVE OF BATTLE

To succeed, such a complex plan had to be clearly understood by all those who were to carry it out and, as was his custom, Nelson took great care to communicate it fully to his captains, few of whom had served with him before. As we have seen, even before the fleet passed Elsinore, he had already begun to talk with the captains whose ships formed part of the squadron under his direct orders. On 1 April, taking advantage of a northerly wind, he moved his attacking squadron to the southern end of the Middle Ground – apparently, the signal to raise anchor and set sail was greeted with three cheers in all the ships now under his command. Then, at about 5 p.m., he gave a dinner party for his 'inner circle' in the *Elephant*'s great cabin. Three members of the old Band of Brothers were there – Foley, Fremantle and Hardy – together with the second-in-command, Rear Admiral Thomas Graves, George Murray of the *Edgar*, who knew Nelson slightly, having served with him briefly in the West Indies over twenty years before, and Edward Riou, the brilliant frigate captain who had already impressed Nelson with his expert surveying of the shoals. Colonel William Stewart, who also attended (later), told Nelson's biographers, Clarke and M'Arthur, that Nelson 'was in the highest spirits and drank to a leading wind.'[41]

After dinner, Nelson sat down with Foley and Riou to prepare his detailed battle orders, while Hardy went out in a small boat to reconnoitre the Danish line. By now, Nelson was extremely tired and his servant, Tom Allen, tried to persuade him to go to bed, but Nelson refused. So, instead, his cot was brought into the day cabin and placed on the deck so that he could lie in it while continuing his dictation. Hardy returned with his data, which further enhanced the precision of the plan, and by 1 a.m. on 2 April the orders were complete. The clerks were set to work making copies for each of the captains, urged on by repeated exhortations to hurry from Nelson, who slept only fitfully. Reports from the deck told him that the fair wind that he had toasted was coming, and he did not wish to lose a moment.

At 8 a.m. the copies were complete, and Nelson signalled for his captains to come on board the *Elephant*, where he handed over the orders personally with further verbal directions. He was obviously impressed by the men he had under his command, for he later told his friend, the Duke of Clarence, 'It was my good fortune to Command such a very distinguish'd sett of fine fellows.'[42] The letter containing these words was suppressed when Nelson's correspondence was published by Clarke and M'Arthur in 1809, because it contained references to the Crown Prince of Denmark, Clarence's first cousin and by then King of Denmark, so the 'distinguish'd sett of fine fellows' phrase has not entered the Nelson canon. But, as an expression of the confidence he placed in his subordinates, and of the generous way in which he always paid tribute to their support, it deserves to stand alongside the more famous 'Band of Brothers'.

Not content only with briefing his commanders, Nelson then summoned all the ships' pilots to the flagship for a personal briefing about the battle plan and about the findings of Hardy's night-time survey. However, this meeting was much less happy. All the pilots, most of whom were civilians, were overwhelmed by the responsibility that rested on them for guiding the squadron into battle safely and, as Stewart remembered, 'a most unpleasant degree of hesitancy prevailed among them all'.[43] Eventually, Alexander Briarly, the Master of HMS *Bellona*, volunteered to lead the fleet and went in a small boat to find and mark the southern extremity of the Middle Ground. He then transferred to the *Edgar*, which was to lead the British line. So, by 9.30 a.m., having done everything possible to prepare his force thoroughly, Nelson was ready to begin the attack.

At 9.45 a.m., Nelson signalled to his whole squadron to prepare to weigh, following this with a succession of orders to specific ships to weigh at intervals.[44] So, right from the start of the operation he was exercising much tighter control over his force than in any of his other battles. By 10.20 a.m., the *Edgar*, commanded by Captain George Murray – later to be singled out in Nelson's dispatch for his 'noble example of intrepidity which was well followed up by every Captain, Officer and Man in the Squadron',[45] was so far ahead of her consorts that Nelson was forced to signal to her to shorten sail. Ten minutes later, she reached her appointed station opposite the two-decked *Jylland* and opened fire. She was followed as planned by the *Ardent*, which took on the gun battery *Sværdfisken* and the frigate *Kronborg*. Next came the *Glatton*, commanded by William Bligh of *Bounty* fame. Although only a 56-gun ship, she was armed with heavy carronnades, and these could be seen wreaking havoc on the Danish ships as she moved slowly up the line to take her position opposite Olfert Fischer's pendant ship, *Dannebrog*, named after the Danish national flag. At about the same time, the British frigate *Désirée* began to manoeuvre to place herself across the bows of the southernmost Danish ship, the massive *Prøvestenen*, where she could pour in a raking fire without herself being exposed to her opponent's heavy guns. A young midshipman, William Millard, who watched this majestic deployment from the quarterdeck of one of the rearmost ships, HMS *Monarch*, recalled:

> We saw [the *Edgar*] pressing on through the enemy's fire and manoeuvring in the midst of it to gain her station; our minds were deeply impressed with awe, and not a word was spoken throughout the ship but by the pilot and the helmsman; and their communications being chanted very much in the same manner as the responses in our cathedral service, and repeated at intervals, added very much to the solemnity.[46]

Then, just as the attack appeared to be developing smoothly, things began to go wrong. At 10.40 a.m., the *Agamemnon* found that she had anchored so close to the Middle Ground shoal the previous night that she could not clear it and was forced to anchor, a great distance away from the battle site. In the meantime, the other ships were encountering great difficulty in discerning where the main channel lay. Thinking that the Danish line was moored actually on the shoal line, the ships' pilots kept edging away to starboard, not realising that this course was taking them ever closer to the western edge of the Middle Ground. Then, at 10.55 a.m., HMS *Bellona* struck a spur of the shoal and stuck fast. From where she lay, she could reach the Danish line with long-range fire but, already, Nelson's attacking force had been appreciably weakened. Worse was to follow. Gunsmoke was beginning to drift across the channel, obscuring the view still further, and the *Bellona*'s next astern, HMS *Russell*, able to see only her consort's masts, continued to follow in her wake and soon found herself aground as well.

Now Nelson was approaching in the *Elephant*. Seeing the *Bellona* so far away from the Danes he signalled to her, 'Engage the Enemy More Closely', following this five minutes later with the same signal to the whole fleet. Surgeon Ferguson of the Rifle Brigade was in the flagship and remembered vividly Nelson's 'extreme' agitation at this moment: 'I shall never forget the impression it made upon me. It was not however the agitation of indecision, but of ardent, animated patriotism panting for glory, which appeared within his reach, and was vanishing from his grasp.'[47] In a letter written to a friend shortly after the battle, Colonel Stewart also remembered Nelson's 'distress at the Pilot's refusing to take the Ship closer to the Enemy was very great, & he called me down at the beginning of the day from the Poop to tell me the indignation he felt at the fellow's refusing to go nearer than to ¼ less 5 – which is within a fathom of what the *Elephant* draws.'[48] There is no evidence to suggest that Nelson was any clearer about the position of the shoals than his colleagues – although, as he himself once wrote, his early experiences as a midshipman in the Thames had made him 'confident of myself among rocks and sands which has many times since been of the greatest comfort to me'.[49] But he was determined to fight the battle at as close a range as possible, and so all his instincts were to steer towards the Danish line and not away from it.

Whatever the reason, he now made his first critical decision of the battle, which averted a major disaster. His own orders required that the *Elephant*, and all the ships astern of her, should pass down the unengaged, or starboard, side of their next ahead. Had she done so she, and the rest of the squadron, would almost certainly have piled up on the Middle Ground, and the battle would have been over almost before it had started. Instead, in a sudden, instinctive decision, Nelson ignored his own orders, and the advice of the nervous pilots, and directed that the

---

SURGEON FERGUSON

Ferguson's account was first published in Vol. 2 of James Harrison's biography, *The Life of the Right Honourable Horatio Lord Viscount Nelson* (London, C. Chapple, 1806), p. 295. Harrison mistakenly said that Ferguson was the Surgeon of HMS *Elephant*, which led some subsequent biographers to cast doubt on the accuracy of his account since, as the ship's surgeon, his battle station would have been below in the cockpit and not on the quarterdeck.

However, it has recently been established that Ferguson was in fact the Surgeon of Colonel Stewart's Rifle Brigade (see Eric Tushingham and Clifford Mansfield, *Nelson's Flagship at Copenhagen: HMS Elephant* (London, The Nelson Society), p. 158). Since the *Elephant*'s casualties were comparatively light, it is unlikely that Ferguson's services would have been required below, and it therefore seems fair to assume that he was indeed on the quarterdeck and thus close to Nelson during the battle, as he claims.

So it is possible to reclaim his version of Nelson's words and to restore them to the narrative.

Elephant should pass to port of the two grounded ships. The rest of the fleet followed him – thus avoiding the underwater hazards.

Now Nelson had to improvise swiftly to cover the gaps in his attacking line, and he acted with characteristic coolness and decision. First, he ordered Captain Foley to place the *Elephant* in the position originally allocated to the *Bellona*, opposite the *Aggerhus* and *Floating Battery One*. He then stood at the head of the *Elephant*'s starboard gangway, where he could be clearly seen, and personally directed the ships following him into their new positions.

First came Fremantle's *Ganges*. As they made their approach her Master, Robert Stewart, had been killed, and her pilot, Isaac Davis, badly wounded in the arm. So now Fremantle himself was directing the tricky manoeuvre of easing the ship into position, while under heavy fire from the massed Danish guns. As the *Ganges* surged past the *Elephant*, Fremantle heard a familiar voice – somewhat high-pitched, with a distinctive Norfolk accent. Glancing across at the flagship, he realised that Nelson himself was hailing him through a speaking trumpet telling him to fill a gap left by one of the grounded ships and take on the ship originally intended as the *Elephant*'s opponent, the 74-gun battleship *Sjaelland*, one of the largest Danish ships in the line. So, as he later told his wife, 'I dropt my anchor on the spot Lord Nelson desired me.'[50]

The same happened as the other ships came within hailing distance. Captain Mosse in the *Monarch* was told to take on the blockship *Charlotte Amelia* and floating battery *Søhesten*, and Rear Admiral Graves in the *Defiance* was allocated the 64-gun *Holsten* and the 64-gun *Infødsretten*. But these changes meant that the ships at the head of the Danish line and the large Trekroner battery were left largely unengaged, so Captain Edward Riou of HMS *Amazon*, to whom Nelson had given overall command of the frigates, completed the British line with his small force.

This glimpse of Nelson personally controlling the exact positioning of his forces, more like a general on land than an admiral, is one of the most telling images of the Battle of Copenhagen. More than any of his other great battles, this was an operation in which his personal intervention and direction during the fighting itself were critical.

'DAMN ME IF I'LL SEE THAT SIGNAL!': 1–2 P.M. – SIGNAL 39

By 11.50 a.m. all the available British ships were in action (see plan on p. 200). But the accidents of the previous hour had materially altered the nature of Nelson's attack. First, instead of being able to bring concentrated fire on the southern end of the Danish line as intended, his slimmed down force was now stretched out over the entire length with some ships, such as his own *Elephant*, taking on two, and even three, opponents. As a result, some of the Danish vessels were able to engage British ships without being subjected to return fire. Second, because of the continuing confusion about the position of the shoals, most of the British ships were some 400 yards from their opponents, and *Bellona* and *Russell*

The Battle of Copenhagen, 2 April 1801. The British fleet (right) begins its attack on the Danish line (left). This study by Nicholas Pocock shows the difficulties with which Nelson and his captains had to contend. The dangerous shoals are invisible and some of the Danish floating batteries are so low in the water they can barely be seen.

were even further away. So the overwhelming close-range fire on which Nelson's plan had depended was no longer available to him.

To add to his problems, the Danish resistance was proving far stouter than he had expected, and soon all of his ships were taking severe damage and casualties. In particular, the floating batteries proved extremely difficult to hit. Stewart, who spent part of the battle firing a carronade on the *Elephant*'s poop, remembered that *Floating Battery One*, with which the flagship was hotly engaged,

> held us a hard rattle for at least an hour or more nor did we make her strike until we discharged Round & grape from all the guns of the ship – her height above water was not above six feet & there was no possibility of hitting her – there were no less than 8 of these formidable batteries afloat and they were all as difficult to subdue, and held us a severer contest than even the hulks of the Line of battleships.[51]

Midshipman Robinson Kittoe, in HMS *Defiance*, who made a detailed drawing of the Danish line during the battle, noted that the floating batteries 'have no mast and are more like a chest than a vessel'.[52]

Whatever his private feelings may have been at this long-drawn-out contest –
far longer than he had somewhat over-confidently predicted – Nelson put a brave
face on it. Later, in 1809, Stewart told Clarke and M'Arthur: 'A shot through the
mainmast knocked a few splinters about us. He observed to me, with a smile, "It
is warm work and this day may be the last to any of us at a moment" and then
stopping short at the gangway he used an expression never to be erased from my
memory and said with emotion, "but mark you I would not be elsewhere for
thousands."'[53] But, in his letter to Clinton written just a few days after the battle,
Stewart had recorded a less polished and, perhaps, more authentic expression:
'Well Stewart, these fellows hold us a better Jig than I expected, however we are
keeping up a noble fire, & I'll be answerable that we shall bole [sic] them out in
four if we cannot do it in three hours, at least I'll give it them till they are sick of
it.'[54] Stewart's recollection of Nelson's words is supported by one of his own
junior officers in the Rifle Brigade, Captain Sidney Beckwith, whose account of
the battle has also recently been discovered. He told a friend that Nelson
observed, 'if he could not beat them in two hours he must take three, or if that
would not do, he must take four hours to do it'.[55]

However confident of eventual victory Nelson may have been, this confidence
was not shared in the fleet flagship, HMS *London*. There, Parker was watching
the developing battle with mounting dismay. It had been agreed between him and
Nelson that he would weigh anchor at the same time as the attacking squadron
and move in to threaten the northern end of the Danish line with his division, thus
deterring them from transferring their ships to reinforce the southern end of their
line. But, hesitant and unenterprising as ever, Parker had not taken advantage of
the northerly wind on 1 April to move his ships closer to Copenhagen. The
southerly wind that had made Nelson's attack possible was now directly against
him, and he was forced to tack laboriously against it while the strong current that
was sweeping Nelson's ships into action was also running against him. As a result,
Parker's division was able to make only about 1 knot over the ground, and so its
advance into battle was painfully slow. By 12.45 p.m., three hours after the signal
to weigh anchor had been made, it was still more than 4 miles away from its
planned position and well out of range of even the closest Danish ships.

Nonetheless, Parker was still close enough to see what was happening, and the
situation looked bleak indeed. Three of Nelson's ships were flying signals of
distress and were clearly out of the action; Nelson's attacking line was now very
thinly stretched and the Danish resistance, which everyone had expected would be
crushed fairly easily, was still apparently unabated even after more than an hour
and a half of heavy firing. So, at 1 p.m., Parker ordered signal No. 39 to be flown,
'Discontinue the engagement.'

There has been disagreement ever since over what he actually intended by this
signal, and since Parker never explained his motives, it is impossible to be
absolutely certain. One of Nelson's earliest biographers, Robert Southey, 'upon the
highest and most unquestionable authority' (whose identity he did not reveal),
claimed that Parker intended the signal to be discretionary – in other words, he was

covering Nelson if he felt that he needed to withdraw.[56] However, the signal was not made to Nelson individually. It was a general signal – in other words, to the entire attacking squadron – and it could therefore only be read as mandatory. It was clearly regarded as such by Nelson's immediate subordinates. Graves repeated the signal, as he was required to do – although he ordered it to be hoisted in a position where it could be seen in the *London* but not by the engaged ships. He also kept Nelson's signal for 'Close Action' flying and continued to take his lead from Nelson. The frigates, which were being very badly mauled by the Trekroner battery, individually obeyed the signal – so their captains clearly saw it as a direct order to them from the Commander-in-Chief. Last to disengage was Riou in the *Amazon*, who said regretfully as she turned away from the battle, 'What will Nelson think of us?' Moments later, he was cut in two by a Danish shot.

Another theory, suggested by Hyde Parker's chaplain and foreign secretary the Revd Alexander Scott (who later became Nelson's chaplain and secretary in the *Victory* in 1803–5), was that the two admirals had agreed beforehand that if the Danish resistance proved too strong, Parker would recall Nelson. Again, this theory is scotched by the fact that Parker ordered the signal to be made general, rather than addressing it only to Nelson.

In any case, all the contemporary eyewitness accounts make it clear that Nelson was not expecting the signal and, indeed, that he was considerably surprised, even angered, by it. It was first seen by Signal Lieutenant Frederick Langford, who duly reported it to his Admiral. Nelson responded angrily, reminding Langford that he had told him to watch the Danish commodore's ship to see when she surrendered. The *Dannebrog* was on the *Elephant*'s port quarter, while the *London* was over her starboard bow, so Nelson was effectively telling Langford to turn his back on the flagship. He then resumed his agitated pacing of the quarterdeck, his 'fin' twitching – a familiar warning signal, to those who knew him, that he was very annoyed.

Langford, however, knew his duty and, as Nelson came level with him again, he asked, 'Shall I repeat it, my Lord?' 'No,' replied Nelson curtly, 'acknowledge it.' If Nelson had repeated the signal, he would have associated himself with the order, and the other ships in the attacking squadron would have obeyed it. By acknowledging it, he was indicating only that he had seen the signal and understood it. He was giving a clear hint to his colleagues that they should ignore Parker's order. Once again, he resumed his pacing; but after a moment's thought he stopped again and called after Langford, who was returning to his station on the poop, 'Is No. 16 [Engage the Enemy More Closely] still flying?' and when Langford replied that it was, said firmly, 'Mind you keep it so.' By keeping No. 16 flying, he was further underlining the message to his captains that he did not intend to obey Parker's order. It is also interesting to note that this story shows that Nelson had kept his earlier operational signal, 'Engage the Enemy More Closely', flying throughout the action. He was now using it as a battle-cry, just as he had at the Nile.

To demonstrate unequivocally to all those assembled on the *Elephant*'s quarterdeck what his intentions were, Nelson now indulged in a characteristic piece of drama. He spoke loud enough for all to hear, and Surgeon Ferguson recorded his words: '"Then damn the signal; take no notice of it and hoist mine for closer battle: that is the way I answer such signals . . . Now nail mine to the mast!" Then turning to Captain Foley he said, "Foley you know I have lost an eye and have a right to be blind when I like; and damn me if I'll see that signal!"[57] In 1809, Colonel Stewart also wrote an account of the scene for Clarke and M'Arthur, and he has Nelson clapping a telescope to his blind eye and claiming archly, 'I really do not see the signal.' His version has been repeated in almost every biography since[58] – but Ferguson's account rings more true. The words he quotes emphasise that Nelson was angrily, even contemptuously, refusing to see the signal, rather than making a joke of it, as Stewart suggests.

There were two main reasons why a withdrawal at that stage of the battle would have been a mistake. First, Nelson as the commander on the spot could sense that the tide of the battle had just begun to swing his way. After the string of early disasters the deadly, accurate and sustained broadsides of his well-trained crews were beginning to tell on their opponents. Between 12.30 p.m. and 1.10 p.m., five Danish ships, including the *Sjaelland*, the powerful linchpin of the northern end of the line, had disengaged; while the pendant ship *Dannebrog* was on fire, set ablaze by inflammable 'carcasses' fired by Bligh's *Glatton*. Indeed, the Danish commander, Olfert Fischer, had just struck his pendant and moved up the line in an open boat to transfer his command post to the *Holsten*. From the *Elephant*'s quarterdeck it would have been apparent that gaps were beginning to open up in the Danish line and that, in places, the Danish fire was slackening.

The second reason for continuing the action was that the northern end of the Danish line, especially the Trekroner battery, was still unsubdued. Given the wind direction, the British could only retreat in a northerly direction, and so they would have had to run the gauntlet of these undefeated units while negotiating the tortuous, unmarked shoals. As Nelson's second-in-command, Thomas Graves, wrote to his brother after the battle: 'If we had discontinued the action before the enemy struck we should all have got aground and been destroyed.'[59] There seems to be general agreement then that Nelson did the right thing in disobeying Parker's order – for the second time that day, he had saved the British from potential disaster.

'A MASTERPIECE OF POLICY': 2–3 P.M. – THE FLAG OF TRUCE AND THE 'CRITICAL HALF HOUR'

Nelson's most important contribution to the British victory was yet to come. Although during the hour immediately following Parker's signal there were no further significant reductions in the Danish line, their fire continued to slacken – for example, the *Edgar*'s log recorded, 'At two the enemy's fire slackened fast.'[60] In view of the gaps that had already been made in the line, and with this further evidence that his opponents were flagging, Nelson now decided that the time had come to put the second stage of his plan into operation. Orders went to the bomb vessels *Sulphur* and *Hecla* 'to get to the Northward to throw Shells at the Crown

Islands and Vessels with them'. At the same time, the remaining five bomb vessels were ordered 'to take stations abreast of the Elephant and to throw shells at the Arsenal'. Additionally, the flat boats with troops were called alongside the *Elephant*, so as to be ready for an assault on Trekroner.[61]

However, the Danes were stubbornly refusing to admit defeat: in a number of instances their fire died away almost completely and then suddenly flared up again as reinforcements arrived from the shore, causing confusion in the British fleet as to whether some of the Danish vessels had surrendered or not. So, as the boats and bomb vessels began to take up their positions, the gun duel was still far from over. Already, according to Stewart, the *Elephant* had fired more than 40 broadsides, which meant that her ammunition was beginning to run low, and all the ships of the attacking squadron were by now severely damaged, especially in their rigging. Nelson always had at the back of his mind the thought that this battle was but the first step in a long campaign. At least two other fleets, those of the Swedes and the Russians, might yet have to be encountered and, thanks to the gallantry and determination of the Danes, his ships were in danger of being so badly damaged that they would have to be sent home for repairs. So, at about 2 p.m., instead of launching his planned second-wave assault, Nelson decided to bring the battle to an end by other means.

What he did next has been a source of controversy ever since the day of the battle itself. Calling for ink and paper, he dashed off a note, standing on the main gun deck of the *Elephant*, and using as a desk the casing over the rudder head, in the area that in normal times was the wardroom. The note read: 'Lord Nelson has directions to spare Denmark when no longer resisting but if firing is continued on the part of Denmark Lord Nelson will be obliged to set on fire all the floating batteries he has taken, without having the power of saving the Brave Danes who have defended them.' It was headed, 'To the Brothers of Englishmen, The Danes.'[62] As Nelson wrote, his secretary, Thomas Wallis, was scribbling a copy. When the Admiral had finished, Wallis folded the note and was about to seal it with a wafer (a small piece of gummed paper) when Nelson stopped him and told him to seal it properly with wax. The necessary implements had to be recovered from where they had been stowed when the ship cleared for action, but the man sent to find them was killed while on his errand. Eventually though, the note was properly sealed, using Nelson's formal seal, which bore his coat of arms. Nelson could not see where his opponent, Commodore Olfert Fischer, was (in fact he was at that very moment in the process of transferring his command post once more – this time to the Trekroner battery) and so he addressed the note to 'The Danish Government'. It was carried ashore in a boat flying a flag of truce by Captain Frederick Thesiger, who spoke Danish. As Thesiger left, Stewart asked Nelson why, at such a moment, he had insisted on sealing the note correctly: '"Had I made use of a wafer," he replied, "the wafer would have been still wet when the letter was presented to the Crown Prince; he would have inferred that the letter was being sent off in a hurry: and that we had some very pressing reasons for being in a hurry. The wax told no tales."'[63]

'To the Brothers of Englishmen, the Danes'. In this romanticised, early twentieth-century lithograph, Nelson seals his letter to the Crown Prince. He was in fact wearing a shabby greatcoat, not full dress uniform.

Nelson's official seal. This is, traditionally, the seal Nelson used on the letter he sent to the Crown Prince. It bears an impression of his coat of arms.

If Fischer had received the note, it is quite likely that he would have rejected it. As it was, Thesiger's boat took just over half an hour to reach the shore, where the Crown Prince of Denmark was directing the operations. And, during that critical period, between about 2.05 p.m. and 3.40 p.m., the whole of the centre of the Danish line suddenly collapsed, with no fewer than seven ships surrendering or leaving the line. At about the same time, Nelson's bomb vessels arrived in position close to the *Elephant*, and some of them even began firing ranging shots into the arsenal. So, as Crown Prince Frederick stood on the quay at Tolboden, just in front of the great citadel of Copenhagen, with Nelson's note in his hand, he could see through a large gap that had opened up in his defensive line to the menacing bomb vessels beyond (see battle plan on p. 201). Scarcely surprising, then, that he seized the opportunity that Nelson had offered him and sent an aide to enquire what Nelson's motives were.

Nelson replied that his 'object in sending on shore a Flag of Truce is humanity' and he continued to make this claim whenever the battle was discussed in the succeeding months, often becoming very annoyed when anyone suggested the contrary. Certainly, his credentials were strong, since he was usually a humane man and famously prayed for 'humanity after Victory' just before Trafalgar. But his colleagues had absolutely no doubt that cunning and policy had also played an important part in his decision to suggest a truce. Stewart wrote to Clinton, 'The armistice was a masterpiece of policy of the little hero's', and an anonymous 'Officer of Rank' who was serving in the *Elephant* agreed: 'Lord Nelson saw their dangerous situation [i.e. the grounded ships] and it was only a cool comprehensive mind like his own that could devise a means of extricating them.'[64] Even his close friend, Thomas Fremantle, agreed with this assessment, writing to his wife Betsey, 'Every merit is due to Lord Nelson for his policy as well as his bravery on this occasion.'[65]

In the past the debate about Nelson's motives has tended to focus on one or other theory – in most accounts, his act is portrayed either as humanity towards a beaten foe or as a ruse to avoid any further damage to his own ships. In fact the two are not mutually exclusive, and the most probable answer is that his decision to end the conflict was influenced by both. What cannot be disputed, however, is that by the time the Crown Prince's aide, Adjutant General Lindholm, arrived on board the *Elephant* with his master's enquiry about Nelson's motives at about 3 p.m., the Danish line of defence had effectively ceased to exist. The British had won the battle and, for a third time, Nelson's personal intervention had been critical. As Lindholm returned through the Danish lines bearing Nelson's response to the Crown Prince he gave orders for firing to cease, and by 3.15 p.m. flags of truce were flying on both sides. The battle was formally over.

But victory had been dearly bought. The casualties on both sides were high – although some of the British ships had suffered appreciably more than the others. Hardest hit was the *Monarch*, which had been opposed to three ships as well as the powerful Trekroner battery. Her captain, James Mosse, had been killed early in the action, along with 56 others, and 163 of her ship's company had been wounded – a casualty rate of about 30 per cent, which Stewart called 'a positive butchery'. Captain Riou of the *Amazon* had also been killed and Captain Thompson of the *Bellona* had lost a leg. *Edgar* and *Isis* had suffered particularly heavy losses. The total British killed and wounded stood at 943, and the Danish losses were about the same – 1,035.

If the human cost was high, so too was the cost to the ships. Few of the British battleships had escaped serious damage, and four were so badly mauled that they had to be sent home for repairs. Moreover, the shoals continued to claim victims. No sooner had the firing ceased than Nelson began to extricate his battleships from their hazardous positions. At once a series of accidents occurred that showed what might have happened had the squadron obeyed Parker's ill-advised signal earlier. First the *Defiance* ran aground, then the *Monarch* and *Ganges* collided, and finally the *Elephant* also stuck fast and could not be freed until some of her water had been pumped overboard and part of her bread supply unloaded into a couple of smaller ships.

All those who had taken part in this bloody action remembered it as a particularly hard-fought contest and, on the British side, there was a strong sense of admiration for the courage and determination shown by the Danes. Nelson wrote to Emma Hamilton (in a letter dated '8 o'clock at night, very tired after a hard fought battle'): 'the French fight bravely. But they could not have endured for one hour what the brave Danes withstood for four.'[66] There also seems to have been a sense among the British that they had not been as successful as they had expected. Graves wrote somewhat defensively, 'Considering the disadvantages of the navigation, the approach to the enemy, their vast number of guns and mortars on both land and sea, I do not think there ever was a bolder attack.'[67] And Nelson himself, in the letter to the Duke of Clarence which was later suppressed, wrote: 'The loss of services in the stations assigned to them of three sail by their getting on shore prevented our success being so compleat as I intended, but I thank God under those very untoward circumstances for what has been done.'[68]

On the other hand, there was no doubt in anyone's mind to whom the credit belonged for the British success. Graves, who had never served with Nelson before, summed up his account of the battle with the words, 'In short it was worthy of our gallant and enterprising little Hero of the Nile. Nothing could exceed his spirit.'[69] Even the soldiers were impressed. Beckwith wrote, 'Nor can I conceive anything more perfect than every part of the fine little Hero's conduct on that trying occasion.'[70] Stewart said simply, 'The conduct of Ld. Nelson, to whom alone is due all praise both for the attempt & execution of the contest, has been most <u>grand</u> – he is the admiration of our whole fleet.'[71]

'I HOPE IT WILL MAKE A RIGHT UNDERSTANDING': NELSON NEGOTIATES

Having opened the negotiations with the Danes, Nelson was now asked by Parker to continue them and so, the day after the battle, he went ashore to meet the Crown Prince, stopping on the way to inspect the ships that had been in action. They talked for two hours, accompanied only by Captain Hans Lindholm, the Prince's aide-de-camp, who had visited the *Elephant* to enquire about the purpose of Nelson's message. The following day, Nelson wrote a short summary of their meeting to the Duke of Clarence. As the letter was suppressed, this version of the conference has only recently been discovered:

> On the 3rd [April 1801] I had a long conference with His Royal Highness the Prince Royal of Denmark and he was so good as to allow me to state fully my opinion on the present state of Denmark and we considered its unnatural and unprovoked alliance agst us. His assurances always went that his Intentions were perfectly misunderstood, that his uncle[72] had been deceived and that he never would be the Enemy of England, that all his object was to protect his Commerce & to be at peace with all the world. However H R Hs requested we would suspend hostilities 'till he could call a Council & endeavour to make some sensible propositions, so we parted and this Evening I expect he will send them to Sir Hyde [Parker].[73]

Nelson and Lindholm appear to have struck up a friendship for, on 4 April, Nelson wrote thanking him for some newspapers and emphasising 'As I only told His Royal Highness plain truths I hope it will make a right understanding between the two countries and that Denmark will no longer be Ally of the enemy of Great Britain.'[74]

Parker now took the lead in the negotiations while Nelson made preparations to renew hostilities, should this be necessary. Although all the attacking battleships had withdrawn, the bomb vessels had been left in position, still threatening the arsenal and dockyard. On 7 April Nelson went and inspected them and ordered soundings to be taken around the northward end of the Middle Ground shoal 'in case the Bombs are forced to retreat'.[75] He was also, as always, concerned for the welfare of his people. Parker had ordered most of the Danish prizes to be burnt, which meant that there would be no prize money, and so Nelson wrote to St Vincent on the 5th to ask him to arrange for a special grant: 'What must be the natural feelings of the Officers and men . . . to see their rich Commander in Chief burn all the fruits of their victory, which if fitted up and sent to England as many of them might have been by dismantling part of our Fleet would have sold for a good round sum?'[76]

He was also keen to move on up the Baltic, still wanting to get at the Russian fleet before it could get out of its winter harbour at Revel. But the Danes were proving difficult and so, on 8 April, Parker sent Nelson on shore once again to arrange an armistice, this time in company with Colonel Stewart and the Revd Alexander Scott, who acted as an interpreter, and the Secretary to the British party. At one point, a Danish commissioner said to a colleague in French that they might have to renew hostilities. But Nelson understood French well enough to know what was being said and immediately turned to Scott, 'Renew hostilities!' he said eagerly. 'Tell him we are ready at this moment; ready to bombard this very night!' Eventually, after what Scott called in his diary 'Five hours of *pour et contre* parler',[77] an armistice of 14 weeks was agreed. Nelson had clearly hoped for longer – in his journal entry recording the negotiations he first wrote '4 months' and then crossed it out and wrote '14 weeks'.[78] With his usual eye for a good man, he had observed Scott's performance during the negotiations and noted him as someone to watch. Stewart carried the news of the armistice home, taking with him letters from Nelson to a number of his friends, including Prime Minister Henry Addington (who had apparently asked him to write directly to him), and Clarence, who was told: 'Since I had the honour of writing to your Royal Highness last, the Truce has produced an Armistice. I hope it will be approved, without it, we should have gone no further. The Government of Copenhagen were afraid absolutely to involve themselves in a New War for one with Russia they considered as Inevitable if they made a hasty peace with you.'[79] In fact the Danes already knew, although the British did not, that Tsar Paul had been assassinated on 23 March – the news had reached them during the closing stages of the armistice negotiations on 9 April. The linchpin of the Armed Neutrality had snapped.

Unaware that the diplomatic situation was changing rapidly, and with the Danes temporarily out of action, Nelson now had to start again the wearisome business of getting Parker to move: this time on the Russians, whom he had always regarded as the prime target. By now the Commander-in-Chief was so unsettled by his responsibilites that he was unable to sleep, and the effects could be seen in his continued inability to take any decisive action. In order to get further up the Baltic, the fleet had to get over a large shoal known as the Grounds. Some of the masters of the fleet had been sent in the *Fox* cutter to make a survey. They returned on 9 April with a rough chart and the news that most of the fleet should be able to get through, but that the two flagships would have to be lightened. The *Fox* was sent back to buoy the channel, and it was not until the 13th that she came back again with the news that all was ready.

Nelson was of course chafing at this snail-like progress. 'All our 74s and 64s ought this day to be over the Grounds,' he told Troubridge on the 12th, 'but I am fretting to death . . . nothing can rouse our unaccountable lethargy'.[80] However, he was still watching over those who had served with him at the battle. Captain Thomas Thompson of the *Bellona* was recuperating after the loss of his leg, and miserably contemplating his future: 'I am now totally disabled and my career is run through only at the age of 35,' he told a friend.[81] Then, on the 12th, he received this wonderful letter: 'I have been so much taken up with the business of the Armistice and together with the Weather and my very indifferent state of health', wrote Nelson, 'that I have absolutely been unable to come to see you, but I rejoice to hear such very good accounts. Patience My Dear fellow is a Virtue (I know it) but I never profest in my life yet I can admire it in others. I will assuredly see you before we part and I beg you will believe me as ever your affectionate friend.'[82] Nelson was also, as ever, keen to encourage young naval officers – even if they were a former enemy: just ten days after the battle, the Commandant of the Danish Naval Academy, Captain Hans Sneedorff, received 'Lord Nelson's Compliments' and a copy of Davison's Nile Medal. 'I send you also a Short account of my life it cannot do harm to youth & may do good, as it will show that Perseverance and good conduct will raise a person to the very highest honors and rewards. That it may be useful in that way to those entrusted to your care is the fervent wish of Your Most Obt: Servt:'[83]

Finally, on 14 April Parker sailed with the main body of the fleet, having first removed stores and guns from the *London* to lighten her and leaving Nelson behind to 'expedite the sailing of the ships for England' – scarcely an essential task. The next day, as the fleet was anchored in Køge Bay, the frigate *Amazon*, which had been sent ahead to the Swedish naval base at Karlskrona, arrived to tell Parker that the Swedish fleet was at sea. With a battle now suddenly likely, Parker sent an urgent message to Nelson, who responded by leaping into the nearest boat and ordering its crew to row the 24 miles to Køge. Alexander Briarly, who had helped pilot the fleet into action at Copenhagen, was with him and remembered that the weather was 'pretty sharp'. The trip took six hours and the boat had no supplies on board, not even any water. 'All I had ever seen or heard of him', commented Briarly, 'could not half so clearly prove to me the singular and unbounded zeal of this truly great man.'[84]

Parker had not sailed and so Nelson hoisted his flag once more in the *Elephant*. Yet again, progress was leisurely, and two days later they reached Karlskrona, to find the Swedish fleet safe behind its batteries. Parker now was seized with uncertainty once more, writing to Nelson, 'Under all circumstances I do not feel I ought to proceed higher up the Baltic until I hear from England,' and, then, in a revealing gaffe, showed that the old tension between them was returning. He started by signing the letter 'Most Affectionately Yrs' but then crossed out 'Affectionately' and replaced it with 'Faithfully'.[85]

Then, on 22 April, news came that gave Parker an excellent excuse for inaction. A letter arrived from the Russian ambassador in Copenhagen to announce that the new Tsar, Alexander, wished to restore friendly relations with Britain. It was the first official news of the dramatic change that had occurred, and Parker immediately, and with evident relief, turned the fleet southwards again and returned to Køge Bay.

The following Sunday, the 26th, was Emma Hamilton's birthday, and a remarkable party took place on board the *St George*. Divine Service was performed, and then Nelson sat down to dinner with Parker and those captains in the fleet who had met Emma. A number of the invitations he sent have survived. Fremantle was told brusquely, 'If you don't come here on Sunday to Celebrate the Birthday of Santa Emma Damn me if I ever forgive you'; while Charles Tyler, who had known Emma in Naples, received the message 'Sunday the 26th being Santa Emma's birth day I beg you will do me the favor of dining on board the St: George as I know you are one of her Votarys.' Chaplain Scott entered in his diary, 'April 26th I have given the people a sermon on board the *St George*. St Emma's Day!', and even Parker entered into the spirit of the occasion, agreeing 'with particular pleasure [to] attend your Saint on Sunday next'.[86]

Parker's good humour was no doubt mainly due to the fact that he had just heard from Britain that his report of the Battle of Copenhagen had been well received. Nelson, too, had been highly praised. St Vincent wrote, 'You have greatly outstripped yourself and all who have gone before you in the late most glorious conflict.'[87] Feeling that, with the news from Russia, his work was done in the Baltic, Nelson applied to Parker for leave on 29 April. He was also feeling particularly unwell: the cold was affecting him badly and he was also suffering one of his regular malarial attacks: as he told Troubridge, 'last night's attack almost did me up and I can hardly tell how I feel today'.[88] Parker agreed to his request – although, with his customary heavy-handedness, he could not resist spoiling the effect by asking for a formal Surgeon's certificate – and suggested that Nelson should return in the frigate *Blanche*, which was sailing for England on 5 May. In the meantime, Nelson was confined to his cabin, where he was visited by Scott and also by Captain Lindholm, with whom he was now corresponding regularly. His servants were packing his belongings, and all was ready for his return home.

Then, at 1 a.m. on 5 May, Colonel Stewart arrived on board the *London* with dispatches and, to his consternation, Parker learned that he was ordered to hand over the command to Nelson and return to England.

The news of Copenhagen had reached Britain in two stages. Parker's official dispatch reporting the battle and the moves immediately preceding it had arrived in London on 15 April, two days after the news of the death of Tsar Paul. It met with a mixed reception. Both Houses of Parliament had passed votes of thanks but there were none of the usual signs of rejoicing for a victory – for example, no illumination of public buildings took place. Nonetheless, St Vincent and his government colleagues were contented enough to send their congratulations to Parker and Nelson. However, three days later, on 18 April, Stewart arrived in town with news of the 14-week armistice – which was not at all what the politicians had been expecting. Moreover, it is clear that he also told St Vincent and others privately about Parker's hesitation (which had anyway been apparent from his dispatches) and, most damning of all, about Signal No. 39. The following day George Rose breakfasted with St Vincent and heard the whole story. 'For these and other causes,' said the old Earl, 'we have recalled Sir Hyde and Lord Nelson is to remain in command.'[89] Forty-eight hours later, Stewart was on his way back to the Baltic.

'WITHOUT A MOMENT'S DELAY': THE COMMANDER-IN-CHIEF

Nelson's reaction on hearing the news of his appointment was mixed. Privately, with Emma, and friends such as Davison, he was bitter and angry, pointing out that the command had come too late, and even in his public letters he emphasised his poor health and asked to be relieved at once: 'My health neither more than less than a consumption . . . makes the high honor conferr'd on me the less pleasant nature as I cannot enjoy it,' he told Nepean.[90] On the other hand, there was little sign of ill-health in the storm of activity that now suddenly burst over the Baltic fleet. His first order was to hoist in all boats, and by the following day the fleet had been completely reorganised and new tasks allocated. An urgent note went off to Rear Admiral Totty, who was expected with reinforcements, to 'join me without a moment's delay'.[91] Pending Totty's arrival, Captain George Murray was ordered to take the smaller battleships and most of the sloops under his command and patrol off Bornholm to watch the Swedish fleet, while Captain Henry Inman was given command of all the bomb vessels, fire ships and gunboats and told to remain in the same area. Murray was ordered not to interrupt Swedish trade or even to prevent small war vessels from sailing. 'But in the Event of the Swedish fleet putting to sea it will become your duty to attack it and to use your best endeavours to take or Destroy the Whole.'[92] The *Speedwell* brig was sent into Karlskrona with a message to the Swedish admiral warning that 'I have no orders to abstain from hostilities should I meet the Swedish fleet at sea' and adding 'I am sure you must take this communication as the most friendly proceeding on my part.'[93] Then, having secured his lines of communication, Nelson set off at last with the main battlefleet for Revel (modern Tallinn), scattering letters to British diplomats in the area to let them know what he was doing. As he told Clarence: 'I am proceeding with 11 Sail of the Line into the Gulph of Finland and I trust to manage matters in such a way that the Emperor of Russia shall take it as a Compliment, at all events We shall get acquainted with the navigation of the Baltic in case we ever have a Northern War.'[94] That last phrase was significant – as he was to show by all his actions in the ensuing weeks, Nelson appreciated that the gathering of intelligence was a vital part of his mission.

Rear Admiral Thomas Graves was now second-in-command of the whole fleet, and the rapport they had struck up before and during the battle continued. Nelson immediately started sending him friendly notes, telling him what he was planning and sharing intelligence with him. By 12 May, the day before they reached the

Rear Admiral Sir Thomas Graves.
Nelson's second-in-command in the Baltic.
He is wearing the insignia of the Order of
the Bath presented to him by Nelson on
board HMS St George *in June 1801.*

Russian naval port, he knew that they were already too late: 'the Russian Squadron: sailed to the Eastward only on the 2nd of May,' he told Graves. He sent the *Kite* ahead with Frederick Thesiger on board to carry a letter to the Governor 'to request that your Excellency will permit the Squadron's being supplied with everything it may want such as Fresh Beef, vegetables &c.'[95] In other words, he was working hard to appear to be making a simple courtesy visit, although everyone knew it was actually a carefully calculated show of strength.

Arriving off Revel on 12 May, Nelson prepared to go ashore to call on the Governor. He invited Graves to accompany him – although since Graves was ill at the time, the note insisted, 'I charge you to Obey Your Doctor.' A diplomatic delay ensued, while the Governor sent to St Petersburg for instructions, which Nelson put to good effect by collecting information about the port and its fortifications and making plans for a future attack. Stewart drew a plan of the bay, which Nelson sent to St Vincent: 'perhaps you will direct a copy to be lodged in the Hydrographic Office.'[96] Eventually, on 16 May, the official reply, from the Russian Foreign Minister, Count Pahlen, arrived, saying that Nelson's letter had been 'an object of the greatest surprise' and adding that 'the only guarantee that [the Tsar] can accept of the loyalty of your intentions is the prompt removal of the fleet that you command.'[97] Nelson knew he had made his point and did not need to press it any further: he had shown that, if necessary, Britain was able to project her power right up to the gates of Russia. So he wrote a courteous and emollient reply, regretting that 'my desire to pay a marked attention to His Imperial Majesty has been so entirely misunderstood', and withdrew gracefully.[98]

From Revel, he moved to Rostock in Prussia, where he organised more fresh provisions for the fleet. At the same time, Murray was sent to Danzig 'to make the necessary enquiries with respect to what supplies of every kind can be procured for the Fleet'.[99] Piece by piece he was building up an infrastructure to enable Britain to maintain a fleet in the Baltic should this be required. At the same time, he was dealing with assured confidence with the local diplomats. James Crauford from Hamburg wrote to say, 'It is my most sincere prayer that you may long continue to adorn that country whose name, already first in the world, you have so greatly exalted.'[100] This was the sort of language Nelson appreciated, and Crauford received warm thanks for his 'very flattering letter', followed by a lucid appreciation of the situation in Denmark and Russia.[101]

By now similarly lucid reports and appreciations were reaching England, and the politicians quickly realised that they were dealing with a very different kind of admiral. Above all, he was a man who got results. On 26 May, the fleet was joined by a Russian lugger, bearing Pahlen's response to Nelson's friendly note of 16 May. Pahlen followed Nelson's lead by dismissing the contretemps at Revel as a misunderstanding, assured Nelson of Russia's desire for friendship and announced that the Tsar had ordered the embargo on British merchant ships to be lifted. As the lugger left the fleet it fired a salute. Turning to his Secretary, Thomas Wallis, Nelson said, 'Did you hear that little fellow salute? Well now there is peace with Russia depend on it; our jaunt to Revel was not so bad after all!' His judicious combination of a show of force and diplomacy had paid off.

This new political assurance in his protégé was not lost on St Vincent as he assessed Nelson's reports back at the Admiralty. Nelson was still insisting that his health was too frail for a long stay in the Baltic, and St Vincent freely admitted that the search for a suitable successor was proving difficult. He then launched into a warm and glowing tribute that is the more remarkable when we remember that less than six months before he had said that Nelson was not capable of filling a commander-in-chief's post. Now all was changed:

> I never saw the man in our Profession excepting yourself and Troubridge, who possessed the magic art of infusing the same spirit into others which inspired his actions, exclusive of other talents and habits of business not common to naval characters.
>
> Your Lordships whole conduct from your appointment to this hour is the subject of our constant admiration; it does not become me to make comparisons. All agree there is but one Nelson.[102]

The reference to 'habits of business' is particularly telling. Clearly Nelson had impressed his crusty old chief not only with his fighting spirit – which had never been in question – but also with his ability to administer a large fleet. A recent discovery among the Nelson papers at the British Library has shown how this was done – naval historian Andrew Lambert noticed that Nelson's system of fleet management in 1801 was based on St Vincent's own standard report forms and orders from his time in command of the Channel fleet, copies of which Nelson had taken with him to the Baltic.[103]

To assist him with all this administrative work Nelson now had, for the first time in his career, a captain of the fleet, or chief of staff. William Domett, who had worked in that capacity for Parker, had agreed to stay on. Nelson also tried to persuade Scott to stay, but the clergyman remained loyal to his patron, Sir Hyde Parker, in his adversity and went home with him. It is also clear that Edward Parker was by now acting as an unofficial aide-de-camp: in a letter to Emma Hamilton, with whom he was now corresponding, he gave her personal details about Nelson, whom he was now calling 'my most valuable Friend'.[104] Nelson had also established a work routine. Stewart noted that he was never out of bed later than six (and usually earlier) and that 'The whole ordinary business of the fleet was invariably dispatched as it had been by Earl St Vincent before eight o'clock.'[105] As Stewart commented, this example created a sense of alertness among the fleet as a whole. He also kept the fleet constantly on the move, telling Stewart that he wanted to keep all hands employed, 'No matter how and no matter where.'

By now, he was expecting his recall almost daily and, eventually, on 13 June, he received the news that another of William Locker's protégés, Charles Pole, was on his way out. He also received orders to invest Thomas Graves as a Knight of the Bath – just a few days before, he had told Edward Berry 'you will see that Graves has got the Red Ribbon and that I am a Viscount, Sir Hyde —'[106] The dash meant 'nothing'. The unfortunate Parker had been completely left out of any honours and was said to be contemplating asking for a court of enquiry in an attempt to retrieve his reputation. Nelson carefully avoided any public criticism of the man whose inertia had caused him so much concern and trouble, but, as he told Clarence: 'I should be very sorry to hear of any enquiry taking place respecting the Baltic fleet, no profit can arise from it and a negative Merit is something very like implied censure.'[107]

The previous day, he had presided over an altogether more congenial occasion when, representing the King, he had dubbed Thomas Graves knight on the quarterdeck of the *St George*. All the captains from the fleet were present in their full dress uniform; there was a guard of honour made up of Royal Marines and troops from the Rifle Corps with Stewart at their head; and the Royal Standard was flying from the main truck. Nelson first tapped Graves on the shoulder with the sword presented to him by the Nile captains, carried for him by Edward Parker. He then put the red ribbon over Graves's right shoulder and fastened the star to the left breast of his coat as, at a given signal, the whole fleet fired a 21-gun salute and the Royal Marines and troops presented arms. Then Nelson made a short speech, ending: 'I hope that these Honours conferred upon you will prove to the Officers in the Service that a strict perseverance in the pursuit of glorious Actions and the imitation of your brave and glorious conduct will ever ensure them the favours and reward of our most Gracious Sovereign.' As Edward Parker reported to Emma, 'it pleased and awed every body'.[108]

For Nelson it must have been a moment of powerful significance. He was representing his sovereign, surrounded by his comrades in arms, many of whom had recently fought with him in the hardest-won of all his battles. And he was knighting a man to whom he had drawn close in the preceding weeks, using a sword presented to him by the Band of Brothers themselves. He even managed to include Emma too – the new knight's ribbon, star and commission were carried in procession on a blue satin cushion she had given to her lover.

Five days later Pole arrived and Nelson transferred at once to the *Kite* before setting sail for England. Ten days after that, Emma received a hurried note, dated 'June 30th ½ past 1 running in for Yarmouth':

> My Dearest friend –
> I hope in God to be with you long before this letter, but whether I am or no believe me Ever Aye for Ever your faithful
> Nelson & Bronte
> Best regards to Sir William I have neither seen or heard of anything like you since we parted, what Consolation to think we tread on the same Island.[109]

She scribbled on the bottom: 'Just Rec'd he will be in Town today' and sent it to her husband.

'My Aid de Camp'. Nelson's Public Order Book for the Channel campaign, 1801. In this order he appoints his protégé, Captain Edward Parker, his aide-de-camp.

CHAPTER IV

The Channel Command: July–October 1801

Nelson arrived in London from the Baltic to find the capital in the middle of an invasion scare. The July edition of the *Naval Chronicle* spoke of 'the immense preparations making all along the French coast for the long-talked-of INVASION'.[1] On 21 July all leave was suspended by the Army, and the following day a parade of nearly 5,000 Volunteers was held in Hyde Park. We now know from recent French research[2] that these preparations were very largely a bluff by Napoleon, designed to bring Britain, his last remaining major adversary, to the negotiating table. In early March 1801, he had appointed one of his favourite admirals, Louis René de Latouche-Tréville, to command at Boulogne with orders to concentrate all the available forces there. But Latouche's means were in any case extremely limited, and it also proved very difficult to move those ships he did have to Boulogne under constant attack from the watchful British scouts. So, by the end of July, he still had only 63 vessels of various sizes under his immediate command, while there were only 2,400 infantry and 600 cavalry camped in the hills above the town – scarcely an impressive invasion force. French historian Rémi Monarque concludes: 'Without seriously envisaging disembarking on the enemy's shores, [Napoleon] wanted the British to fear the eventuality. For this, a minimum of preparatory effort was needed to render the threat credible.'[3]

Certainly, however, the threat was taken very seriously by the Government, and nowhere more so than at the Admiralty. On 24 July, Lord St Vincent, by then six months into his appointment as First Lord, wrote to Admiral Skeffington Lutwidge, commanding in the Downs: 'The state of the enemy's preparations on different parts of the coast of the Channel particularly opposite to you, beginning to wear a very serious appearance, and all the intelligence agreeing that a descent on some part of the coast is actually intended, it has naturally been a matter of consideration what measures would be most advisable to be taken for our defence.'[4]

At that time, Lutwidge was one of three admirals commanding British forces opposed to the French in the Channel – the other two being Admiral Archibald Dickson, Commander-in-Chief North Sea, and Vice Admiral Alexander Graeme, Commander-in-Chief at the Nore. However, each of these was an independent command, and so it was difficult to coordinate their efforts. St Vincent now decided that the best way to deal with the threat was to create a new, unified force of small vessels to act as a mobile and independent first line of defence. Additionally, he and his political colleagues wanted to show that they were doing all they could to prevent invasion. So, in a conscious act of public relations, they gave the command of this new force to the victor of the Nile and Copenhagen. The *Naval Chronicle* approved: 'Every person must rejoice to see Lord Nelson, whose courage, enterprize and vigilance are so pre-eminent employed in such a service.'[5] Nelson was formally appointed on 24 July and remained in post for almost three months, until 22 October.

When set alongside the other great campaigns in which he was involved, Nelson's brief service in the Channel can appear almost as an interlude and, certainly, this is the way in which it has been treated by most of his biographers. However, as regards his career as an admiral, it deserves rather more attention than it has received hitherto.

To begin with, it is important to remember that this was the first time he had been appointed to command a new fleet at the outset of a campaign. The Nile squadron had been a specially selected detachment from St Vincent's already well-established fleet, and by the time Nelson succeeded to the Baltic command, that fleet had already been in being for two months. Moreover the Channel fleet was, at least in terms of numbers of ships, by far the largest force he had ever commanded. The composition was never wholly static but at one point he had 143 vessels, mounting 2,124 guns and with 11,416 men under his orders.[6] Even in the first few weeks, when he and his men were most active, there were over seventy ships and vessels at his disposal. The most he ever had under his command at the height of his career, in the Mediterranean in 1803–5, was fifty.

The force was drawn from many different sources, and the various vessels were chosen to suit the nature of the operations they were likely to undertake and the coastal waters in which they would be working. In early August, there were six ships of the line, including three – *Ardent*, *Glatton* and *Isis* – from the now largely disbanded Baltic fleet, and all of them small 64- or 50-gunners. There were seven bomb vessels – half the Navy's available force – a clear indication that shore bombardment was likely to feature high in the new fleet's priorities. There were seven frigates and eleven sloops, ranging from large fifth rates, such as *Amazon* and *Unité*, to the small 14-gun *Gier*, captured from the Dutch in 1799. However, the core of the force, some thirty in all, were small, handy gun brigs and gun vessels. About half had been built in 1797 to deal with an earlier invasion threat and the remainder had been hurriedly constructed in 1801 to meet the present emergency.[7]

A few of the captains had served with Nelson before. John Gore of the *Medusa* had served ashore with Nelson in Corsica and had later commanded

HMS *Windsor Castle* in Hotham's actions in 1795. Sam Sutton had commanded the *Alcmene* at Copenhagen and transferred to HMS *Amazon* to replace Edward Riou. And John Conn, who commanded the bomb vessel *Discovery* at Copenhagen, had now brought her to join Nelson. However, the ships of his large and scattered force were never in company long enough for a new Band of Brothers to be formed.

'CORDIAL UNANIMITY': NELSON TAKES COMMAND

The day after the appointment was announced, Nelson and St Vincent met at the Admiralty. Characteristically, Nelson had already roughed out a plan for the defence of the Thames, which he took along with him. Bearing in mind that he had learned of his new command only a few days before, it was an astonishingly detailed and lucid appreciation, displaying a striking familiarity with the geography of the estuary and the best means for defending it. Clearly, he was drawing on the memories of his long days of boat work in the Thames estuary as a boy. As always with him, it was not a dry official document. Instead it was shot through with his aggressive spirit: 'the moment the enemy touch our Coast, be it where it may, they are to be attacked by every man afloat and on shore this must be perfectly understood. Never fear the event.'[8] St Vincent was impressed with the plan, and it formed the basis of Nelson's official orders, issued on 26 July.[9] In them, the limits of his command were set from Beachy Head to Orford Ness, and he was given two main objectives. First, he was to make arrangements for the defence of the Thames and Medway and the coasts of Essex and Suffolk and, second, he was to station his forces in the best position 'for blocking up or destroying, if practicable, the enemy's vessels and craft in the ports where they may be assembled, or if they should be able to put to sea, for destroying them.'

Despite the size of his fleet and complexity of his command, Nelson was not given a captain of the fleet. Once more, as in the Mediterranean, he had to improvise his own staff. Frederick Langford, his Baltic signal lieutenant, accompanied him, and he also applied to the Admiralty for permission to employ Edward Parker as his aide-de-camp. By now, Parker was the protégé to whom he was closest – so much so, that both of them described their relationship in terms of father and son. Parker had accompanied his patron home from the Baltic and stayed with him throughout his brief period of leave, even joining him and the Hamiltons on a fishing excursion to Shepperton, near Staines, shortly before Nelson was recalled to active duty. Now he became Nelson's official right-hand man – at times literally so, for, as Nelson told Emma, 'Parker sits next to me to cut my meat when I want it done.' Parker himself continued to write regularly to Emma, as he had from the Baltic, with reports of Nelson's health and doings, laced with a fair amount of flattery.

It was Parker, therefore, who now took responsibility for distributing Nelson's orders to his new command. As in the Mediterranean in 1798–9, one way in which this was done was through a Public Order Book; Parker was responsible for maintaining this book and, indeed, wrote many of the orders in it himself.[10]

Accompanied by Parker, Nelson travelled to Sheerness on 27 July, hoisted his flag temporarily in the frigate HMS *Unité* and promptly exploded into action. Orders were issued to over thirty captains to place themselves under his command. Any captains who were not ready to take their ships to sea were required immediately to explain 'for what reasons they are retarded'. Then, having dined with Admiral Graeme, to make sure that he was content with the new arrangements, Nelson moved on down the Dover Road to the pleasant port and market town of Faversham, with its prosperous merchants' houses and busy quays and warehouses along the banks of the creek. It was the headquarters of the Kent division of the Sea Fencibles, sea-faring men, such as fishermen, who had been allowed immunity from impressment on the understanding that they would come forward in time of emergency to man the vessels designed for the defence of the rivers and coastline. However, now that the emergency had actually arrived, they were proving reluctant, and Nelson found that he was expected 'to get up and harangue like a Recruiting Sergeant'.[11] Reporting on their visit, Parker told Emma: 'We were received by the acclamations of the people who looked with wild but most affectionate amazement at him who was once more going to step forward in defence of his country.'[12] Nelson was of course used to this sort of adulation and even enjoyed it. But this was the first time since he had shot to fame that he had been on active service so close to home, and he was soon to find that working in the full glare of public attention had its negative side.

On 29 July, he arrived at Deal, the port closest to the great anchorage at the Downs, which was to be his headquarters for the campaign. There, he and Parker dined with Skeffington and Mrs Lutwidge, and he renewed his acquaintance with his former Arctic captain. Although Nelson was still technically the junior, he clearly had the more important command, but the old affection held and the two worked happily together for the rest of Nelson's time in the area, Lutwidge loyally supporting his former pupil. Having hoisted his flag temporarily in the 64-gun battleship *Leyden*, more orders shot from his desk like rapid gunfire. Divisions were created and placed in strategic positions: one at Margate Sands, one off Flushing and two right on the enemy coast – one to cruise between Calais and Dieppe and the other off Étaples. Trusted men were placed in command, and each received clear, detailed orders outlining their task and with the assurance that their admiral relied on their 'Judgement and Zeal'. As a measure of how hard he was working, Nelson also signed an urgent request to the Victualling Office for more stationery, 'as I am much in want of the same'.[13]

All these documents were shot through with his trademark energy: everything was to be done 'with as much expedition as possible', 'as speedily as possible'. In every order, he sought to impress his new subordinates with the urgency of the situation and the need for vigilance. As he told Edward Berry on 28 July: 'You are likewise to keep the Crews of the Vessels under your Orders constantly exercised at the Great Guns and small arms &c in order to make them fit for real Service and to strongly enjoin them that the strictest lookout be kept, as well by Night as by day to prevent any Surprise of the Enemy.'[14] At the same time, there was a strong emphasis on the need for such a disparate and widely scattered force to pull together. On 31 July, Nelson issued a General Order to his senior commanders that is worth quoting more fully, since it perfectly captures his leadership style:

> As much of our success must depend on the cordial unanimity of every person, I strongly recommend that no little jealousy of Seniority should be allowed to creep into our Minds, but that the directions of the Senior Officer or the judicious plans of the Senior should be adopted with the greatest cheerfulness.
>
> As it is impossible that I can be at all times in every part of my extensive Command I rely with confidence on the Judgement and Support of every Individual under my Command, and I can assure them of my readiness to represent their Services in the strongest point of view to the Admiralty.[15]

It was a bravura performance – a classic demonstration of how to galvanise a new command, and to impress one's personality and style on subordinates right at the outset of a campaign or operation. It was also one of his best: the only time he bettered it was off Cádiz, in the weeks before Trafalgar. Edward Parker told Emma, 'He made everyone pleased, filled them with emulation and set them all on the qui vive.'[16] That is an excellent summary of Nelson's command methods.

Having energised his own force, Nelson was now ready to announce his presence to the enemy. On 1 August, he went on board the 32-gun frigate *Medusa*, which was to be his temporary flagship until the slightly larger *Amazon*, which had been officially allocated to him, arrived. So, for the first time since early 1797, he had to get used to the more cramped quarters of a fifth rate. He occupied the great cabin, of course, which meant that the captain, John Gore, had to move out. Typically, Nelson was conscious of the trouble he was causing and asked Emma to arrange for a silver tea kettle to be prepared as a gift with a suitable inscription of gratitude. 'He is very rich,' he told her, 'therefore I must take care not to offend.'[17] Arriving off Boulogne on 2 August, he found that Latouche had moored a line of some twenty-four vessels outside the harbour to defend the approaches. Having first carried out a close reconnaissance in person, on board the aptly named *Nile* lugger on 3 August, he then ordered his bomb vessels to try some ranging shots on the defensive line. On the same date he began a full bombardment lasting most of the day, during which some 900 shells were fired. The bomb vessels anchored to carry out the shelling, while the supporting ships kept under way, 'to be of effective use should the enemy's vessels should make any movement.'[18] Nelson spent the entire day in his barge, moving from vessel to vessel, encouraging his men, and so became the object of the French return fire. As he told Emma: 'The French have been very attentive to me for they did nothing but fire at the boat and the different vessels I was in but God is good.'[19]

Estimations of the effectiveness of the bombardment varied widely. In his official report to Lord St Vincent, Nelson claimed that ten vessels had been 'entirely disabled', while in his report Latouche claimed that only two had been damaged.[20] A report from a neutral vessel suggests that the truth lay somewhere

Boulogne, c. 1804. Although drawn some years after Nelson's attack, this view of Boulogne nonetheless gives a good impression of how the town looked in 1801.

between – '5 gunvessels sunk, 6 or 7 greatly damaged'.[21] In truth, however, the numbers sunk or damaged mattered very little: as Nelson told the Duke of Clarence, the main purpose of the operation was 'to show the Enemy that, with impunity, they cannot come outside their Ports'.[22]

More importantly, close examination of Boulogne had convinced Nelson that the invasion was not going to come from there. He and his staff had counted no more than 'fifty or sixty' boats inside the harbour and, as he told Lutwidge, 'of the Craft which I have seen I do not think it possible to <u>row</u> them to England and sail they cannot'.[23] So he decided to make a tour of the Channel ports, trying to discover where the feared invasion army was based. Lieutenant William Cathcart, a nephew of Sir William Hamilton serving in the *Medusa*, wrote to his father: 'We are now going to Flushing and if the enemy are not in more force there the people are all fools to dream of an invasion . . . I really fear our Government have bad information.'[24] Clearly, little more than a week after he had taken up his command, Nelson and his staff were beginning to suspect that the invasion threat was an empty one.

A strong easterly wind prevented the proposed reconnaissance of Flushing and so Nelson decided to turn his attention instead to his other pressing problem – persuading the Sea Fencibles to serve at sea. Characteristically, neither St Vincent nor Troubridge had much sympathy with them – so far as they were concerned, the men had undertaken to serve in an emergency and, if they would not honour their pledge, they should be pressed into service. But that was not Nelson's way – instead, he decided to meet with the men and listen to their point of view. One of the largest groups of Fencibles – 414 men, according to the return submitted by the area commander for Essex, Captain Isaac Schomberg[25] – was based at Harwich, which happened also to be at the northernmost limits of Nelson's command, and where there was a small naval dockyard. So he decided to go there on a tour of inspection in the *Medusa*, arriving on 9 August. The local militia turned out to welcome him, together with the town dignitaries, but he preferred to stay afloat, transferring to the *King George* cutter, which took him close into the town for a conference with Schomberg and the other Fencible captains.

Basing his opinion on their reports, he assured the Admiralty that the loyalty of the men and 'their readiness to fight' was not in question, but that they were worried about their livelihoods and so did not want to go to sea until it was absolutely necessary. His solution was simple: instead of requiring the men to report to the Nore, where they could be allocated to ships, he would send the ships to them, so that they could embark quickly, as soon as the alarm was given. So orders went out to ships waiting at the Nore to sail to various key embarkation points at Brightlingsea, Harwich, Orford, Woodbridge, Gorleston and Lowestoft.[26] He also issued a general Order to all his captains emphasising that the Fencibles were to be treated sensitively: 'It is my particular directions to the several Captains and Commanders who may be ordered to receive them . . . that they be extremely careful of their Conduct towards them, taking care that they are treated with as much kindness as possible, and to give all due Encouragement to those who display Zeal and Interest for the Service they are embarked in.'[27]

Nelson returned to the *Medusa* and gave orders to sail to the Nore. However, the wind had changed, so that the frigate was pinned within Hoseley Bay, and the Downs pilots on board did not feel confident enough among the unfamiliar shoals to try to extricate her. Into the breach stepped the local maritime surveyor, Graeme Spence, who knew of a channel running under Walton Naze, through which he undertook to navigate the *Medusa*. Nelson accepted his offer, the passage was duly made successfully – and the channel has been known as 'the Medusa Channel' ever since. Nelson's own navigational eye was as keen as ever: spotting that the local guardship was anchored in a dangerous position, he sent an order to her commanding officer telling him exactly where he wished him to place her: 'Bring Little Oakley Church a little open to the right of Harwich [*sic*: should be Walton] Naze Cliff and Great Holland Church Tower a little open to the left of Frinton chapel on Frinton Cliff in five fathoms at least of water.'[28] All the landmarks he mentioned are still there, and reading those precise directions conjures up a vivid impression of him standing on the *Medusa*'s quarterdeck, watching the coastline keenly as she edged her way through the shallow waters off the Naze. Reporting the incident to St Vincent, Nelson commented, 'It is necessary I should know all that is to be known of the navigation'[29] – yet another example of his thorough approach to information-gathering. The First Lord wholeheartedly approved, telling him that his reports about his voyages in the Thames and the Medway 'convey greater information to us than any we have received from other quarters'.[30] Indeed, St Vincent's regular letters to Nelson during this period show the old man's growing appreciation of the businesslike qualities that his protégé was now displaying.

Reaching the Nore, Nelson found more dignitaries waiting for him: the Mayor and Corporation of Sandwich came on board to present him with the Freedom of the town and invited him to dine with them, but he turned them down. 'I shall be attacked again when I get to the Downs,' he told Emma, 'Oh how I hate to be stared at.'[31] But, as Parker noted in a letter to Davison: 'The Blue flag at the fore [Nelson's flag as a vice-admiral of the blue] triumphantly display'd on our ship gives Confidence to the eager Thousands who with Enthusiasm behold it.' He also added, 'That B. will play the devil with Him, She is endeavouring to persuade Him that the Ministry are jealous of his proceedings at Boulogne' – an interesting insight into the way that Nelson's closest colleagues actually felt about Emma.[32]

Also awaiting him were intelligence reports that increased his suspicion about the emptiness of the French threat. Information from Boulogne confirmed that the French had no more than 2,000 troops stationed there. A reconnaissance of Ostend and Blankenberge by Captain Richard Hawkins in HMS *Galgo* had revealed that there were only sixty or seventy boats in the ports – scarcely enough to transport 3,000 men. 'Where, my dear Lord,' Nelson asked St Vincent, 'is our Invasion to come from?' Even so, he was still actively looking for a target at which to launch a major offensive blow: 'To crush the enemy at home was the favourite plan of Lord Chatham and I am sure you think it wisest to carry the war from our own doors.'[33] His first preference was for an attack on Flushing, at the mouth of the River Schelde; but this required the support of a significant force of troops, and none were available. So, eventually, almost by process of elimination, the idea grew of a full-scale boat attack on the French flotilla defending the approaches to Boulogne. It was the only place where another demonstration could be made of the British ability to strike at French forces on their own coast.

'PERSEVERING COURAGE': THE ATTACK ON BOULOGNE, 15 AUGUST

Nelson arrived back in the Downs on 13 August, and at once a flurry of activity began. Orders went out to assemble a flotilla of flat boats, and the commanders of the bomb vessels, together with their artillery officers, were ordered to fit each one with a howitzer. Arrangements were also made for them to be towed to Boulogne. The boats of the squadron were assembled, along with their crews, who were to be armed with cutlasses and pikes and provided each with a blanket. As usual, the orders bristle with Nelsonian phrases: 'with all possible expedition', 'without delay', 'make all the haste you can'.[34]

Nelson's battle orders, issued in the morning on 15 August[35] (see p. 202), envisaged a concerted attack on Latouche's line of defence by some 900 men. They would be carried in 55 ships' boats organised in 4 divisions, each of 13 to 15 boats, supported by a fifth division of flat boats armed with howitzers. The enemy's line was divided into four segments, and each division was allocated a segment – the idea was that the attacks should all arrive at once so that the whole

French line would be engulfed and overwhelmed. Two boats from each division were to be prepared for cutting the cables of the enemy vessels and towing them away or for setting them on fire should this not prove practicable. The men from the other boats, armed with pikes, cutlasses and tomahawks, were to board the vessels and attempt to capture them. The howitzer boats were to cover the attack by firing on the French camp and shore batteries. Each division would have a captain in command: the eastern division was under Philip Somerville; Edward Parker and Isaac Cotgrave commanded the two centre ones; and Richard Jones the westernmost. John Conn controlled the howitzer boats. In a classic passage, Nelson emphasised that once a French vessel had been captured or destroyed 'the business is not to be considered as finished; but a sufficient number being left to guard the Prize, the others are immediately to pursue the object by proceeding on to the next, and so on, until the whole of the Flotilla be either taken, or totally annihilated.' He also gave the captains commanding the various divisions 'permission to make any additional arrangements in the mode of attack they may think will more easily facilitate it.'

These highly detailed and clearly expressed orders challenge the suggestion made in some modern accounts that the attack on Boulogne failed because of careless preparation or because Nelson's judgement was impaired.[36] There is little sign of impaired judgement in the careful plan that he devised and, as always, his preparation and forethought were exemplary. However, on this occasion he was opposed by an officer who matched him in professional skill. Knowing that Nelson was in command, Latouche had predicted that he would return to Boulogne to renew the attack and had made his preparations accordingly, strengthening his defensive line and securing his ships firmly to each other. He had installed his headquarters in a tower on the hills above Boulogne and, from this vantage point, he was able to watch the arrival of Nelson's force and to observe the sudden flurry of activity around the flagship as the attacking force of boats gathered on the evening of 15 August. He therefore stationed watch-boats well ahead of his line to give advance warning of an attack and had his men alert and ready at their posts.[37]

Around 11.30 p.m.[38] on the 15th the attacking force left the *Medusa* – the challenge was 'Nelson' and the answer 'Bronte' – and, for the second time in his career, Nelson was left waiting for news of a major operation while others carried out his orders. He had not enjoyed the experience at Tenerife and he liked it even less this time. He later told St Vincent it was an experience he had vowed never to repeat: 'my mind suffers much more than if I had a leg shot off in the process.'[39] He tried to pass the time by writing to Emma. She was looking for a house for him, and he started by discussing prices with her. Then, almost in mid-sentence, he changed course: 'my mind feels for what is going forward this night it is one thing to order and arrange an attack and another to execute it.'[40] About 1.30 a.m. there was a sudden fierce crackle of musketry which lasted for about 15 or 20 minutes before all fell silent again, and still they waited for news. Eventually, about 2.15 a.m., the *Medusa*'s barge came alongside with eight killed and wounded on

board; they were taken out and the boat sent back to assist. Then, at 3 a.m., just
as the distant gunfire flared up again, came a small group of boats all laden with
casualties. Soon there was a steady flow of them – in all, 45 killed and
128 wounded. The attack had been a bloody failure.

Piecing together later what had happened, it became clear that the four
attacking divisions had become separated in the dark and swept eastwards by a
strongly flowing tide. As a result, they had arrived at their objective piecemeal,
instead of in an overwhelming wave as Nelson had planned. Parker's division had
arrived first, and he attacked the French brig *Etna*, flying the pendant of
Commodore Périeux. However, the brig was well-prepared, with anti-boarding
netting rigged, and her heavy fire caused huge losses in Parker's boat. His second-
in-command, the *Medusa*'s First Lieutenant, Edward Williams, was the most
successful of all the attackers, capturing a lugger and storming another large brig:
as he later reported, 'nothing could surpass the zeal, courage and readiness of
every description of officer and man under my command.' But as the rest of the
attack faltered, they were driven back with heavy losses.

Elsewhere, little had gone right. Isaac Cotgrave, with the other centre division,
had attacked another French brig, but his own boat was sunk when a heavy shot
was dropped straight through its bottom and, as he later reported, he and his men
found the French fire too strong and so were forced to withdraw. Meanwhile,
Somerville's eastern division was swept away from its objective by the tide and
was only able to reach the French line at about 3 a.m. – thus provoking the second
wave of musketry that had been heard on board the *Medusa*. They succeeded in
boarding and capturing a brig, but when they tried to cut her cables, as Nelson
had planned, they found that the French had used chain rather than hemp cables.
By now the shore batteries could see them and were pouring in a heavy fire, so
Somerville was forced to withdraw. As he did so, he met with Robert Jones's
westward division. They had been unable to make any progress at all against the
strongly flowing tide and had failed altogether to reach their objective. Having
struggled with their oars until dawn, they gave up and dropped down the line to
help Somerville's division but, meeting them returning, they joined them in retreat.
Throughout all these attacks John Conn's howitzers had been firing on the French
camp and batteries 'until', as he later claimed, 'the enemy's fire totally slackened'.

Certainly, Latouche's forces had been fully prepared and on the alert – the
watch-boats he had stationed ahead of his line spotted the attackers and sounded
the alarm in plenty of time.[41] Nelson later told St Vincent, 'it was their misfortune
to be sent on a service which the precautions of the enemy rendered impossible to
succeed in'.[42] But the tide had been another important contributor to the British
failure and the question remains why the problems it caused were not anticipated.

There was still worse news to come. As the wounded were carried back, it was
discovered that among them was Edward Parker. While attempting to board the
Commodore's brig he had suffered a multiple fracture of his thigh and had been
on the verge of capture. However, William Cathcart, commanding the *Medusa*'s
cutter, came alongside, took Parker's boat in tow and dragged her clear of the

French fire. Also among the wounded was Frederick Langford who, like Parker, had suffered a serious leg wound.

Nelson's public response in the immediate aftermath of this disastrous repulse was positive and reasonably upbeat, given the circumstances. As at Tenerife, he accepted sole responsibility and, in his official dispatch to the Admiralty, he highly praised the 'determined persevering courage' of his men. He also mentioned the chains that Somerville and his men had discovered, and St Vincent picked up the hint in his reply, writing: 'The manner in which the enemy's flotilla was made fast to the ground could not have been foreseen.' Nelson then circulated the First Lord's message to his men, telling them: 'The moment the enemy have the audacity to cast off the chains which fix them to the ground, that moment Lord Nelson is well persuaded they will be conducted by his brave followers to a British port, or sent to the bottom.' Three days after the repulse, he sent Conn in again with his howitzer boats to try to set fire to Commodore Périeux's pendant ship. He also continued to look for possible targets for other attacks, telling St Vincent, 'I have real thoughts of attacking the Enemy at Flushing.' Captain John Russell of HMS *Gier* was sent to Calais to see if the vessels sheltering there could be bombarded.[43]

Privately, however, the repulse at Boulogne and especially the appalling wound suffered by Parker unsettled Nelson. He told Emma, 'You will believe how I am suffering and not well into the bargain.' On 18 August, he attended the funeral of two of the *Medusa*'s midshipmen, William Gore and John Bristow, and then visited the wounded in the hospital at Deal. By now Parker and Langford had been transferred to rooms in Deal, where they could be personally attended by Dr Andrew Baird, whom St Vincent had sent down as soon as he heard the news. At first, it looked as if Parker was recovering but, even so, when Nelson came to leave him, 'he got hold of my hand and said he could not bear me to leave him and cried like a child.'[44] In the end, however, the young man's leg could not be saved and, having endured the torture of an amputation close to the hip joint, he then lingered for four agonising weeks, fighting death at every stage, rallying and then sinking again, until finally he died on 27 September. Nelson visited him whenever his duties permitted, living on a perpetual emotional see-saw: rejoicing when the signs were good and cast down when the prospects were less favourable. They were drawn together even closer during this terrible period, each acknowledging their affection to the other – and to Emma, who received letters from both. Nelson sent her reports on Parker's progress almost daily, and Parker told her that Nelson was 'my Friend, my Nurse, my Attendant, my Patron, my Protector, nay Him whom the world cannot find words sufficient enough to praise.'[45] When the young man was buried, with full military honours, in the graveyard of St George's, Deal, Nelson finally broke down in public and was seen leaning against a tree, sobbing inconsolably.

This was now the second time in his career that Nelson had lost a much-loved young companion in arms and protégé, and in a defeat for which he felt personally responsible. Parker had also been far closer to him than John Weatherhead, who had died in similar circumstances in the attack on Tenerife in 1797. It was a devastating emotional blow and it clearly affected him deeply. 'I scarcely know how I got over it,' he told Emma after the funeral. 'I could not suffer more and be alive. God forbid I should ever be called upon to say or see as much again.'[46]

'This curious command': the campaign winds down

An immediate result of Nelson's grief over Parker was that he appeared to lose his taste for risky operations. In the days immediately after the Boulogne defeat, he was actively contemplating an assault on the enemy forces at Flushing, encouraged in his planning by some very favourable reports by the man on the spot, Captain Edward Owen, another energetic, enthusiastic young officer in Parker's mould. On 24 August Nelson went over to Flushing with a force of some thirty ships, including three bomb vessels. He gathered information with his usual thoroughness. First, he interviewed the local pilots and then undertook a close personal reconnaissance in a small cutter, the *King George*, getting within 3 miles of the defences. He concluded that an attack was impossible, and explaining this to Lutwidge he used a telling phrase: '[Captain Owen's] Zeal, I am afraid, has made him overleap sandbanks and tides and laid him aboard the Enemy but I must clear away these little obstacles before I could give him scope for his intentions.'[47] The man who had overleapt sandbanks many times in his career, and whose carefully laid plans at Boulogne had been ruined by tides, had suddenly learned caution.

He had also learned that fame has a negative face. His postbag now contained begging letters and details of ingenious inventions for which his patronage was sought. The man who asked barefacedly for £300 to set up a school in Yorkshire was ignored; the friend of an inventor of a 'machine for keeping a Gun at one continuous Elevation' received a thoughtful and thoroughly 'Nelsonian' reply: 'it might be very useful but . . . I am rather of the Opinion it will not be brought into use. The best and only mode I have found of hitting the Enemy afloat is to get so close that whether the Gun is pointed upwards or downwards, forward or aft, that it must strike its opponent.'[48]

He was also beginning to feel oppressed by the number of well-wishers who kept trying to catch a glimpse of him whenever his ship was in port or at anchor in the Downs – on one occasion, he counted fifty boats rowing round the *Medusa*, 'to have a look at the one-armed man'. Better-connected people would actually come on board visiting, as if he was living at home ashore. 'The devils here want to plague my soul out,' he told Emma. 'The Countess M., Lady this that and t'other came alongside a Mr Lubbock with them to desire they might come in. I sent word I was so busy that no person could be admitted as my time was employed in the Kings service . . . I will not be shewn about like a <u>beast</u>.'[49]

Worse, he found that his professional deeds were being openly criticised in the press. He was especially castigated for the heavy casualties at Boulogne. As he told Nepean: 'every means even to posting up papers in the Streets of Deal had been used to sett the Seamen against being sent by Lord Nelson to be butchered, and that at Margate it was the same thing whenever any boats went on shore, <u>what</u> are

Merton Place, c. 1807. Thomas Baxter captures some of the beauty and peace that made Merton 'paradise' for Nelson and Emma.

you going to be slaughtered again.' He concluded sadly, 'as I must probably be from all the circumstances I have stated not much liked by either Officers or men I really think it would be better to take me from this Command.'[50]

In addition to all these pressures, Nelson was missing Emma. Repeated requests for a few days' leave were firmly refused by St Vincent: 'The public mind is so very much tranquilised by your being at your post that it is extremely desirable that you should continue there . . . give up at least for the present your intention of returning to town which would have the worst possible effect at this critical juncture.'[51] He wrote to her almost daily, and it is clear from references in his letters that, once again, she was giving him a hard time. Any reference to his going ashore had to be carefully justified and, in some cases, he even went so far as to ask her permission. He had to explain to her that, for reasons of security, he could not tell her in advance where he was going. And it would appear that she even started begging him not to expose himself to danger, just as Frances had done. After Boulogne almost every letter to her contains an assurance 'I will not run any unnecessary risk. No more boat work I promise you.'[52] She had been house-hunting for him and found a suitable property in the village of Merton, to the south-west of London and close to the Portsmouth road. So he was also distracted by surveyors' reports and the usual delays of house purchase. He did see Emma briefly in September when she and Sir William paid him a visit at Deal, accompanied by brother William and his wife Sarah. While they were with him he was happy, but when they left reaction set in: 'I came on board but no Emma. No no my heart will break . . . My dearest wife how can I bear our separation?'[53]

Finally, to complete Nelson's distraction, there were persistent rumours that peace was imminent. Secret negotiations with France had begun even before he took up his command in late July, and as early as 11 August St Vincent had told him, 'Our negotiation is drawing near its close and must terminate one way or another in the course of a few days.' In fact the negotiations dragged on for another two months, and so long as they continued, Nelson was kept prominently in the front line as a symbol of Britain's continuing determination not to give away

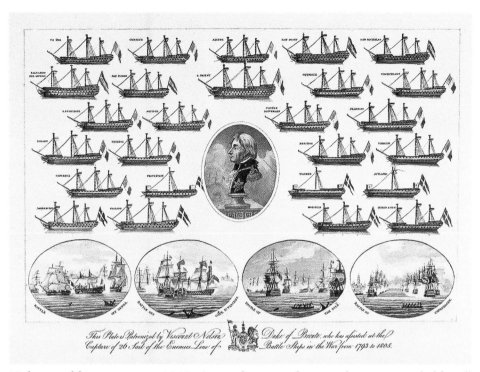

Nelson and his captures, c. 1802. A popular print shows Nelson surrounded by all the ships he had helped to capture between 1793 and 1801. He was involved in the design and chose the central portrait himself, a version of his favourite likeness by de Koster (see Colour Plate 9).

too much. He was bombarded with letters urging him to stay at his post. On 28 August Nepean wrote him a private letter telling him 'as a friend' not to think of hauling down his flag; as late as mid-October, Prime Minister Addington was still begging him not to relinquish his command.[54] He continued to protest at being used in this way, writing to Alexander Davison: 'I am trying to get rid of my Command but I am to be forced to hold it to keep the Merchants easy until Hostilities cease in the Channel.' He told St Vincent, 'I own I do not think it a command for a Vice Admiral,' and in a frank letter to Lord Keith he remarked 'this curious command is not giving me much strength'.[55]

It was no longer giving him much scope for action either. Despite his own doubts and depression, and despite the inevitable slackening of discipline caused by the rumours of peace, he did his best to keep his force motivated and at full alert. He was still accumulating navigational information and rearranging the disposition of his forces accordingly: with winter approaching, he wanted to find stations for them that combined safety with an ability to react quickly to any attack.[56] He was still looking at ways of attacking the enemy without excessive danger to his men. On 1 October he told Captains Rose and Somerville: 'It is my

The Peace of Amiens. *In this caricature celebrating the peace, Nelson is one of the figures taking part in the dance.*

intention to send the Nancy fire brig to attempt the Destruction of the Enemy in Boulogne.' This was another of the enthusiastic Edward Owen's ideas: on 26 September he had reported that the vessels in Boulogne were so placed that 'it appears a fire vessel may be used against them'.[57] But then, just when all was ready, and waiting only for a fair wind, Nelson received a formal letter from the Admiralty telling him that preliminaries of peace had been signed. So he was forced to write to St Vincent to ask 'whether it would be right, under our circumstances with France to do a violent thing?' St Vincent agreed that any such attack would be 'an ill omen of the sincerity of our professions'[58] and so the plan was abandoned. Even now, with peace imminent, and hostilities suspended, Nelson insisted that his force should remain vigilant, telling his captains that they should 'keep the Ships and Vessels under your Command in every respect ready for putting to Sea at the shortest possible Notice and to exercise your Men at the great Guns and small Arms very frequently.'[59] On 14 October, he formally requested permission to go ashore and, finally, on 20 October, St Vincent wrote giving him permission to do so. Even then, however, he made it clear that Nelson would be continued in pay, and thus officially in command, until the Definitive Treaty was signed. On 22 October, he finally struck his flag and set off to join the Hamiltons at his new home in Merton.

HMS Victory: *the Great Cabin. Nelson's dining-cabin is in the foreground, with pictures of Emma and Horatia on the bulkhead. In the background is the day cabin, where he worked with his secretaries.*

CHAPTER V

The Mediterranean Campaign: 1803–4

'I AM AT LAST AFLOAT': TAKING COMMAND

The Peace of Amiens, signed on 25 March 1802, was always fragile and, by April 1803, it was becoming clear that war with France was again likely. Although Nelson publicly supported the peace policy of Addington and his government, that did not prevent him from privately advising the Prime Minister on ways in which he could prepare for war. Manning the fleet was always a problem at the outset of any conflict and, in October 1802, he sent Addington a short paper outlining 'the quickest Mode of bringing our naval force into action', in order to give 'an early and knock down blow to the Enemy'. His proposals were bold and ruthless: 'an embargo on every port on the Kingdom . . . Every Soldier, every Magistrate and every good Man to exert themselves in taking up every seafaring Man in the United Kingdom.' A few months later, when war was eventually declared, a very similar scheme was operated, the so-called 'Hot Press'. It caused an outcry – but Nelson had foreseen such opposition, 'although it may not be palatable to all at the Moment, yet in a Week I expect the whole Country will approve it'.[1]

After weeks of waiting in the wings, as the politicians agonised over whether to renew the conflict, Nelson was formally appointed commander-in-chief of the Mediterranean fleet on 16 May 1803 when war was eventually declared. He was ordered to hoist his flag in the *Victory* – although he was also told to make contact with his old friend William Cornwallis, who was commanding the Channel fleet, to see if he needed the three-decker, before proceeding to his station. At 44, he was the youngest man ever to hold the Mediterranean command, and he owed the appointment to St Vincent, who was still First Lord of the Admiralty.

As in 1798, St Vincent chose Nelson over the heads of older and more experienced admirals, including Lord Keith, who had held the position at the close of the previous war and expected to be appointed again. Clearly, St Vincent's doubts about Nelson's suitability for higher command had now been completely removed by his protégé's remarkable services in 1801.

Nelson had spent the waiting weeks making contact with various key people whom he wanted for his 'team'. Thomas Atkinson, who had been the Master of the *St George* in the Baltic, was appointed Master of the *Victory*, which had been named as Nelson's flagship. John Scott, whom he wanted as his public secretary, had to organise a transfer from the *Royal Sovereign*. The Revd Alexander Scott, whose excellence as a linguist Nelson had noted during the Baltic campaign, received an urgent summons to join him in Portsmouth. Scott was Rector of Southminster, and he had to pack his bags and leave his parish in just four days. Not surprisingly, his Bishop objected to this abrupt abandonment of his clerical duties, but Scott was able to call Nelson to his defence:

> If my friend the Revd: Mr: Scott has got into any scrape with Your Lordship I much fear that I have been the innocent cause of it. I wish'd to have with Me a Clergyman of sound morals and of that respectability of character who I could always have near my person and to be my guest, in addition to this, Mr: Scott is I will venture to say one of the most learned Men of the Age and of great Observation of Men and manners. He is My Confidential private Foreign Secretary which on this station where so many languages are to be corresponded in is a place of very great importance.[2]

At the same time, Nelson set his own personal affairs in order. One of his Merton neighbours, Benjamin Patterson, was told in April: 'I am much obliged by your kind letter & should I unhappily be called from Merton by the conduct of that Insolent Scoundrel Buonaparte, I shall be happy in accepting your kind offer of assistance for much of my farming affairs at Merton.'[3]

At about 10 a.m. on 20 April, he put off from Portsmouth 'in a heavy shower of rain' and hoisted his flag in the *Victory*, writing to Addington: 'I am at last afloat and shall sail about 4 OClock to proceed off Brest . . . If I get safe to my Command you may rely that my most Zealous endeavours shall be used to assist all in my power our friends and well wishers and to distress our Enemies.'[4]

Then he was off, in company with the frigate *Amphion*, speeding down the Channel with a brisk northerly wind behind him. On board too was Hugh Elliot, the new British ambassador to Naples, who was taking passage with him. Nelson's departure was so sudden that one of the *Victory*'s lieutenants, William Crockett, was left behind. On 31 May he wrote to Sir Evan Nepean to explain:

> Having been on shore on some Mess concerns when Lord Nelson embarked on the 20th: instant; His Lordship sailed in such a sudden and unexpected haste that I had the misfortune to be left behind; when I saw the Victory under way

I hired a wherry with all possible dispatch to get on board, but the weather proving hazey, and a breeze springing up Eastward I could not get up with her.[5]

He then hired a packet vessel to Plymouth, in the hope of catching up with his ship there, but eventually had to return to London. He never joined the *Victory*.

Arriving off Ushant on the 22nd, Nelson searched vainly for Cornwallis and his fleet for a few agitated hours and then, almost in a fever, as if a major battle was imminent, transferred a few belongings to the *Amphion*, leaving the *Victory* behind him to search for his friend. Hardy and Sutton exchanged places rapidly, and Ambassador Elliot was bundled hurriedly, together with the members of Nelson's rentinue, out of their spacious quarters in the three-decker and into the cramped confines of the frigate, where some of them were obliged to sleep six or seven in a cabin. And then they were off again, pushing south against contrary winds, with Nelson complaining to Emma, 'I am very anxious to get to my station. This is all lost time and the sooner to get to work the sooner please God I shall return.'[6] By 4 June, less than a month after he had been told to start his preparations by St Vincent, he was at Gibraltar, taking up the reins of his new command. He paid an official visit to the Lieutenant Governor, Sir Thomas Trigge, and then personally inspected the dockyard, ordering the Naval Store Keeper, Edward Pownall, to ensure 'that the most strict attention is paid to the preservation and issue of every description of Naval Stores under your charge.'[7] Then, after only seven hours ashore, he was off again into the Mediterranean, leaving a galvanised garrison and dockyard behind him. It was a wholly characteristic start to his appointment, similar to the energetic way he had begun in the Baltic in May 1801 and again in the Channel in July the same year. He exuded determination and purpose, telling Addington: 'Buonaparte . . . I am sure is alarmed at our resistance to his Will and dreads the Event and that he may have reason to repent his rashness Insolence & folly is the fervent prayer and shall be the strenuous endeavour of N& B.'[8]

Nonetheless, despite his eagerness to join his new fleet and start his 'strenuous endeavour', he first took time to make a tour of the key strategic points of his new command, starting with Malta. Then the *Amphion* proceeded northward through the Straits of Messina and, on 25 June, arrived in familiar waters: 'Close to Capri the view of Vesuvius calls so many circumstances to my mind that it almost overpowers me', Nelson told Emma. Despite such strong personal feelings, he did not go ashore, contenting himself with exchanging letters with Ambassador Elliot, who had been sent on direct from the Straits of Gibraltar in the frigate *Maidstone*. From him, he learned that the French had marched an army into Calabria and appeared to be threatening Naples itself, or perhaps planning an invasion of Sicily. Nelson sent assurances to Sir John Acton that the defence of Naples was a high priority for him and promised to keep a warship always at Naples in case it was needed to evacuate the royal family. But he did not stop in his headlong voyage.

Eventually the *Amphion* arrived off Toulon on 8 July and found there Rear Admiral Sir Richard Bickerton with the main fleet – eight battleships, four frigates and a number of sloops.[9] It was still very much a peacetime fleet – as Nelson told Emma, 'the ships themselves are a little the worse for wear'.[10] None of the battleships was larger than a 74-gunner – although these included the *Superb* and the *Renown*, both fine, relatively new ships. However, two were 64s, East Indiamen converted on the stocks in 1796 to meet an acute shortage of ships. As Nelson told St Vincent, they 'sail very ill and in these times are hardly to be reckoned'. Others were in a poor state: 'the *Triumph*'s bowsprit is in such a dangerous state that I am sending her to Gibraltar.'[11] He also had to send the *Kent* into Malta to refit and, as he told Lord Hobart, 'that place is at such a distance [from the navigation] that oftentimes we could sooner communicate with Spithead'.[12] The smaller vessels were a similar 'mix', including fine, new ships such as his former flagship, the *Medusa*, and the smaller *Seahorse*, the frigate that had brought him home from Tenerife, and older, more infirm ships such as the *Camelion*.

The ships' captains, however, were in much better shape and, although few of them had served with him before, Nelson quickly appreciated that he had inherited an excellent team, writing to Troubridge on 20 October, 'more Zeal and attention with good humour I never saw exceeded, it is like the Nile fleet without Davidge Gould'.[13] There were well-known 'stars', such as Richard Keats of the *Superb*, who had made his name at the Battle of the Gut of Gibraltar in July 1801, when he attacked two Spanish three-deckers in HMS *Superb* and set them on fire before moving on to capture a French ship. Nelson quickly recognised Keats's worth, gave him a number of important detached operations and, the following April, told his patron, the Duke of Clarence, 'the more I know of him the more excellent qualities I find not only as a Sea Officer but as a man who knows much of the World'.[14] Another man with 'excellent qualities' was Sir Richard Strachan of the *Donegal*, and soon he too was being allowed to make his own command decisions, 'I leave you at liberty to run up to gain a laurel in the battle which will soon be fought . . . I do not expect you but leave that to yourself'.[15]

There were old comrades – such as John Gore of the *Medusa*, who had been with Nelson in the Channel, and of course Samuel Sutton, who finally brought the *Victory* to join the fleet on 30 July, exchanged once more with Hardy, and returned to the *Amphion*. Among the commanders of the smaller ships, there was a scattering of Nelson's personal 'followers' – for example, the Hon. Bladen Capel of the *Phoebe*, who had carried home Nelson's duplicate dispatches from the Nile in 1798, and the Hon. Courtney Boyle of the *Seahorse*, who had been one of the *Boreas*'s midshipmen. Many years earlier Nelson had written to Boyle's father, the Earl of Cork, 'he is amiable in the truest sense of the word . . . In the professional line he is inferior to none.'[16] Now Boyle received one of his patron's characteristic notes:

My dear Boyle
I am very happy to have you in so fine a frigate under my
command for I am yours most faithfully
Nelson & Bronte.[17]

Rear Admiral Sir Richard Bickerton.
Nelson's second-in-command throughout
the Mediterranean campaign.

Second-in-command of the fleet was Rear Admiral Sir Richard Bickerton. Expecting that Bickerton would not wish to serve as a subordinate, having held the chief command, St Vincent had ordered Rear Admiral George Campbell out to the Mediterranean in HMS *Canopus*. But at their first meeting, Bickerton made it clear to Nelson that he wanted to stay and so, apart from a short break in Malta towards the end of 1803 while the *Kent* was refitted, he remained with the fleet throughout the campaign. Soon, Nelson was writing warm and friendly notes to him, sharing information and explaining decisions, just as he had done with Thomas Graves in the Baltic. 'I am always at all times days & hours glad to see you,' he told him in October 1804.[18]

The strategic situation in the Mediterranean was strikingly different from that which Nelson had known in 1799–1800. Then, most of the places demanding his attention had been in the south – Egypt, Naples and Malta – which is why Palermo had been an appropriate base for him strategically, as well as desirable for personal reasons. Now, with an increasingly powerful French Mediterranean fleet based at Toulon, the focus had shifted decisively to the north. Moreover, as well as controlling the entrance of the sea from Gibraltar, Britain now had a secure base at Malta, which reduced the importance of Naples – although still valuable as an ally and a source of food supplies, Naples and her dockyard facilities were no longer needed as urgently as in the previous campaign. Moreover, Malta was placed conveniently at the narrow pass between the eastern and western basins. As a result, so long as the enemy battlefleet could be confined in the western area, the control of the remainder of the theatre could safely be left to squadrons of frigates and sloops. So, instead of being forced to move constantly between objectives, as in 1799–1800, Nelson was able to keep his main fleet concentrated in the northern part of the western basin, within striking distance of Toulon. Meanwhile, behind the battlefleet screen, his cruisers could extend British influence to the widest limits of the Mediterranean, including the Adriatic.

The French, by contrast, were limited and confined by British seapower. Although their army in Calabria was an ever-present threat, it could only operate independently within the Italian peninsula. To campaign anywhere else, it had to cross the sea, which meant that it would need a naval escort. So, once again, holding down the main French fleet in Toulon was the best way of preventing this. As Nelson explained to Spiridion Foresti, the British Consul in the Ionian Islands (based at Corfu) in June 1804: 'I have effectually prevented the surprise from the only port from whence it could happen and the only way for a naval force to protect the Ionian Republic is by watching the Enemy in their own Ports.'[19] As a result, for the next two years the French fleet was to be his constant concern.

The one thing he could not prevent by seapower was a French conquest of Naples. For this he needed troops – of which there were too few in the area. The only sizeable British land force, the Army of Egypt, had returned to Britain by 1803, leaving only a few thousand men stationed in Malta under Nelson's former colleague in the Corsican campaign, Major-General William Villettes. Nelson's immediate plan was to use these men to garrison Messina, thus hopefully deterring the French from attempting a crossing to Sicily, but Villettes's orders were only provisional and in the end nothing was done, despite Nelson's personal pleas in private letters to Lord Hobart, the Secretary at War. His early dispatches home contained the first of many pleas that the government would send a detachment of troops into the Mediterranean.

So, since the fleet was Britain's sole source of power in the area, Nelson's most pressing task was to keep his ships afloat and in as good order as possible, given that the nearest dockyard facilities were at least two weeks' sailing away. In August 1803, St Vincent told him airily: 'I have no idea under the vigour of your character that there will be an imaginary difficulty; real ones cannot exist. In short, cordage may be manufactured at sea; caulking and every other refitment which in England requires dock yard inspection your Lordship knows is much better performed by artificers of the squadron.'[20] The old Admiral's trust was not misplaced. Within a few months Nelson was telling Troubridge: 'I shall so far put your mind at rest that the Ships here have no complaints which the Captains cannot remedy, their bottoms & rotten masts they cannot help.'[21]

But this was only achieved by constant, careful husbanding of stores and incessant paperwork, and Nelson's files for this period are filled with detailed descriptions of the unremitting work that went on daily to keep his tottering ships constantly at sea.[22] He found the continual battle to tease jealously guarded stores out of careful dockyard officials so wearing and time-consuming that eventually, in January 1805, he came up with a strikingly modern solution. Orders went to Commissioner Otway at Malta to send out to the fleet a transport – aptly named the *Camel*! – which, said Nelson, 'must be considered as a floating Store House and consequently well furnished with Stores to answer all our Wants . . . It is my determination not to send any more [ships] to Valette Harbour, but constantly to have Stores sent out and the different Ships defects made good at Sea, or at the Anchorage occasionally used by the Fleet.'[23]

Similar care and attention was paid to the provision of fresh food for the men. As Nelson told his former colleague of the Nicaraguan campaign, Dr Moseley:

> The great thing is health and you will agree with me that it is easier for an Officer to keep men healthy than for a Surgeon to cure them . . . <u>onions</u> I find the best thing which can be given to Seamen, having always good mutton for the sick, cattle when we can get it and plenty of fresh water . . . These things are for the Commander-in-Chief to look to and shut very nearly out from Spain and only getting refreshments by stealth from other places my task has been an arduous one.[24]

From the moment he took up the command, Nelson searched constantly for new sources of fresh food. For example, in September 1803, he wrote to Mr Clark, the British Consul at Tunis: 'I shall likewise be glad to be informed what supplies can be procured at Tunis or its environs for the fleet during the coming winter, and what the Prices of cattle will nearly come to, and what quantitys can be procured at short notice.'[25]

However, Nelson soon realised that this method of obtaining supplies was far too erratic, so he requested that a single 'agent victualler afloat' should be appointed to his fleet. Richard Ford was duly sent out to the Mediterranean by the Victualling Board, arriving off Toulon in February 1804 with his assistant, John Geoghegan. At the same time, a small fleet of transports – eighteen by the middle of 1804 – was organised to carry the supplies they had obtained out to the fleet wherever it happened to be stationed.[26] Often this was done at sea – 'replenishment at sea' was not invented in the Second World War! As a result of this administrative innovation, supplies began to flow regularly, and the health of the sailors was markedly improved. In August 1803, the *Gibraltar* landed 135 scurvy cases on the island of La Maddalena in northern Sardinia, where all but one were cured in ten days by a diet of fresh meat and vegetables.[27] Nine months later, Nelson was able to tell Dr Andrew Baird, 'the health of this Fleet cannot be exceeded.'[28]

The nearest British base was of course at Malta, where the splendid Grand Harbour and the naval dockyard at Valletta offered a safe anchorage and excellent facilities for ship repairs and supplies. But it was too far away from Nelson's regular cruising grounds off Toulon. As he told Tom Fremantle in January 1804: 'I would much rather undertake to ansr: for the Toulon fleet from St Helen's [the anchorage at the eastern end of the Isle of Wight] than from Malta, it is a place I never dare venture to carry the fleet.'[29] He solved the problem by using three anchorages in Sardinia: the Gulf of Palmas and Pula Roads in the south and the magnificent Agincourt Sound, in the shelter of the island of La Maddalena on the north coast, overlooking the Strait of Bonifacio. The great advantage of La Maddalena was that it was less than 250 miles from Toulon. So he felt able to take the whole fleet in there for replenishment and repairs, knowing that he could be back on station in less than two days if required. He spoke highly of it in many of his letters, telling Fremantle for example that it was 'a very fine anchorage' and on one occasion even comparing it favourably to Trincomalee in Sri Lanka, which he had seen as a boy in HMS *Seahorse*.

Sardinia was of course a neutral state, and so the anchorages had to be used circumspectly, and great care was taken to maintain good relations with state officials. At that time the island was ruled by an absentee King, Vittorio Emanuele I, with his court at Turin on mainland Italy exercising government through a Viceroy, his brother the Duke of Genoa, who was based at Cagliari. Nelson maintained a regular and friendly correspondence with the Viceroy – but in such secrecy that the letters did not appear in his official letterbooks. The originals have only recently been located and transcribed.[30] The series started with his first visit to La Maddalena in November 1803, when he announced his arrival 'to obtain refreshments for my fleet' and went on to assure the Viceroy that 'if this island is attacked by the French I have orders to furnish every assistance possible'.[31] And it continued until just a few weeks before Trafalgar, when he assured the Viceroy that 'whether I was at Pulla or in the West Indies the interest and welfare of your Royal House was always near my heart.'[32]

He took similar care to maintain good relations with the local population, using Alexander Scott as his agent. For example, in October 1804, Nelson presented a silver altar cross and matching candlesticks, obtained by Scott in Barcelona, to the local church at La Maddalena, writing to the priest: 'I have to request that I may be allowed to present to the Church at Maddalena a piece of Church Plate as a small token of my esteem for the Worthy inhabitants, and of my remembrance of the hospitable treatment His Majestys fleet under my Command has ever received from them. May God Bless us all.'[33] Scott also befriended Lieutenant Pietro Magnon, the commandant of the tower of Longdon Sardo, a fortification close to La Maddalena. In December 1803 Magnon was invited on board the *Victory* and Nelson presented him with a Nile medal.[34] He became an ardent anglophile, writing to Scott: 'I do not believe dear Doctor it is an offence against our neutrality, nor at all immoral, to send good wishes . . . for the triumph of your generous nation.'[35] Magnon's superior, the commandant of the area, by the name of Millelire, was also treated to dinner on board the *Victory*, and Nelson took similar pains with the local inhabitants near the Gulf of Palmas and Pula Roads. Once again, Alexander Scott paid a number of private visits ashore, and some of the local officials were entertained on board the *Victory*.

As a result of these careful efforts, La Maddalena became Nelson's forward base. Nelson took the fleet there eight times between October 1803 and January 1805, and during the same period he used the anchorage at Palmas three times and Pula Roads five times. As Richard Ford's reorganisation of the supply system began to take effect, storeships from Malta and Gibraltar would be waiting when the fleet came in, and there were good sources of fresh water at both locations. This meant that, although individual ships were sent from time to time into Malta

Revd Alexander Scott. Nelson's Chaplain and 'foreign' Secretary, seen here in old age.

or Gibraltar for refits or more extensive repairs, the battlefleet almost always remained confined within a triangle between Palmas, Barcelona and Toulon (see plan on p. 206). So it was seldom more than a week's sail away from the main opponent.

'A CORRECT AND CLEAR CORRESPONDENT': THE BUSINESS OF THE FLEET

Until the French ventured out, however, the routine work of the fleet went on. And, as always, high on the list of matters demanding Nelson's attention was the question of patronage. Although as Commander-in-Chief he had some power of rewarding his followers, as he constantly reminded them and their supporters who filled his postbag with requests for favours, 'All Admiralty vacancies are filled up by the First Lord of the Admiralty . . . Nothing is left to the Commander in Chief of the Present day but Deaths & Dismissals by Court Martials.' So, as he told Lieutenant Hamilton, who was pressing for promotion: 'My disposition to serve you stands at this moment the same as when your father wished me to receive you as the tenth Lieut: of the Victory but I can neither kill captains nor will the French to Oblige you.'[36]

Indeed, he went so far as to spar with Lord St Vincent about the number of names on the Admiralty List, many of which he could see were designed to please the Earl's political supporters, and reminding him how he had complained about the length of the list when he had held the same position back in 1795–7. But St Vincent was having none of it: 'perhaps your Lordship does not know', came the crushing reply, 'that I carried to the Mediterranean a much longer list than I have troubled you with.'[37]

Nonetheless, by 1803 Nelson knew the system intimately and was usually able to work it to benefit those he favoured. An Admiralty request in October 1804 to promote Lieutenant Henry Duncan, son of Admiral Lord Duncan, to commander released a lieutenant's place in Bickerton's flagship, into which one of Bickerton's own protégés, George Mowbray, was promoted. This in turn released a place in the *Seahorse*, which Nelson filled by promoting Midshipman Charles Yonge, a relative by marriage of his brother William. The Admiralty note on the official letter confirming Yonge's appointment made clear what was going on: 'Appointed in consequence of his being a young man of great merit and an Elevi [*sic*] of Admiral Viscount Nelson.'[38]

The Mediterranean command brought with it immense responsibility for the man in the top post. On almost every other major station, ministers could directly influence operations, as Nelson had found in the Baltic and Channel in 1801. In the Mediterranean, news and dispatches took weeks to reach the fleet, and on at least two occasions during 1803–5 communications were disrupted for months at a time after dispatch vessels had been captured. As a result, Nelson found himself handling complex diplomatic matters as well as the more straightforward administration of his fleet and operations against the enemy. He dealt with all these wider tasks confidently and with a statesmanlike touch that impressed all the politicians and diplomats with whom he came into contact.

Although Nelson himself remained mostly in the western basin of the Mediterranean, and although most of his correspondence related to events in that area, the eastern limits of his command stretched as far as Egypt and Palestine, and also included the Aegean and Adriatic Seas. He maintained a small force of frigates stationed in the Adriatic under Captain William Cracraft, and he kept in regular touch with British diplomats in the area, such as William Drummond, the Ambassador at Constantinople. Because of his victory at the Nile in 1798 and the lavish rewards bestowed on him afterwards by the Sultan of Turkey, he felt a special personal affinity with the Turks. In June 1803, he wrote to the Grand Vizier announcing his arrival and adding: 'I have also the pleasure to communicate to Your Highness that one part of my Instructions is to afford every assistance in my power to the Sublime Porte should that restless ambition which before gave such troubles to it[39] again attempt to Molest the Ottoman Empire.'[40] Drummond wrote that: 'The Turkish government has heard with particular pleasure that your Excellency has the chief command of the Mediterranean, your name stands no less here than it does everywhere else.'[41]

One of Nelson's key contacts in the area was the British Consul at Corfu, Spiridion Foresti, whom he had first met in the previous war. They corresponded officially on a regular basis, but recently located private correspondence shows that they also became warm friends:

I have to thank Mrs Foresti and yourself for your kindness to me. I have it is true wished to be useful to you but I fear I have never succeeded equal to my wishes, nor allow me to say equal by any means to your deserts for long and most faithful Services, and for your great sufferings incurred in serving the State

. . . Your Public Service I never fail remindg: Government of for you are
certainly one of the Most correct & clear correspondents I ever met with.[42]

By contrast, Nelson's correspondence with Hookham Frere, the British
Ambassador to Spain, was markedly less warm. Frere was cautious, circumspect
and not given to definite pronouncements – qualities guaranteed to irritate
Nelson. He wanted clear answers and unequivocal advice on whether, and if so
when, Spain would enter the war: 'I rely with perfect confidence on your early
information of what is likely to be the result of the present negotiations with Spain
as I keep all the fleet collected until I either know that all is amicably settled or
that I may be prepared to meet the Spanish fleet before they can form a junction at
Toulon.'[43] Private letters to the former Prime Minister of Naples, Sir John Acton,
show how Nelson's faith in Frere declined. On 18 March 1804 he wrote,
'although Mr Frere has sent circular letters for us to be on our guard yet I believe
he knows nothing of the matter'.[44] Then, less than a week later, 'My opinion of
Mr Frere is confirmed for in any case he ought to tell us that a change has either
taken place or that the same hostile appearances continue.'[45]

Perhaps the best evidence of Nelson's increased experience and confidence in
diplomatic matters was the way in which he handled relations with Naples. Never
again would he allow his conscience to be 'Sicilified', and Naples was now treated as
but one of a number of important allies to be watched over and assisted as required.
Indeed, an analysis of his diplomatic correspondence in this period shows Nelson
gave more of his attention to the affairs of Sardinia than to those of Naples. Urgent
invitations to go ashore and recover his health in Naples or Palermo were politely
rebuffed: 'I have wrote to Mr: Elliot upon the impossibility of my going ashore to
either Naples or Palermo, and it is possible that I may render Your Majesties cause
more service in conversing with the Ministry in London than even by remaining here
the Winter and to be forced to retire for ever next summer.'[46]

In sharp contrast to his former deferential, even obsequious, behaviour, he also
wrote frankly to the Neapolitan leaders about delicate diplomatic matters as if he
was an equal. He told the Queen of Naples, Maria Carolina: 'I most sincerely
hope that the House of Austria[47] will not unite itself against Russia but I fear I see
cause for Jealousy in the conduct of Russia in the Ionian Republic and in the
Morea, if that should unfortunately be the case the coming forward of Russia will
be of the greatest disservice to the cause of Europe.'[48] He even lectured Acton on
the need to reform the Kingdom's antiquated feudal system:

Perhaps Sicily is in a more perilous situation than you are aware of. The French
I have great reason to believe have made it understood in Sicily as well as in
Sardinia that the feudal System and the Oppressive Laws of Vassallage
attendant on that system shall be done away when they take Sicily . . . Turn this
over in Your Enlightened Mind. Mankind have more enlarged ideas than in
former times. I will not say more, but that something must be done, or those
Countries where the feudal System prevails will be lost.[49]

Nelson's mastery of the complex Mediterranean diplomacy is one of the most impressive aspects of this crucial period in his career – and offers tantalising glimpses of the level of statesmanship he might have attained had he survived Trafalgar.

Recent research has established that Nelson's diplomatic activity, as well as his operations, was supported by a complex and widespread intelligence system.[50] As before in his career, he maintained and nurtured a network of personal contacts in strategic points all over his command. Sometimes these were old colleagues, such as James Duff at Cádiz, whom he reminded in October 1803 'next January it is 27 years since our first acquaintance',[51] which means they must have met when he visited the area in 1777 as an acting lieutenant in the battleship HMS *Worcester*. Duff and his superior at Madrid, James Hunter, maintained a regular and most useful stream of information – at one point, for example, Hunter even sent, at Nelson's request, full details and a sketch of the road from Barcelona to Madrid. Another useful contact was Henry Blanckley, the British Consul in Minorca, a friend of Nelson's father. In August 1803, he wrote to Nelson suggesting that a boat should be sent regularly to cruise off the island, so that he could send off intelligence of the Spanish defences.[52]

Sometimes the contacts were new ones, such as Edward Gayner, a Quaker merchant in Barcelona. While Spain remained neutral, Gayner arranged supplies for the fleet quite openly; recently located private letters make it clear that he also supplied Nelson with intelligence. For example, in a letter dated 10 February 1804, he tells Nelson: 'Our accounts from France agree that the French are manning their Fleets. It is said they have nine sail of the line and altogether 23 Sail Vessels at Toulon.'[53] Gayner got his intelligence to Nelson in a number of ways. When it was routine material, he simply waited for the next British warship to call at Rosas for supplies. When he judged that the information was more important, he hired a local boat owner, Pira Marti, paying him to seek out one of Nelson's frigates and then either hand over the documents 'or continue with the frigate until he finds the fleet'. On at least one occasion he visited the *Victory* herself when she was patrolling near to Rosas, writing on 16 January 1804 to 'My friend Lord Nelson to acknowledge my gratitude to him for the kind reception I met on board the *Victory'.*[54] There is, however, a sad ending to his story. A note from one of Gayner's colleagues has recently been found in which it is stated that the Quaker merchant was put in prison by the Spanish authorities in Barcelona in late 1804. We do not know exactly why he was sent to prison – but it seems likely that it was because his intelligence-gathering activities had been noticed.[55]

Another most useful source of intelligence was intercepted mail. Right at the start of the war, in June 1803, Nelson's favourite, William Layman, who had been with him in the Baltic, scored an intelligence coup when he was put as prizemaster into a captured French frigate, *L'Ambuscade*. While on board, he discovered a treasure trove of official French naval papers which the French captain had omitted to destroy or throw overboard. These included: signal codes for the fleet and shore telegraph installations; a complete list of French signal flags and pendants; official naval tactical documents and memoranda; and details of a

1. *Rear Admiral Lord Nelson, 1800. This portrait, painted in Vienna by the court portraitist Heinrich Füger, captures Nelson's ruthlessness and capacity for concentration.*

2. *Nelson at the Battle of Cape St Vincent. In this rather stylised view of the scene by Daniel Orme, Nelson accepts the sword of the Spanish Admiral Winthuysen, on board the* San Josef.

3. *The Battle of the Nile, 1 August 1798. The French flagship,* L'Orient, *explodes at the height of the action.*

4.& 5. Celebrating the Nile. (Top) James Gilray celebrates Nelson's victory with a vivid image of the admiral belabouring tricoloured crocodiles with a club marked 'British Oak'. (Bottom) A more sedate engraving depicts the thanksgiving service on the Vanguard's quarterdeck, led by the Revd Stephen Comyn (left).

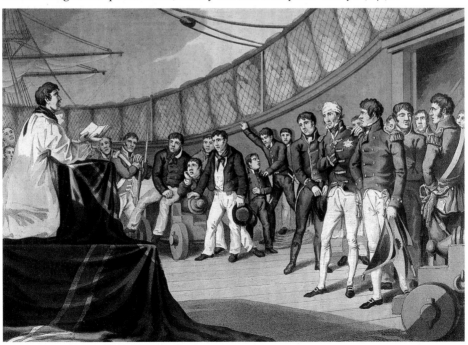

6. *Rear Admiral Lord Nelson, 1800. John Hoppner's original sketch for his full-length portrait, painted at the time of the break-up of Nelson's marriage, shows him looking haunted and unhappy.*

7. *Emma, Lady Hamilton, c. 1795. Miniature in a locket that Nelson wore round his neck. It contains a lock of her thick, richly auburn hair in the back – a reminder, like the image, of Emma's voluptuous sexiness.*

8. *Horatia Nelson, c. 1803. Horatia captured in the garden at Merton by Henry Edridge. Nelson took this painting with him to sea and it hung on the bulkhead of his cabin in the* Victory.

9. & 10. 'The most like me'. (Top) The portrait Nelson thought was most like him, based on a pencil sketch by Simon de Koster. It belonged to Sir William Hamilton. (Bottom) A later miniature, c. 1802, based on Lemuel Abbott's famous 1798 portrait, which is probably the best-known likeness of Nelson.

11. The plum pudding in danger. *James Gilray neatly sums up the international situation in 1805. Napoleon (right) carves off a portion marked 'Europe' while Pitt (left) prefers the 'Ocean'.*

12. The Battle of Trafalgar, 21 October 1805, c. 12.45 p.m. *Nicholas Pocock's superb aerial view shows the moment when the* Victory *(centre) forced her way through the Franco-Spanish line.*

13. Truth and falsehood. *A British caricature contrasts the way in which the news of Trafalgar was dealt with in Britain and in France.*

14. *The state funeral of Lord Nelson, 9 January 1805. The scene in St Paul's Cathedral during the closing stages of the service. All Nelson's family, friends and naval colleagues are gathered around the coffin.*

detached French squadron at that time operating at San Domingo in the West Indies and expected back any day in the Mediterranean.[56] This was by any standards a remarkable haul to land on the desk of a new commander-in-chief at the very outset of a war, and Nelson was obviously very grateful to the bright young man who had given him such an invaluable insight into the organisation of his opponent. No single subsequent capture ever quite matched this one but, even so, Nelson continued to gain valuable information as a result of the actions of his cruisers, and his correspondence is full of references to intercepted letters captured in prize ships.

Finally, there were straightforward routine naval reconnaissances, which kept Nelson regularly informed of the state of the fleet in Toulon together with any indications of its likely movements. There were also special intelligence-gathering operations. Only occasional, and guarded, references to these missions appear in Nelson's official dispatches and letters; but we can now reconstruct them from material located in his own files and those of his associates. So, for example, between March and October 1804 he organised a mission to the Black Sea by Lieutenant Henry Woodman, the agent for transports in Malta. Woodman's very thorough report, located recently, includes not only factual details about the Russian fleet and its supplies and harbours, but also some colourful character sketches of key Russian officials. There was the Governor of Odessa, who 'makes much use of his Butler's wife who is very pretty'; or the Governor of the Naval Academy, who 'has all the portraits of distinguished English admirals hung around his study'.[57]

Convoys remained a constant worry and required much thought and carefully synchronised planning. Nelson was always being asked to provide them, but he never had enough ships to act as escorts. 'What can I do, I have not the ships,' he wrote despairingly to Bickerton in January 1804 after listing all the people who were demanding them from him.[58] The following month, he replied patiently to a complaint from Francis Wherry, the British Consul in Smyrna: 'you may rely that the protection of our Commerce is always in my thoughts. But as you justly observe the preparation for the Invasion of England, which stagnates the trade, likewise keeps at home our Ships of War, therefore I have not that number of Ships which otherwise the Government would give me.'[59] At the same time, he was receiving similar complaints from the opposite end of the Mediterranean. Sir Thomas Trigge at Gibraltar was told firmly: 'it is Vain My Dear Sir to try to please everybody – some Merchants who have lost their ships do not approve of the way the Brigs are stationed . . . I am always sorry when I hear of a Capture but my mind feels easy that none of the Captures are owing to any inattention of mine.'[60] On the other hand, his efforts were at least appreciated by his closest colleagues. Rear Admiral George Campbell, the third-in-command, wrote in February 1804: 'I wish from my heart you had more Frigates, as in my Humble Opinion, Your Lordship employs them as a Commander in Chief ought to do, for the Countrys Service and not for private Lucre.'[61]

Malta was the linchpin in the system. Merchantmen would be escorted there from the eastern basin and the Adriatic by Nelson's thinly stretched force of smaller ships to form a large convoy, which was then passed under a more powerful escort – sometimes, for example, a battleship on passage home – to Gibraltar. There, the Malta convoy would be joined by vessels gathered from the western basin and the convoy, by now numbering dozens of ships, would then be escorted northwards. A similar system operated in reverse for vessels sailing into the Mediterranean. The slightest delay or accident to one ship could disrupt the entire, delicately balanced system. In March 1805 Captain Frank Sotheron, commanding the battleship HMS *Excellent* stationed at Naples, agreed to the request of Ambassador Elliot that HMS *Seahorse* should be diverted from her planned course in order to take urgent dispatches to the Commander-in-Chief. As a result, a vital convoy from the Levant to England was held up at Malta for want of a proper escort, and, as Nelson told the inexperienced young captain wearily, when he wrote to explain to him the knock-on effects of the decision, 'our Merchants will call loudly against me'. However, this lesson in wider command was given lightly and with an assurance of continued trust: 'I am truly sensible that you ever act in the most correct manner . . . yet I have only mentioned my situation to you to prove to you the impossibility of any of the small ships being allowed to remain in Port longer than is absolutely necessary.'[62]

'UNTIRING ENERGY': THE ADMIRAL IN HIS OFFICE

All this correspondence created a vast amount of paper – most of which passed through the Great Cabin of HMS *Victory*. Nelson and his immediate staff occupied the spacious admiral's quarters on the aftermost part of the upper gun deck. The suite was entered by a door on the port side, leading to an anteroom, which also served as a mess and sleeping area for the clerks and servants. From here, a second door opened into the dining-cabin, stretching across the full width of the ship. It was handsomely furnished, with special sea-going furniture designed and produced by Gillows – a long mahogany table with a concertinaed base that enabled it to be folded up small, and a matching sideboard that broke down into small parts for easy stowage. The dining chairs, similarly, were collapsible. A heavy, green-baize-lined chest contained the Admiral's sea-going silver – only a fraction of the complete collection presented by Lloyd's of London for the Nile and Copenhagen, but still capable of making an impressive show when the table was laid for a formal dinner. Separating this area from the Admiral's day cabin beyond was a bulkhead, on which hung two portraits: a fine pastel of Emma painted in Dresden in 1800 by Johann Schmidt, which Nelson called his 'Guardian Angel' (see illustration on p. 44), and a delightful little watercolour of the 2-year-old Horatia in the garden at Merton by Henry Edridge (see colour plate 8).

The day cabin was a more workmanlike room. Lit in daytime by a beautiful set of curving, sashed windows stretching right across the stern, and by night with special hanging candlesticks on gimbals, it was both an office and a drawing-room. Nelson's desk stood there, together with specially designed armchairs with

*Rear Admiral George Murray. Nelson's Captain
of the Fleet in the Mediterranean, 1803–5.*

large pockets let into the upholstery of each arm, designed to hold the papers on
which the Admiral and his secretaries were working. Doors at either end of the
windows led to the quarter galleries, small enclosed spaces jutting out slightly over
the water – one contained the Admiral's lavatory and the other was for washing.
Another smaller space, on the starboard side of the ship just forward of the dining
cabin, was Nelson's sleeping cabin and contained his cot, with hangings lovingly
embroidered by Emma, and large chests in which his clothes and other belongings
were stored. All the furniture, fittings and bulkheads could be quickly removed
when the ship cleared for action and the entire space became part of the gun deck
once more, with 12-pounder cannon in the gunports.[63]

   To assist him in dealing with his business, Nelson had what would now be
regarded as a wholly inadequate staff – especially when one bears in mind that
every letter had to be written and copied by hand. The Captain of the Fleet, and
thus effectively the chief staff officer, was Captain George Murray, an old
shipmate from HMS *Bristol*, and the man who had led the British line at
Copenhagen. Nelson's first choice for the post had been Thomas Foley, but he was
too frail for active service, and Murray's first instinct on being asked had been to
refuse, because he feared that such a role could lead to tension and threaten their
friendship. Nelson's reply was characteristic: if there were any disagreements, he
would waive his rank as admiral and talk to Murray as a friend. Murray gave way
and brought to the job what the *Naval Chronicle* called 'the utmost suavity of
manners blended with an immovable firmness of decision', adding: 'without
detracting in the slightest degree from the credit which is due to the deceased
admiral there is scarcely a man who served in his Lordship's fleet that knows not
how to appreciate the merits of Captain Murray.'[64]

Murray dealt with the general administration of the fleet, and his correspondence shows that his 'utmost suavity of manners' had constantly to be applied to deal with harassed captains driven over the edge by the shortage of supplies. But, sometimes, even Murray was not able to deal with the situation and Nelson had to be called in. 'My dear Keats,' he wrote to the Captain of the *Superb* on 30 March 1805, 'I felt most exceedingly last night at finding your friend Admiral Murray[65] so exceedingly hurt at some conversation which had passed between you and him about hammocks . . . I wish, my dear Keats you will turn this in your mind and relieve Admiral Murray from the uneasiness your conversation has given him.'[66]

The main burden of the secretarial work was borne by the two Scotts, assisted by a small team of clerks. John Scott, Nelson's 'Public Secretary', dealt with the public correspondence and with the time-consuming matter of prize money. The Revd Alexander Scott, the 'Confidential' or 'Foreign Secretary', handled all Nelson's foreign correspondence and also helped him with the intercepted material, much of it of course in French, Spanish or Italian, all of which languages Scott spoke and wrote fluently. As we have already seen, Scott also had another important role – as Nelson's agent ashore – and not just in Sardinia but in Naples and Spain as well. As his daughter later remarked:

> As a confidential agent he was exactly the man required – full of observation – agreeable wherever he went – able to understand all that he heard and saw – whilst his condition as an invalid and his pursuits as a scholar facilitated his opportunities. Often therefore as he was sent to Spain, to Naples &c apparently for his pleasure or for the benefit of his health, it was never without some special purpose.[67]

A lady who met him on one of his visits to Naples recalled that he was 'pale, thin and tall in person, very romantic and enthusiastic'.

A large amount of the paperwork they handled between them has survived, and so it is possible to reconstruct their working methods with some precision. Work usually started immediately after breakfast at about 7 a.m. and continued until 2 p.m., when everyone would disperse to prepare for dinner, which was served at 3 p.m. Nelson and Alexander Scott would work through the foreign material together, seated in the specially designed armchairs, 'into the roomy pockets of which Scott, weary of translating, would occasionally stuff away a score or two of unopened private letters found in prize ships although the untiring energy of Nelson grudged leaving one such document unexamined.'[68] Nelson would then dictate replies, or sometimes draft them in his own hand, handing them to John Scott or one of the clerks to prepare a fair copy for his signature. Often, however, Nelson would write the fair copy in his own hand. If the letter was to a foreign dignitary, Alexander Scott would prepare a translation in an appropriate language to accompany the original. John Scott would go through a similar process with the other 'public' correspondence: the in-letters would be read out, to save Nelson's eyesight, and Nelson would then either dictate or draft a reply.

Nelson's writing slope. Nelson used this portable desk daily, especially when writing his own letters.

Once the reply had been prepared, John Scott or one of the clerks would then copy it into the official letter books – large, ledger-like volumes in which the letters were entered chronologically and then indexed by name of recipient, to make reference easier. The original letters were also arranged chronologically and stored in loose files. As well as these more traditional methods, Nelson's team also had at their disposal equipment for producing 'pressed copies', then a comparatively new invention and not in general use. Using this, direct impressions of the original letter were obtained by pressing them onto moistened tissue paper, which was then reversed, so that the writing could be read, and stuck into books containing blank pages of light grey paper, against which the faint impression stood out more easily. Sometimes the letters copied in this way were also copied into the official letter books, but a significant proportion of them were not. Analysis of the letters that were omitted has shown that they tended to be ones that were either private or secret.[69]

Let us take the output of a typical day: 4 October 1804.[70] As well as signing some dozen routine orders relating to the fleet and its administration, Nelson also dictated or drafted, and then signed, a further eight letters written out for him by

John Scott and the clerks. Most of these were official orders to his captains – for example, to Captain William Cracraft commanding the Adriatic squadron about an intelligence mission in the area by Captain Leake of the Royal Artillery (although it was nowhere explicitly stated that it was an intelligence mission – we know this from other secret correspondence). Additionally, Nelson wrote nine more letters completely in his own hand. Some of them were private – for example, the friendly letter to Spiridion Foresti quoted above (see p. 110), or a personal note to Governor Ball. Some were secret – for example, one to General Villettes about troops to garrison Messina. Twenty-nine letters in all – and that is only the out-mail! He obviously impressed John Scott: 'I have heard much of Lord Nelson's abilities as an officer and statesman but the account of the latter is infinitely short. In my travels through the service I have met with no character in any degree equal to his Lordship: his penetration is quick, judgement clear, wisdom great, and his decisions correct and decided.'[71] Even when allowances have been made for the fact that Scott was writing to Emma Hamilton, that is a remarkable tribute from one man of business to another.

'PERFECTLY AT EASE': NELSON AND HIS CAPTAINS

Scott also remarked that Nelson was always 'cheerful and pleasant', and this judgement was echoed by many of those who served with him at this time. When Captain William Parker, a nephew of Lord St Vincent, joined the fleet at La Maddalena in the frigate HMS *Amazon* on Christmas Day 1803, he told his mother: 'I met with a most gracious reception. All the captains and officers of the squadron are delighted with His Lordship and I think I have a prospect of being very happy under his command.'[72] Captain James Hillyar, another young frigate captain and one of Nelson's protégés, talked of his patron's 'extreme kindness and attention', and it is clear that Nelson was unusually free of any sense of rank or pomposity. Alexander Scott remembered that: 'even for the most important naval business he preferred a turn on the quarterdeck with his captains, whom he led by his own frankness to express themselves freely, to the stiffness and formality of a council of war.' Captain Edward Codrington only met him a few times in the weeks before Trafalgar. Nonetheless he was able to sum up his method shrewdly: 'The predominant feeling was not fear of censure, but apprehension of not gaining his approbation.'[73]

   He also continued to use social occasions, such as dinners, as a way of getting to know his colleagues better, and of sharing his own ideas with them. Dr Gillespie, who served as the *Victory*'s surgeon during part of the campaign, remembered these evenings with pleasure: 'If a person does not feel himself perfectly at ease it must be his own fault, such is the urbanity and hospitality that reigns there, notwithstanding the four orders of knighthood worn by Lord Nelson and the well-earned laurels he has acquired.'[74]

   For really the first time in his career, Nelson was appreciably older than most of the captains under his command, and it is clear that he continued to enjoy the company of younger men, tending to behave like a youngster himself when he was with them. They brought out his natural boyishness and playfulness. When Parker and Capel were sent off on a mission together, Nelson first gave them a stern lecture about not taking risks, and then laughingly told them, 'I daresay you think yourselves a couple of fine fellows and when you get away from me you will do nothing of the sort but think yourselves wiser than I am!'[75] On another occasion, Parker was allowed an even more intimate glimpse of his commander. A dinner party in the *Victory*, while cruising off Toulon, was interrupted by the news that the French fleet appeared to be coming out of harbour. All the captains present scrambled for their boats and Parker, as the most junior, was left until last. When they were alone, Nelson returned to the abandoned table, filled a glass to the brim with claret, lifted it above his head, saying, 'Here is to Lady Hamilton! She is my guardian angel!' and drank off the wine.[76] Nor had he lost his gift for encouraging the very young. Midshipman James Dalton of HMS *Renown*, who dined with him in the *Victory* on 13 December 1803, received a Davison Nile Medal, which, said the wonderful accompanying letter, 'will serve to remind you that on 13th December I first had the pleasure of being known to you. A wish to imitate successful battles is the sure road by exertion to surpass them, which that you may do for your own honour and the advantage of your Country is my sincere wish.'[77]

None of the young men in the Mediterranean ever came as close to Nelson as Edward Parker – perhaps that was a gap in Nelson's emotional life that could never be filled again after the trauma of his favourite's death. But there was one who did stand out from the rest – William Layman. He was of course the fisherman who had caught the turbot that won over Sir Hyde Parker in March 1801 and he had also been at Nelson's side at Copenhagen. Given command of the sloop HMS *Weazle*, he wrecked her on a rock near Gibraltar, was exonerated by the court martial and given another sloop, the *Raven* – which he succeeded in wrecking as well. This time the court martial was less lenient and ordered him to be censured and placed at the bottom of the commanders' list – which prompted a passionate letter in his defence from Nelson to the First Lord: 'You must, my dear Lord, forgive the warmth which I express for Captain Layman; but he is in adversity and therefore has the more claim to my attention and regard. If I had been censured every time I have run my Ships, or Fleets under my command, into great danger, I should long ago have been *out* of the Service and never *in* the House of Peers.'[78]

Clearly Layman was a bright and engaging young man: just the sort of pushy – even cocky – youngster that Nelson most liked, presumably because they reminded him of the way he had been at their age. As he told Emma indulgently, 'His tongue runs too fast, I often tell him neither to talk nor write so much' – which would have been excellent advice to the young Captain Nelson in the West Indies. But Layman was also imaginative and inventive. It was he who delivered the major intelligence coup at the outset of the war when he found the important French naval documents on board *L'Ambuscade*. In September 1803, he submitted to Nelson a plan for cutting out a French corvette at Marseilles with words calculated to delight his patron: 'The carrying out of Ships from under the Fortifications of the Southern Capital of France could not fail to strike

Above and right: *Nelson's dining-table and tableware. Nelson's special folding dining-table, made by Gillows, and a few items from the fine collection of silver and glass tableware he used for entertaining on board HMS* Victory.

at the commencement of the War which would intimidate Frenchmen and impress on them a belief that every person under the Commander in Chief had imbibed from him superior skill & intrepidity.'[79] Following the loss of the *Raven* in 1804, while a prisoner of war in Cádiz he not only managed to obtain up-to-date information on the state of the port's defences and of the Spanish ships stationed there but also devised a complete plan of attack for capturing the port. Nelson always valued, and sought to encourage, this sort of initiative in his subordinates.

None of this is to suggest, however, that Nelson was soft with his young officers: on the contrary, they were constantly reminded that he had his eye on them. Within five days of arriving at La Maddalena in December 1803, William Parker learned just what an eye for detail his new admiral possessed when he received a rap over the knuckles for some victualling vouchers he had issued, including six bags of hay for bullocks: 'I see no reason for the purchase of hay for bullocks which have been killed so immediately.'[80] Robert Pettit, another favourite, who had wasted a 'plum', a detached cruise in the *Termagant*, was treated even more roughly: 'I wished to have given you a chance to pick up something in the Termagant and most particularly told you not to heave her

down. You will now receive an order to join me that Captain Hillyar may go into the ship . . . if you have not put yourself in fortunes way it is your own fault and not of him who wish'd to be your sincere friend.'[81]

Once again, as we have seen throughout his career as an admiral, it was Nelson's instinct for the personal touch that made him so loved. When Captain Mark Robinson (the son of his former captain in HMS *Worcester* in 1776) was about to take the battleship HMS *Swiftsure* into Agincourt Sound for the first time in January 1805 he received a letter from the Admiral carried by one of the *Victory*'s lieutenants stating, 'As you must feel more comfortable to have an officer on board who has been at Madalena I send you Lieutenant Brown', and then continuing with a wish that his gout was 'removed' and an invitation to dinner.[82] When Rear Admiral George Campbell was forced to apply for sick leave Nelson sent an immediate private reply to assure him of his understanding and support, before dealing with his case officially: 'You may be sure of my anxious wish for your speedy recovery. The very first frigate which Joins if you do not find yourself better shall waft you in a trice to the happy shores of Old England.' The official order to Campbell, couched in more formal language, was sent the following day.[83]

Examination of the originals of these notes has shown that none of them was written by a secretary: all those cited are in Nelson's own handwriting. This was a man who preferred above all to have personal contact with his subordinates. If a face-to-face meeting was not possible, then a personal note was the next-best means of communication. Failing that, there were still the Public Order Books, which he had used before to keep in daily touch with his subordinates. Sadly, no such book for the period 1803–5 appears to have survived, but we know that Nelson continued this method of communication, since the personal order books of Captain Sir Robert Barlow of HMS *Triumph* and Captain Richard Thomas of the *Etna* have survived, both of which contain a number of Nelson's public orders. This suggests that, like Captain Darby in 1798 (see p. 25), they had seen the orders in a central Order Book and copied them down. Like the orders in all the earlier books, the ones seen and copied by Barlow and Thomas convey a vivid sense of Nelson's eager, combative presence. But he could also be calm when required. Recently, the Royal Naval Museum acquired some letters written by Nelson's steward, William Chevallier, to Alexander Davison and they contain a vivid description of an incident in March 1805 that is not mentioned in the *Victory's* log.

> Once the Victory took fire near the Powder Magazine, the whole of the terrified Crew run'd up the riggin[g] and at that dreadful moment when every Man thought it his last hour, Lord Nelson was then as cool and composed as ever I saw him before. He orders every man below to put out the fire, and such is the confidence and respect the sailors have for him that everyone obeid and in twenty Minutes the fire was got under. Thus from the Admirals fortitude and the readiness his Orders were Obeid, was the Victory saved and All Souls on board. [84]

'THE BUSINESS OF AN ENGLISH COMMANDER-IN-CHIEF': BATTLE ORDERS AND SHIP MOVEMENTS

Nelson's combative spirit can be seen in the battle orders that he issued during this period, of which two have survived. One, dated 28 April, envisaged an attack on the French fleet at anchor in one of the many bays and harbours to the east of Toulon (see transcript on p. 207). Starting with Nelson's trademark statement of aggressive intention – 'As it is my determination to attack the French fleet in any place where there is a reasonable prospect of getting fairly alongside them' – it went on to give very detailed orders for fighting at anchor, clearly based on Nelson's experiences at the Nile and Copenhagen and including a list of the special equipment that was required.

The second was a plan for a full-scale fleet action at sea (see transcript on p. 205). It is undated and so we cannot be sure exactly when it was issued, but the internal evidence suggests strongly that it probably dates from the spring or summer of 1804. Once again, Nelson began by emphasising his main aim: 'The business of an English Commander-in-Chief being first to bring the Enemy's fleet to Battle on the most advantageous terms to himself (I mean that of laying his Ships on board that of the Enemy as expeditiously as possible) and secondly to continue there without separating until the business is decided.' As in 1798 and 1801, he planned to achieve this by concentrating his attack on one part of the enemy line, overwhelming it before the remainder could come to the aid of their comrades. As he put it, he would: 'engage with all our force the six or five Van-ships of the Enemy, passing certainly if opportunity offered through their Line . . . the second or third Rear-ships of the Enemy would act as they please and our Ships would give a good account of them should they persist in mixing with our Ships.'

However, he went on to introduce some new elements to his tactical thinking, telling his subordinates that he was sure that they 'will, knowing my precise object, that of a close and decisive battle, supply any deficiency in my not making signals'. Indeed, he went so far as to say that, once the battle was joined, 'Signals from these moments are useless when every man is disposed to do his duty.' Moreover, speaking of the opening movements before the battle, he wrote, 'If the two Fleets are willing to fight but little manoeuvring is necessary, the less the better, a day is soon lost in that business.'

So the lessons Nelson had learned during his frustrating experiences under Hotham in the two battles in those same waters in 1795 were now bearing fruit. Nelson was making it clear to his subordinates that he wanted to avoid any unnecessary manoeuvring before battle was joined. One way in which he achieved this was by making the order of sailing, in which his ships customarily cruised, the same as the order of battle, in which they attacked, thus avoiding any delay in forming a line of battle when the enemy were sighted. A list of the ships of the squadron dated 13 February 1804 and headed 'Order of Battle and Sailing' shows the ships grouped in two divisions – one of five ships under Nelson himself in the *Victory*; the other, of four ships, under Bickerton in the *Kent*.[85] From the organisation of the ships and the disposition of the admirals within the list it is clear that in the event of a battle the first division, which included some of the most powerful ships of the fleet, such as the *Victory* and the even heavier *Canopus*,[86] would form the van, Bickerton's ships forming the rear.

DATING THE 1804 BATTLE PLAN

The battle plan under discussion here was first printed by Clarke and M'Arthur in 1809, who claimed it was drawn up during Nelson's chase to the West Indies. But, as both J.K. Laughton and Julian Corbett (see *The Campaign of Trafalgar* (London, Longmans, Green & Co.) 1910, p. 155) pointed out, the numbers of ships mentioned in the memorandum do not correspond with the numbers of ships in either the British or the Franco-Spanish fleets in May–June 1805. On the other hand, they are close to the numbers we know the two sides had with them in the Mediterranean in the spring and summer of 1804.

For this reason, most authorities now agree that the plan belongs to Nelson's Mediterranean deployment and not to the Trafalgar Campaign.

Similarly, the dangerous moment at Cape St Vincent when Thompson in the *Britannia* failed to take in Jervis's order for the rear division to tack had also had its effect: Nelson now told his captains that they should not wait for his signals but act on their own initiative. In these two key elements of the 1804 plan we can see the origins of the famous battle plan that he developed before Trafalgar.

Before a battle could be fought, however, the enemy had to be enticed out of port. Nelson always maintained that he was not blockading Toulon and became irritated when anyone suggested that he was. When the City of London formally thanked him as the officer commanding the fleet blockading Toulon, the Lord Mayor was told firmly: 'I beg to inform Your Lordship that the Port of Toulon has never been blockaded by me: quite the reverse – every opportunity has been offered to the Enemy to put to sea for it is there that we hope to realise the hopes and expectations of our Country.'[87]

In fact, Toulon was a particularly difficult port to blockade closely. This was partly due to the weather. Nelson's private journal and letters to Emma mention constant storms and gales in the Gulf of Lyons and so, in the winter months of 1803–4, he found it easier to patrol some 30 miles to the south of Cap San Sebastián on the Spanish coast. There the highlands of Spain gave a little shelter from the sharp northerly winds. 'My plan', he told the Duke of Clarence, 'is to spare the Ships & Men and to be ready to follow the Enemy if they go to Madras but never to blockade them, or prevent them from putting to sea any day or hour they please. The pleasure of this fleet would be to have them out.'[88] Additionally, the lie of the land at Toulon favoured the French – from the heights to the north of the port they could see the patrolling squadrons at a great distance. So Nelson kept his ships at least 40 miles out to sea, and he also kept them constantly on the move. As he told Dr Moseley, this had the additional advantage of keeping his ships' companies active and made sure that the 'sameness of prospect' did not 'satiate the mind'. Keeping his battlefleet mostly out of sight meant that his own movements were not watched, and so the French were not able to tell for sure when he was absent from his station. He, on the other hand, was able to keep a regular watch on them by sending frigates on regular reconnaissances. So, for example, the log of Parker's *Amazon* shows that she looked into Toulon twelve times between 6 March and 23 May 1804, sometimes alone and sometimes in company with other frigates.[89]

Even the battleships were used to glean information. For example, when Richard Keats was sent in the *Superb* on a mission to Naples in July 1803, he was ordered to go via the Strait of Bonifacio between Corsica and Sardinia and to survey the channel. On 14 July he sailed east on the southern side of the Strait and returned on the 31st keeping to the northern side. On both occasions, he had boats out at a half mile from each beam, sounding as they went. He was able to report that 'no doubt remains of there being a good and safe passage through, and sufficient room for a ship to work in'.[90] This was important information: Nelson already knew from a survey carried out by Captain Ryves that Agincourt Sound at La Maddalena offered a good anchorage for his fleet; now he knew he could sail into and out of it from both directions. As a result, as we have seen, he shortly afterwards began to use the Sound as his forward base. There remained just one other channel to check – the narrow eastern entrance, known as the 'Biche Channel' and said to be too narrow for battleships to use. In February 1804, Nelson deliberately took the battlefleet into Agincourt Sound by that route, noting in his Journal: 'The Fleet ran in under reefed foresails through the eastern passage which looked tremendous from the number of rocks and heavy seas breaking over them but it is perfectly safe when once known.'[91] This was all part of his meticulous preparation. As we saw earlier, when he commanded in the Channel, he believed it was necessary that he should know his theatre of operations thoroughly, so that he and his fleet would be prepared for any opportunity that presented itself.

With his smaller ships constantly away on reconnaissance or convoy duties, and even individual battleships occasionally away on missions or refitting, Nelson needed to keep in as close touch as possible with his widely scattered forces. To do so, he used a rendezvous system developed by the Royal Navy over many years of constant patrols at sea. Locations were chosen, spread right across his command, and each was allocated a code number. Sometimes these were places close to land, such as La Maddalena (No. 60), where letters and orders could be left with contacts on shore for ships calling there. Sometimes they were at sea, such as off Cap San Sebastián (No. 97), or off the Hyères Islands (No. 102), in which case a small vessel would be left on station to act as the postbox. Nelson was thus able to leave orders for his captains, including details of his own movements in the immediate future, and they could leave reports for him.

So, for example, in February 1804, Captain Ross Donnelly of the frigate *Narcissus* was sent on a reconnaissance mission to Toulon, 'for the purpose of ascertaining whether the Enemy's squadron is still in port', and was then ordered to rejoin Nelson at a new rendezvous, to which the battlefleet would move while he was on passage.[92] Similarly, here are orders to Nelson's nephew by marriage, Captain Sir William Bolton, giving him instructions for an intelligence-gathering voyage: 'You will go to Barcelona & give my letter to Mr: Gibert[93] and as I expect letters from Madrid you will receive them, and you will then proceed to Roses[94] to get all the papers for Me and join Me as soon as possible on Rends: No: 102 but be very careful how you approach the Hieres Islands for we have been drove in the late Gales far to the Eastward of them.'[95] These orders give a vivid impression of the fleet at work – the battlefleet moving slowly from rendezvous to rendezvous, the smaller ships darting in with news and sailing off again with fresh orders. This system was tested to the limit when the French finally emerged from port in January 1805 and the Trafalgar Campaign got under way.

'EQUAL TO THE MOST ACTIVE SERVICE': THE FLEET IN ACTION – 1804

Before then, however, there were many alarms and a number of occasions when Nelson and his men thought that a battle might be imminent. The first came in early January 1804. One of Nelson's sloops intercepted two letters from

Maréchal Berthier, Napoleon's Chief of Staff, to officials in Corsica which suggested that the French were planning to land an army in Corsica for an invasion of Sardinia. This coincided with intelligence from Nelson's frigates about the movements of the French fleet that indicated they were preparing to put to sea. And, about the same time, Nelson received confirmatory intelligence from the British Consul at Turin, Thomas Jackson: 'An armament is preparing at Toulon. Sardinian agents are saying it is destined for Corsica – but other reports say Sicily.'

So all the signs were that a major operation was at last under way, and on 26 January Nelson wrote to the Sardinian government: 'I am on my way to La Madelena having received from my frigates information on the movements of the enemy. The troops are already close to embarking at Nice and Toulon, 10,000 at least, and one of their objects, for it is not the only object, is to take possession of the Island of Sardinia. On the 19th the fleet had not set sail but was completely ready.' In fact, the French attack did not materialise,[96] but the Sards were now thoroughly alarmed and asked formally for assistance. So, when he sailed from La Maddalena, Nelson left HMS *Termagant* under Captain Robert Pettit at the anchorage, with orders to 'keep a strict watch during the night and have your guns loaded with grape'.[97] On 17 February Nelson wrote to the Viceroy of Sardinia: 'It is my intention always when in my power to have a corvette for the protection of this part of the coast and if you chuse at any time to place your gallies under the orders of the English officer he has my directions to take them under his Command and at any time to give their Commanders his best advice and assistance.'[98] The Viceroy politely declined to place his forces directly under English control: 'as we are not openly at war with France I cannot take such a step on my own authority,' but he added, 'the best measures for opposing the enemy might be secretly concerted with the officers charged with your instructions.'[99] As a result, for the remainder of the campaign, Agincourt Sound was effectively a British naval base. Meanwhile, Nelson renewed his attempts to persuade the British government to send troops into the Mediterranean, this time to assist with the defence of Sardinia.

In fact, this incident marked the beginning of a period of more intense activity off Toulon. As Nelson and his ships returned to their patrol ground from La Maddalena in early February 1804, a new French commander was settling into his post at Toulon. Far to north, on the Channel coast, Napoleon's latest plans for invading Britain were beginning to take shape. Once again, Boulogne was the centre of a build-up of troops, but this time there was no bluff. Knowing that he would need his fleets to cover the crossing, Napoleon appointed to the Mediterranean command his favourite admiral – and Nelson's former opponent at Boulogne – Louis de Latouche Tréville.

Latouche gave a new sense of purpose and vigour to the French fleet. Almost at once, Nelson's scouts began to notice increased activity within the harbour and, by the middle of March, he was telling Evan Nepean at the Admiralty that they were 'in a perfect state of readiness to proceed to sea . . . eight sail of the line are in the outer Road.'[100] Then, in early April, two of their battleships were seen exercising outside the port and, on the 5th, the whole fleet came out for the first time since Nelson had taken up his command. He was then off Cape Corse with the main fleet, but the French movement was seen by Campbell in the *Canopus*, accompanied by the *Superb* and *Active*, who fell back on the main fleet to report. Nelson at once sailed north and, for a second time that year, the talk in the fleet was of an imminent battle. However, not wishing, as he put it, 'to baulk their inclinations of a battle by our superiority in numbers',[101] Nelson ordered Bickerton (who had just transferred his flag into the three-decker HMS *Royal Sovereign*) to stay out of sight over the horizon with his division. By the time they arrived off Toulon, the main French fleet was safe within its batteries once more but, on 9 April, four of their battleships made another sortie to try to cut off the *Amazon*, which had cheekily captured a French merchantman right under the guns of Cap Cépet at the entrance to Toulon. Nelson countered by sending in the *Donegal* and *Superb* but, at their approach, the French once again withdrew.

For the next few weeks, the patrol off Toulon did indeed become almost a close blockade, with Nelson constantly on the watch, and closer inshore than before, but always concealing his true numbers in the hope of persuading Latouche to make a decisive move that might lead to a full-scale battle. To do this, he needed to entice him to the leeward of Toulon, so that he could not easily retreat into his secure base. As he said, 'my mind is fixed not to fight them unless with a westerly wind outside of the Hyères and with an easterly wind to the westward of [Cape] Sicie'. Around this time, too, he issued the special memorandum about fighting a battle at anchor (see transcript on p. 207). Clearly he was anticipating that, if the trap worked, Latouche might make a dash for the nearest friendly bay, and he wanted to prepare his fleet for this contingency. So he had decided on his ideal battleground; he had worked out ways of enticing his opponent onto it by concealing part of his own force; he had prepared in advance a plan for dealing with him if he retreated; and he had fully briefed all his subordinates. As always, the detail – and the imagination – of his forward planning was impressive.

But, as he had shown at Boulogne, Latouche was a wily opponent worthy of Nelson. He continued to exercise his ships and to make teasing darts at any British ships that appeared to be vulnerable, especially the watching frigates. But he refused to be drawn into Nelson's traps. So, on 24 May, the *Canopus*, *Donegal* and *Amazon* were sent to reconnoitre Toulon. It is, incidentally, very likely that Nelson had chosen the two battleships deliberately to irritate, or tempt, his opponent – they were both former French ships. The wind was light and the sea calm, and they were attacked by French gunboats. Hearing the firing, Latouche sent a detachment of five battleships and three frigates to assist, upon which, in accordance with Nelson's plan, Campbell fell back to where he knew the main battlefleet was waiting. The French pursued, and one of the frigates even managed to get onto the *Canopus*'s quarter and open fire. But, shortly afterwards, the signal

came from the shore to withdraw. Clearly Latouche had guessed what was going
on – indeed, he may even have spotted Nelson's division from his command
headquarters in a tower high on Cap Cépet.

Still the probing went on by both sides – William Parker later remembered that
'during May and June scarcely a day seems to have passed without some
exchange of shots with the French batteries, or [the *Amazon*'s] boats manned and
armed going in shore'.[102] And then, in mid-June, all Nelson's careful planning
nearly led to the battle for which he longed. On the 13th two French frigates and
a brig were seen outside the harbour close to the Hyères Islands. Nelson sent two
frigates after them and, shortly afterwards, the battleship *Excellent*. On the
afternoon of the 14th, he headed for the entrance himself in the *Victory*, with
Canopus, *Belleisle* and *Donegal* in company. This time, Latouche appeared to
accept the challenge and emerged from harbour with eight battleships, upon
which Nelson shortened sail with his five battleships and lay to, in line of battle,
about 20 miles south of Cape Sicié. He was occupying the position he had
planned: to leeward of Toulon, with Bickerton and the rest of the fleet out of
sight over the horizon. But before the trap could be sprung, Latouche had
thought better of his move and returned to Toulon.

Nelson thought little of the incident at the time, dismissing it in a letter to
Ambassador Elliot as 'merely a gasconade',[103] and telling Emma '[Latouche]
sometimes plays bo-peep [*sic*] in and out of Toulon like a mouse at the edge of
her hole'.[104] However, he had taken the opportunity to observe his opponent
closely: on 1 July, he told Lord Melville, who had succeeded St Vincent as First
Lord of the Admiralty:

> Monsr: La Touche we know is full manned and by the handling of his ships
> apparently well manned. Nothing swimming can have more health and Zeal
> than the fleet I have the honor of Commanding and it [is] our anxious wish to
> get Monsr: La Touche outside the Hieres Islands that he may not be able to
> get his crippled Ships into Toulon again, for it is our wish to have them
> repair'd at Portsmouth.[105]

Two months later he discovered that Latouche had reported to Napoleon that the
English admiral had 'run away' and that 'I pursued him until night, he ran to the
southeast.'[106] Nelson was furious, promising his brother William that he would
keep his copy of his opponent's dispatch 'and if I take him, he shall *eat* it'.[107] But
Latouche continued to elude him – just ten days after Nelson had written those
words, his opponent died on board his flagship, the fine new 80-gunner
Bucentaure. Nelson heard the news some three weeks later and wrote to Emma,
'I grieve to think he died a natural death, it was more than I bargained for.'[108]

In the same letter, he told her that he planned to come home on sick leave:
'I shall not stay three minutes in Portsmouth but fly to dear Merton where all in
this world which is dearest to me resides.' He had already applied to the
Admiralty for leave, having warned Melville in July: 'I am very sorry to tell you

that my State of Health is such that I much fear before the Winter that I shall be obliged to write to the board for some months rest. A <u>half</u> man as I am, cannot expect to be a Hercules.'[109]

While he waited for the necessary permission to arrive – he expected to be home for Christmas – the pace of the campaign slowed down. The death of Latouche put a stop to the French sorties: by early November, Nelson was telling Melville 'On this very day I reconnoitred Toulon, not a ship outside the harbour. They are not so active as under la Touche.' The regular routine of the fleet continued but he clearly felt the anticlimax after the excitement of the early summer: as he wrote to the Duke of Clarence on 18 August, 'we have a uniform sameness day after day, and month after month – gales of wind for ever and ever'.[110]

Nonetheless, an important change was imminent. Relations with Spain had been worsening gradually throughout 1804 and, on 5 October, before war had been formally declared, a British squadron of frigates intercepted the inbound Spanish treasure *flotta* and captured it after a fierce and bloody fight. When news of this pre-emptive strike reached Nelson in early November, all thought of returning home left his mind. A young diplomat, Lambton Este, who was on board the *Victory* waiting to take passage home with the Admiral, was summoned to the Great Cabin and told abruptly, 'Oh my good fellow! I have abandoned my idea of going to England at present. I shall not go yet and when I go is quite uncertain.' On the 15th, acting on intelligence from his own network, he ordered his ships to seize all Spanish vessels. As he told Emma: 'by management and a portion of good luck I got the account from Madrid in a much shorter space of time than I could have hoped for and I have set the whole Mediterranean to work.'[111]

However, he decided to repeat the practice he had adopted off Cádiz in 1797, of exempting fishing and market boats from capture, knowing that they were useful sources of information as well as of supplies for his ships. He wrote to the Governor of Barcelona: 'I feel it is the duty of Individuals to soften the horrors of war as much as may lay in their power . . . I have given orders that neither the fishing or Market boats should be detained by the fleet under my Command.'[112]

The sweep for Spanish vessels yielded one particularly useful prize, almost as significant as Layman's coup at the start of the war with France. On 21 October a mail packet, intercepted en route to Barcelona, was found to be carrying mail from Minorca and Majorca, among which was important intelligence regarding the defences of both islands. It included, for example, a report from the commander of the Spanish troops in Majorca – the Regimento de Españoles de Huares – with lists giving his exact strength (693 infantry, 389 cavalry).[113] Similar information was found regarding Minorca. On 28 November Nelson wrote privately to General Villettes at Malta: 'the Spaniards are deficient in every thing for its defence. The 2000 Troops at Malta with the Marines I think ought to secure its fall in 24 hours . . . I have the Governors demand for stores, sandbags, shovels, Balls, flints handspikes sponges &. in short every thing.' So, as he told

Villettes, 'I should hope for orders every moment to possess ourselves of the Island of Minorca.' Here, at last, was the opportunity for action – and one that, if successful, would solve many of his logistical problems. Minorca, with its fine natural harbour and well-equipped naval dockyard – much of it built by the British during earlier occupations – would provide him with a secure base, relatively close to Toulon, where his ships could be refitted and stored. Any thought of returning to England was driven from his mind, and his letters to Emma began to talk of a return in the spring – perhaps.

In fact, although he did not know it, permission to return home on leave was already on its way out to him. However, rather than replacing him altogether, the Admiralty had decided to appoint Bickerton as a caretaker commander-in-chief until Nelson returned. At the same time, in view of the outbreak of war with Spain, it had been decided that a squadron would be stationed off Cádiz under the command of Sir John Orde. Since Orde was considerably senior to Bickerton, the decision had also been taken to give Orde a separate command, covering the area from Cape St Vincent to the Straits of Gibraltar – formerly part of the Mediterranean command. Unfortunately, the Admiralty dispatches explaining all this were delayed, and so the first that Nelson heard of the plan was from Orde himself, in a letter that he received on 15 December. Nothing could have been more unfortunate: Nelson still thought of Orde as a rival, and he immediately suspected a plot, pouring out his bile in a series of letters to friends and colleagues in which he complained bitterly of being ill-used by the Admiralty. As he told Captain Pulteney Malcolm, who now commanded the *Donegal*: 'Sir John Orde is for the present placed in Command of a Squadon outside the Streights which is for the present occasion lost from my Command when there was nothing to be got I had it, when the prospect of money comes forth it goes to another.'[114]

However, he did not have long to brood on his wrongs. For, even as he read Orde's ill-fated letter at anchor in Pula Roads, other much more important information was reaching him. A month before, while on a standard reconnaissance, Capel had had an interesting encounter: 'I was close in with Marseilles on Monday the 18th: when a Pilot came off accompanied by only one Man both in a most wretched state and only keeping the Sea from apprehension of being prest for the fleet in Toulon. They assured me that 3 or 4 nights past every individual in the Shape of a Seaman both from the Vessels & houses were seized and sent to the fleet.' He concluded, 'this looks like a Move'.[115] On 16 December, the *Active* learned from a neutral vessel out of Marseilles that 7,000 troops had embarked in the French ships and, about the same time, Nelson heard from the King of Sardinia that the French were assembling troops near Toulon, including a corps of cavalry. He told Malcolm, 'The Toulon fleet is certainly embarking Troops & my reporter says cavalry but this I much doubt but if it is so they are destined for Egypt.'[116]

So all his key sources of intelligence agreed: a major French operation was imminent. Reporting these developments to Melville he indulged in a little flourish: 'Well My dear Lord be assured that I had rather have the French Admiral alongside of Me than the Mines of Peru, for if it be a Sin to Covet Glory I am the most offending Soul alive[117] so said Shakespeare and so says from his heart Your Lordships Most faithful Servant.'[118] Then he was back off to Toulon again to check on the state of the French fleet, reporting to William Marsden that they were still in port and that 'The fleet is in perfect good health and good humour unequalled by anything which has ever come to my knowledge and equal to the most active service which the times may call for or the Country expect of them.'[119]

As he and his comrades were about to demonstrate, that was not an empty boast.

In search of the French. HMS Victory *pauses briefly at Gibraltar during the great chase of the French and Spanish fleets in the summer of 1805.*

CHAPTER VI

The Trafalgar Campaign: January–August 1805

On 19 December 1804, Latouche Tréville's successor returned to Toulon after attending Napoleon's lavish coronation as Emperor, in Notre Dame Cathedral, Paris. He was Pierre-Charles-Jean-Baptiste-Silvestre de Villeneuve – the man who had led the two surviving French battleships out of the carnage of Aboukir Bay in August 1798. He now had new orders: to escape from harbour, elude Nelson and then cross the Atlantic to the West Indies, where he was to rendezvous with other French and Spanish squadrons which had received similar orders. Napoleon was now contemplating a major naval operation in support of his invasion plans. He hoped to unite his fleets in the Caribbean, bring them as one large force to the mouth of the Channel, sweep aside the British defenders and then cover his invasion flotilla as it made its hazardous crossing.

At the same time, in Britain, William Pitt the Younger, who had returned as Prime Minister in May 1804, was constructing a new coalition with the Russians against France. One of the conditions demanded by Russia was that Britain should deploy an army in the Mediterranean and, even though the British forces were already fully stretched in defending Britain's coasts against the threatened French invasion, Pitt agreed. So plans were in preparation for sending out an expeditionary force under the command of Lieutenant-General Sir James Craig.

The scene was set for one of the largest-scale maritime campaigns ever mounted in the Age of Sail. It involved the fleets of three nations – Britain, France and Spain – numbering over one hundred battleships; and it lasted over ten months and covered a huge area – from the Mediterranean to the West Indies and into the Channel. And Nelson played a central role in every stage.

At the start of 1805, Nelson was with his fleet at La Maddalena off Sardinia. Having patrolled off Toulon when the news reached him in December 1804 of an impending French move, he had now retired to his forward base to meet his transports and take on stores. With him were eleven battleships.[1] This was only two more than he had taken command of in July 1803, but in fact this was a much more powerful fleet than his earlier force. There were two three-deckers – HMS *Victory* and HMS *Royal Sovereign* – which contemporary naval opinion regarded as the equivalent of at least two standard 74-gun battleships.[2] He also still had with him the powerful, former French 80-gun *Canopus* which, although only a two-decker, was in fact as large as the three-deckers, and with a powerful lower battery of 36-pounders. Of the remaining eight all were 74s, three were brand new and the oldest dated from 1795. Some of them were in poor condition after the long months of constant patrol at sea – the *Superb*, in particular, was in need of a major dockyard refit. But others, like the *Swiftsure*, were fresh from the dockyard. Of the original 1803 fleet only four survived: *Victory*, *Donegal*, *Belleisle*, and *Superb*.

The battleship captains with Nelson at La Maddalena were a similar mix of old comrades and new recruits. Bickerton was still second-in-command – although now flying his flag in the *Royal Sovereign* instead of the dilapidated *Kent* – and Richard Keats of the *Superb* and Sir Richard Strachan of the *Donegal* were still with him, strangers no longer but trusted and valued new members of the Band of Brothers. Other, longer-standing comrades from former campaigns had joined them – Ben Hallowell in the *Tigre* and John Conn of the *Canopus*. And there were new faces too, including two who would later follow him into battle at Trafalgar: William Hargood, who had succeeded Whitby in command of the *Belleisle*, and Henry Bayntun, who had brought the *Leviathan* out to the Mediterranean in 1804. But so great had the turnover of captains been that, of the original eight, only three remained – Hardy, Keats and Strachan. Nonetheless, Nelson was, as always, highly satisfied with his team and confident in their abilities: as he told an unknown correspondent on 16 January, 'this fleet will send [the French fleet] to Hell let who will Command and I am not so arrogant as to suppose its success in the least depends upon my presence.'[3]

Arriving at the Agincourt Sound anchorage on 12 January, the fleet found the transports waiting, and the laborious work of transferring stores and refilling water barrels ashore began. A large batch of letters and dispatches had recently arrived from England, so Nelson and his staff were busy with this correspondence. Thomas Louis's son was given his first command, the brig *Childers*: 'I am very glad not only on your own account but as I know that it will give pleasure to your Worthy and Gallant father.'[4] Ambassador Elliot received a long and detailed appreciation of the international situation and a moan about the appointment of Sir John Orde, 'now he is to wallow in wealth whilst I am left a beggar'.[5] And Lord Camden received a report on the conclusion at last, at the third attempt, of the Algiers mission – Keats had succeeded in landing the new Consul-General – together with a recommendation that the Revd Alexander Scott, who had assisted as Secretary and Interpreter to the mission, should be given a Crown living.[6] In short, it was business as usual, and as it had been for twenty months before.

'I HOPE TOMORROW TO GET HOLD OF THEM': THE FIRST FRENCH BREAKOUT:
JANUARY–MARCH 1805

Then, at about 3 p.m., on the afternoon of 19 January, the frigates *Seahorse* and
Active tore headlong into the anchorage on the wings of a north-westerly gale,
flying the signal 'Enemy at Sea'. Rushing on board the *Victory*, Courtney Boyle of
the *Seahorse* and Richard Moubray of the *Active* made their report: the French
fleet had sailed from Toulon early on the previous day on a south-south-west
course, and the two frigates had shadowed them until about 10 p.m., when they
were in the latitude of Ajaccio in Corsica, before breaking off to report.
Immediately, the signal was made from the *Victory* for the whole fleet to unmoor[7]
and weigh anchor. Then, as the shrill of the bosuns' pipes echoed around the
Sound and the ships' companies began the laborious, back-breaking process of
hoisting in the boats they had been using for transporting stores, raising anchor
and setting sail, Nelson reviewed his options.

In fact, in their excitement the two young frigate captains had already made a
serious mistake. Instead of both coming to report, one of them should have
continued to shadow the French for as long as possible, trusting that they would
find a way of getting further news to the Admiral. As a result of their over-
eagerness, Nelson's intelligence about the enemy's course was already nearly
20 hours old, and the French could easily have altered direction after the frigates
left them. All the same, the strong north-westerly gales meant that the French were
unlikely to have got to the westward. Moreover, all the intelligence Nelson had
received in December had suggested that they were planning an attack on Naples
or Sicily, and the course they had set suggested that they were aiming to round
Cape Carbonara, at the southern end of Sardinia. To be sure of intercepting them,
therefore, he needed to reach Cape Carbonara first.

The direction of the wind meant that it would have been difficult, possibly
impossible – and certainly time-consuming – to beat the fleet out of the usual
western entrance to the Sound. The only alternative was the hazardous eastern
channel – Biche – and the dusk of a short January day was already falling. But, as
at the Nile, Nelson never hesitated: as the great ships finally catted home their
anchors and began to move at about 4.30 p.m., he sent the *Seahorse* on ahead
and then led the way in the *Victory* down the narrow channel, burning blue lights
at regular intervals to illuminate the scene. Behind came the other ten battleships
in line, each following the stern lights of their next ahead, with the *Active*
bringing up the rear. By 7 p.m. they were clear of all hazards and running
southwards down the eastern coast of Sardinia. The whole operation had taken
less than four hours.

It was a remarkable feat of navigation – but it was of course not so spontaneous
or as hazardous as it appears in the telling. For, as we saw earlier (see p. 125),
Nelson had foreseen that he might have to use the Biche Channel and had
deliberately tried it out with his battlefleet nearly a year before. But this simply
serves to emphasise yet again where his true genius lay – when the moment of

crisis came, he had the information he needed to enable him to take a bold and potentially risky decision, with reasonable confidence that the risks involved were acceptable. It is worth remembering, too, that the ships he led so confidently through Biche were well-stored and ready for a long voyage, thanks again to his careful planning and that of his staff. And finally, he had known about the French intention to break out for over a month, so he was ready to react, literally in minutes, as soon as it happened. All this constitutes a truly remarkable achievement of forward planning, logistics and intelligence. The departure from Agincourt Sound on 19 January 1805, with its mixture of drama, daring and the rewards of meticulous preparation, deserves to rank with any of Nelson's battles as an example of his skills as an admiral.

Nelson was also sure that he knew at least the general direction in which the French were going – and in this important particular his intelligence was of course wrong. As in 1798, no one on the British side had guessed at the breathtaking audacity of Napoleon's strategic schemes. Villeneuve's southerly course had been designed to give the shadowing frigates the wrong scent, and he intended to strike west and head for the Straits of Gibraltar, in accordance with Napoleon's latest plan. However, during the night of 18/19 January the same north-westerly gale that Nelson experienced some hours later at La Maddalena hit the French fleet, and with catastrophic results. The fleet was dispersed, and when dawn broke Villeneuve found himself with only four battleships in company – and each of those had received severe damage to the masts or sprung leaks. Disconcerted by this blow so early in his voyage, he decided to put back into Toulon for repairs, and by 21 January all his ships were assembled again in the safety of the inner roads. Had either Moubray or Boyle remained with their quarry for a few hours longer they might have seen this disaster and been able to report it to Nelson.

In the meantime, Nelson was battling against south-westerly gales, often under only storm staysails, down the easterly side of Sardinia in a fever of impatience. As soon as he cleared the Biche Channel, he sent Boyle in the *Seahorse* on ahead to the Isola di San Pietro off the south-western tip of Sardinia, to watch out for the French – his hurriedly scribbled note telling him to 'Proceed without a moment's loss of time' has survived, and the sprawling handwriting bears eloquent witness to the tension he was under.[8] 'I am a little anxious naturally,' he told Bickerton the next day – taking characteristic care to brief his second fully: 'but no Man has more cause to be happy, I hope tomorrow we shall get hold of them and the result I ought not to doubt. You will be a Peer as sure as my name is Nelson. I shall most probably bring them to battle in the Night if opportunity offers.'[9] He went on to tell him that he had ordered *Leviathan* and *Spencer*, two of his faster ships, to form a detached squadron, and his personal note conveying this command to Robert Stopford of the *Spencer* has also survived. A model of how to write a short, clear battle order, even when under pressure, it is worth quoting in full:

> As I think that you and Leviathan are our fastest sailing Ships I have separated
> You from the Order of Sailing in case opportunity should offer of making a

push at any Separated Ship of the Enemy, or for bringing their Rear to action should they be inclined to run. Therefore you will not be far from us that no mistakes of Signal may take place or of the Telegraph.[10]

I shall bring them most probably to action in the night as well as the day therefore You may expect the Signal if we see them. The distinguishing Lights must be carefully attended to.[11]

Eventually, on 22 January they reached Cape Carbonara, with all the ships cleared for action, expecting a battle within hours. Shortly after they arrived, Boyle in the *Seahorse* rejoined with the news that the previous day he had seen a French frigate in Pula Roads – but the weather was so thick that he had not been able to detect if any other enemy ships were present. Nelson's immediate concern was that the French might be attacking Sardinia, and so Moubray was sent to Cagliari in the *Active* to glean information. Once again, however, Moubray was over-eager: finding no ships in the bay he returned immediately to Nelson, without sending onshore for information. So he was sent back again to do the job properly, bearing a letter from Nelson to the Viceroy of Sardinia, in which the first signs of stress were beginning to appear: 'I remain in a state of perfect doubt of [the French] destination. I am all anxiety for the return of the officer who I entrust Your Royal Highness will not detain one moment.'[12] Another letter went to Francis Magnon, the British Consul and a long-standing contact: 'have you heard of them, pray tell the Officer for I am all anxiety to meet them.'[13]

Already, Nelson's mind was turning to other possible targets, and the same day he sent off Boyle again in the *Seahorse*, this time to Naples, with letters to his contacts there that betrayed the same tension. 'You will believe my anxiety,' he told Captain Frank Sotheron of HMS *Excellent*, stationed there at the time, 'I shall die if I do not meet them of a brain fever.'[14] Moubray returned with negative answers from Cagliari, and so at last Nelson was able to move on again, first to Palermo, which he reached on the 28th, and then to Messina, which he reached the following day. Notes went ashore to the Neapolitan Governor and the British Consul: 'I would recommend being very much on your guard.'[15] Also, using the system he had developed throughout the long preceding campaign, he left a note for his cruising ships, indicating his intended route by a series of numbered rendezvous and with the characteristic warning, 'I shall delay nowhere.' Amazingly, the original note has survived, conveying a vivid sense of the urgency of this pivotal moment in the campaign. It is worn and grubby with use, each captain who called there having opened it, signed and dated it and then resealed it.[16]

On 31 January, the *Seahorse* returned with the news that Naples was unharmed and that no sign had been seen of the French in that area. There were now two possibilities remaining in Nelson's mind: as he told William Marsden at the Admiralty, 'one of two things must have happened, that either the French fleet must have put back crippled, or that they are gone to the eastward, probably to Egypt'.[17] He later told Melville his thought processes as the fleet waited off Messina: 'I considered the character of Bonaparte and that the orders

HMS Victory *and the fleet off Stromboli. Nicholas Pocock shows the fleet searching for the French during the first breakout in January 1805.*

given by him on the banks of the Seine would not take into consideration winds or weather.'[18] In that judgement he was certainly right; but he then went on, 'nor indeed could an accident of three even four Ships alter in my opinion a destination of importance', and in that he erred, judging his opponent by his own standards.

So he took his decision and, for the second time in his career, committed a fleet under his command to a long voyage to the east. However, before he did so, he took care to cover the other eventuality he had considered. As he waited off Messina, a number of his cruisers joined him, and so, on the 31st, he dispatched them to all corners of his command to search in various places in which the French might have taken shelter – such as Elba, San Fiorenzo in Corsica, and even La Maddalena – and then to rendezvous at Toulon. Then, in the second navigational feat of the campaign, the fleet beat through the Straits of Messina, 'a thing unprecedented in nautical history', as he proudly told Marsden.[19] Ahead went Capel in the *Phoebe* with orders to call first in the Morea (modern mainland Greece) with a letter to the Pacha of Coron: 'I send a frigate not only to put you upon your Guard against any surprize from them, but also to gain information that I may know their destination.'[20]

Once Capel had rejoined him with the news that the French had not gone there, he pushed on for Alexandria. As always, he was both thinking ahead and building on his experience in earlier campaigns. Capel went ahead once more, taking with him a warning note to the British Consul at Alexandria, Samuel Briggs, outlining the situation and asking for information. Another, to the Governor of the city, suggested that he should sink ships in the harbour to prevent the French from entering the port to land their troops, as they had done in 1798. 'May Victory crown your endeavours against these Common Enemies is the Most Sincere Wish of Your Excellencys Most faithful and Obedient Servant,' he ended, the proliferation of capitals bearing eloquent witness to his continuing excitement and tension.

Alexandria, which he reached on 7 February, was of course empty of Frenchmen, and so Nelson at once began the voyage back. But the winds that had favoured him for much of the voyage were now foul, and so it was not until 19 February that he finally reached Malta, where for the first time he received definite news of the French and learned that they had been back in Toulon for nearly a month. He poured out his disappointment to friends and senior officers alike, writing to Bickerton: 'This foul wind has almost killed Me. I feel very anxious as you may suppose, not for myself for I am satisfied I have done perfectly right in going to Egypt but my anxiety is for the mischief these fellows may do in my protracted absence but I cannot help it, as it pleases God.'[21] Once he knew for sure where the French were, he told Melville:

> Buonaparte himself cannot be more disappointed and grieved at the return of the french fleet crippled into Toulon than I am, and I am sure every Officer and Man in the fleet under My Command . . . Those gentlemen are not used to a Gulph of Lyons gale, which we have buffeted for 21 months and not carried away a Spar . . . You will observe everybody has an Opinion as to the destination of the Enemy, mine is more fully confirmed that it was Egypt to what other Country could they want to carry Saddles & Arms.[22]

And to Emma he confided, 'nothing can be more miserable, or unhappy, than your poor Nelson'.[23] As the reaction set in, he fell into one of his black moods, writing extended justifications of his decision to various correspondents and even at one point going as far as to recommend to Melville that he should be replaced if the Admiralty thought he had judged wrong. But in truth every command decision he had made since 19 January had been justified, given the information he had before him. The way he handled his fleet in those tense weeks was exemplary: patiently (although not calmly!) waiting for intelligence, instead of rushing impetuously from place to place as he had in 1798; carefully assessing his next move in the light of that intelligence; making sure that key people were kept informed of developments; and, when the situation demanded it, moving swiftly and even taking large risks.

'I FEEL VERY ANXIOUS, AS YOU MAY SUPPOSE': THE SECOND BREAKOUT – MARCH–MAY 1805

Nelson's disappointment at the French fleet's inability to withstand the first storm it encountered was echoed in Paris. 'What is to be done', wrote a furious

Napoleon, 'with admirals who allow their spirits to sink and determine to hasten home at the first damage they receive?'[24] Nonetheless, he continued to devise ever more elaborate plans for covering the invasion – his fifth, issued on 2 March, envisaged a meeting at Martinique of the three main French fleets, from Brest, Rochefort and Toulon, together with Spanish ships from Cádiz. This united fleet was then 'to return to Europe without wasting a moment' and to arrive off Boulogne between 10 June and 10 July.[25]

At about the same time, the British plans for Craig's expeditionary force began to take final shape. On 28 March, the General received his formal orders. He was to sail with six battalions of infantry to the Mediterranean in a convoy of forty-five transport ships, escorted by two battleships under Rear Admiral John Knight. Two battalions were to be left at Gibraltar while the rest pushed on to Malta, where, together with the men that could be released from the defence of the island, they would make up a force of some 8,000 seasoned troops. Craig was then authorised to use this force where it could be of most use: in the defence of Naples, or in Sicily.

Nelson, meanwhile, was still completely unaware of the plans for the expedition. Arriving at Pula Roads, his base in southern Sardinia, on 2 March, he learned that yet another dispatch vessel had been lost – this time the sloop HMS *Raven*, commanded by his favourite, Captain William Layman. The *Raven* had been wrecked off Cádiz on 29 January, but Layman assured his patron that the dispatches he was carrying had been safely disposed of over the side before she struck. As a result, as Nelson told Melville, the last official letters he had received from England had been as far back as 2 November.

He had, however, received some letters from home from Emma and his family, sent overland via Naples and in Sam Sutton's frigate, HMS *Amphion*, but these did not make very happy reading. Emma's letters have not survived, but Nelson's reply to her has – from which it is clear that he had received an angry ticking off for not returning home for Christmas, as he had promised. Now she was threatening to come out to the Mediterranean herself, just as Frances had done in 1799. The mistress received the same answer as the wife: 'never write me about your going abroad to change the climate &c &c then you give me up entirely.' But he did try to reassure her as well: 'You are for ever uppermost in my thoughts day or night Calm or full wind You are never absent from my thoughts. Therefore I trust by all the love you bear me that You will not either fret Yourself or write fretful to Your own Nelson who assures you that I shall come and stay more than a month with You.'[26] But her anger had obviously thrown him, for three days later he wrote again, to assure 'my Dearest beloved Emma of My eternal love affection and adoration, you are ever with me in my Soul, your resemblance is never absent from my mind, and my own dearest Emma I hope very soon that I shall embrace the substantial part of you as well as the Ideal, that will I am sure give us both real pleasure and exquisite happiness.' Even brother William had been enlisted in Emma's campaign to get him to come home: 'it was my full intention to have eat my Xts: dinner at Merton but obstacles intervened that I could not foresee,' explained Horatio wearily.[27]

Letter from Nelson to Emma Hamilton, 13 March 1805. Nelson writes to Emma to explain why he has not been able to keep his promise to come home on leave for Christmas.

At the same time he was once again dealing with the routine correspondence of the fleet. Dr Sewell of the Admiralty Prize Court in Malta was congratulated on 'the Regularity of the proceedings at Malta'.[28] Admiral Sir Roger Curtis was assured that his son, Lucius, over whose career Nelson was watching, was 'an Excellent attentive officer and with the good sense and propriety of conduct which does not always fall to the lot of one of his years'.[29] Lord Moira was told that his protégé, Captain Francis Austen, would be looked after: 'You may rely upon all attention in my power to Capt. Austin . . . I know a little of [him] before he is an Excellent Young Man.'[30]

Austen had come out with an old comrade, Thomas Louis, now a rear admiral, who hoisted his flag in the ship he had helped to capture at the Nile, HMS *Canopus*. This meant there were, once again, two subordinate admirals in the Mediterranean, and so Nelson could have returned home on leave if he had wished. But all his scouts and intelligence contacts were telling him that the French appeared to be making ready to go to sea again and that they had not disembarked their troops. Nelson had noted the course that Villeneuve had taken in the earlier sortie and decided to set a trap for his opponent. As he told Henry Bayntun of the *Leviathan*, in a 'Most Secret memorandum', 'I shall if possible make my appearance off Barcelona in order to induce the Enemy to believe I am fixed upon the Coast of Spain, when I have every reason to believe they will put to sea as I am told the Troops are still embarked. From off Barcelona I shall proceed direct to Rendezvous 98.'[31] Rendezvous 98 was at Palmas in southern Sardinia – so Nelson was intending to trick Villeneuve into taking a course that would take him down the west coasts of Corsica and Sardinia and thus straight into his waiting arms.

In fact, of course, Villeneuve was once again ordered to head westwards out of the Mediterranean but, even so, the trap very nearly worked. Nelson appeared off Barcelona on 17 March, and this was duly reported to Villeneuve, who emerged from Toulon on 30 March sailing directly south, shadowed by two of Nelson's frigates, the *Phoebe* and *Active*. Nelson, meanwhile, had crossed to Palmas, where he was waiting for news. About 10 a.m. on 4 April the *Phoebe* arrived to tell him that the French were heading his way, followed about five hours later by the *Active* confirming the news. It was a model scouting report, and once again excitement rose in the British fleet as the battleships cleared for action and stood out to westward on an interception course.

But, once again, their enemy eluded them. On the morning of 1 April Villeneuve encountered a neutral vessel from Ragusa, whose captain told him of Nelson's true whereabouts. Immediately he altered course and steered for the Balearic Islands, heading for Carthagena, where he had been ordered to rendezvous with a Spanish force. So, even as Nelson cruised confidently off the island of Toro to the southwest of Sardinia, expecting a battle at any moment, his quarry was already many miles away to the west.

So the weary, tense pattern of the January breakout was repeated once again. First, Nelson held his position off Toro, sending out scouts to various key points to look for signs of the French. Then, as it became clear that they were not coming round the south of Sardinia, he moved to Sicily, sending Ben Hallowell in the *Tigre* ahead to Palermo to find out what was happening there. Meanwhile, George Munday was sent off in the *Hydra* to find out whether the French had passed through the Strait of Bonafacio, with Nelson's trademark envoi, 'as this is a service of great importance, I rely on your exertions to execute it'.[32] The same day he sent a hurried note to Emma telling her of 'my present misery at not having yet fallen in with the French fleet'.[33] Already he was beginning to justify himself again, writing to Melville on 5 April: 'I have taken everything into my most serious judgement yet Your Lordship may rely that I will do what I think is best for the honour of my King and Country and the protection of his Majesty's Allies.'[34]

Hallowell rejoined him off Palermo on 10 April, bringing with him the news that there was no sign of the French – and also a bombshell. Acton had heard about Craig's expedition and, of course, assumed that Nelson knew all about it. Nelson's reply has survived and, reading it, we can watch the stages of his incredulous realisation of what was happening. The first half of the letter was written when Hallowell was still sailing towards him and thus able only to signal brief details of the news he was bringing, using the new telegraph system. Nelson began his reply by dismissing the idea of an expedition altogether: 'I have not a Syllable of such a thing happening,' he wrote firmly. A few hours later, after Hallowell had come on board and reported more fully, the implications of the news were beginning to sink in, and Nelson added a postscript: 'I am rather inclined to believe that the French fleet may be bound down the Mediterranean to try and Intercept them.'[35]

It must have been a bitter moment. Here, at last, was the force of troops for which he had pleaded ever since he had arrived in the Mediterranean, and now it was arriving at the moment of greatest danger and could, even then, be about to fall into the hands of the enemy. Nonetheless, he managed to remain cheerful: 'Nothing can be finer than the fleet I command, God Bless our Joint Exertions,' he told Acton. He also resisted the temptation to go charging to the westward in search of Craig. Instead, he sent out more scouts to check that the French were not still lurking somewhere in the area and went himself with the battlefleet to Toulon to make sure they had not doubled back once more.

Then, on 16 April, he received the first definite news of the French whereabouts – another neutral vessel reported having seen them off Cabo de Gata (to the south-west of Cartagena) on 7 April. By now Ambassador Elliot had confirmed Acton's report about Craig's expedition and, like Acton, Elliot assumed that Nelson knew about it already. 'I most solemnly declare', came the exasperated reply, 'my entire ignorance as to the force or destination, or even that <u>one</u> Soldier is intended for the Mediterranean'.[36] But he now had enough information to decide on his next move – the fleet was ordered to set a course for the Straits of Gibraltar. He took with him the whole battlefleet apart from the *Excellent*, which was left on duty as guardship at Naples. To protect the trade and to cover the troop convoy should it enter the Mediterranean he organised a force of frigates and sloops under Thomas Bladen Capel, who was fast becoming another of his favoured protégés.

Just when speed was required, it took him nearly two weeks to get to the Straits. 'My fortune seems flown away, I cannot get a fair wind. Dead foul! Dead foul!' he lamented to Ball,[37] and to Commissioner Otway at Gibraltar, 'I believe easterly winds have left the Mediterranean.'[38] But eventually, on 4 May, he reached Tétouan in Morocco, where his ships put in to replenish their water. Up to this point he had assumed that the French were heading for Brest, or possibly even for Ireland – as had happened in 1797. But he now began to hear rumours that they had gone to the West Indies.

In fact Villeneuve had been lucky with the winds and, after a swift passage, had arrived off Cádiz on 10 April. Sir John Orde was there with his small squadron, taking on stores, but luckily Villeneuve was spotted on his passage through the Straits by Sir Richard Strachan in HMS *Renown*, who brought the news to Orde just in time to allow him to withdraw to the north as the French fleet arrived off

Waiting for a wind. Nelson's fleet, in pursuit of Villeneuve, pauses briefly at Gibraltar to await a favourable wind to take them out through the Straits.

the port. There they were joined by Spanish reinforcements under Don Frederico Gravina y Napoli and continued, without stopping, on out into the Atlantic. Realising that the combined fleets were now a considerable force, Orde decided to fall back still further, taking his ships to join the Channel fleet far to the north.

It was the classic response of British naval commanders in the sort of crisis that was developing. In time of danger, the usual practice was to fall back on the mouth of the Channel, so as to concentrate as large a force as possible for the defence of the Western Approaches. So Orde's decision to retreat was technically correct. What, however, cannot be excused is that he took his frigates with him as well as his battleships, instead of instructing them to shadow the combined fleets and find out their course. Nor, it would appear, did he make any attempt to send news to Nelson – unlike Nelson himself, who always made a practice of keeping all his key colleagues informed of developments in his sphere of command. As a result, when Nelson finally arrived in the area nearly three weeks later, the scent was cold and he had very little information to enable him to decide where the enemy had gone. Orde's cautious and unimaginative conduct off Cádiz in April 1805 confirms how right St Vincent had been not to entrust him with the special expedition in 1798. Indeed, when he reached Britain he was ordered to strike his flag and come ashore. He never served afloat again.

Having completed his watering at Tétouan and taken aboard some cattle, Nelson then took the fleet across to Gibraltar to await a favourable wind to enable them to get through the Straits. The officers sent their linen ashore to be washed – a welcome opportunity after the long weeks of patrol and sea-water washing. However, always weatherwise, Nelson spotted the signs of an impending change in the wind, and the Blue Peter was hoisted in the *Victory*, emphasised with a gun. The officers and men came rushing back on board, cursing 'one of Nelson's mad pranks', but, sure enough, the wind did change shortly afterwards. So, thanks to Nelson's wary eye, the fleet was able to get under way immediately it was sufficiently favourable – but all the linen was left behind.[39]

Eventually, on 9 May, Nelson brought his fleet into Lagos Bay, on the south coast of Portugal, where he found Orde's storeships sheltering. As his crews began emptying them, he considered his options. Although he had no definite intelligence, he did have the negative evidence that there was no sign at all that the enemy had gone north. It was therefore a fair supposition that they were heading for the West Indies. However, he had also learned that Craig's expedition had not yet passed through the area – having sailed from Portsmouth on 19 April it was now approaching from the north. So, fretting with impatience, he moved to a position off Cape St Vincent, to cover the convoy until it had passed safely through to the Mediterranean. Once again, his natural impulsiveness had to be held in check.

In the meantime, he sought to replenish his depleted stock of small ships by issuing a general order to all warships in the area to join him, and, as was his usual custom, he sent out those already with him to get news. The *Amazon* had gone to Lisbon to follow up a rumour that Craig's force had taken refuge there: on 9 May, William Rutherfurd was sent in HMS *Swiftsure* to communicate with her and to order 'any Ships of war from wherever they may be come, or to wherever bound, to join me immediately'.[40] Also, he began to think ahead to the West Indies. On 11 May, the sloop HMS *Martin* was sent with a warning to the Governor of Barbados, Lord Seaforth, and the local naval commander, Rear Admiral Alexander Cochrane. Seaforth was requested to 'cause an Embargo to be placed upon all Vessels at Barbados in order that the Enemy may not be apprized of my arrival'. Cochrane received a classic Nelsonian order to 'weigh upon my fleet's being seen in order that we may get at the enemy before he is aware of my junction with you'.[41]

Even in these most trying circumstances, his care for the detail of other people's lives remained as strong as ever. Remembering that the Vice Consul at Tétouan was probably out of pocket, having ordered cattle especially for the fleet, he wrote to his agent victualler, James Cutforth, asking him 'to make him a reasonable recompence'.[42] And Emma Hamilton received a formal letter requesting her to take Horatia under her guardianship. With it went a private one explaining, 'I send you the enclosed that no difficulty may arise about My Dear Horatia in case any accident may happen to me', and with the reassurance, 'these arrangements do not hasten our death I believe quite the contrary as it leaves nothing to corrode the mind in a sick bed'.[43]

By the time that these letters were sent, the uncertainty in his own mind had been resolved. Craig's convoy hove into sight, having continued on its voyage, rather than putting into Lisbon as Nelson had feared. The two forces sailed in company long enough for Nelson to communicate with Craig and Knight. He reassured Craig that Bickerton, whom he was leaving behind in command, 'is as well acquainted with every circumstance relative to the Mediterranean as I am',[44] while Knight was given one of Nelson's customary lucid appreciations of the local situation, with advice on how to keep the convoy safe from Spanish gunboats during its passage through the Straits.[45] He also received a considerable reinforcement: to make the convoy more secure, Nelson gave Knight the three-decker *Royal Sovereign*. It was a major increase in his force – and it was also a remarkably selfless gesture that few other admirals would have made. Far from being obsessed with his own objectives, Nelson was able to appreciate the vital importance of Craig's mission and did what he could to assist it.

While the admirals and the general conferred, Chaplain Scott was also at work, visiting the Marquis di Circello, the Neapolitan ambassador to Britain who was on board Knight's flagship, HMS *Queen*. 'He will tell you how things stand at Naples,' Nelson told Circello, 'and you may confidentially tell him what you think proper for my information.'[46] By now, however, his final preparations were complete and so, as soon as he had concluded his discussions with Craig and Knight, he was at last able to give the order to set off to the West Indies. He still had no definite information that this was the French fleet's destination: he was acting on his own intuition. Long afterwards, Scott remembered Nelson's words to him as they began the voyage: 'If I fail, if they are not gone to the West Indies, I shall be blamed: to be burnt in effigy or Westminster Abbey is my alternative.'[47]

The following day was a Sunday, the fourth after Easter, and so Scott performed Divine Service on the *Victory*'s quarterdeck under a cloudless sky and with a strong following wind driving the fleet westwards. As he stood there with his men, listening to the prayers, the Collect for the Day may have brought a rueful smile to Nelson's lips: 'O Almighty God, who alone canst order the unruly wills and affections of sinful men . . .'.[48] Certainly he had been forced to order his own unruly will in the preceding weeks. Now, at last, he was able to concentrate on a single objective – driving his force at its best speed across the Atlantic in pursuit of the enemy.

'WE SHALL YET GET AT THE ENEMY': THE CHASE – MAY–AUGUST 1805

Nelson's chase of the combined fleet to the West Indies has been much misunderstood. It has been depicted as the typical, unthinking action of a naturally impulsive man, and it has even been suggested that it was a 'wild goose chase'.[49] In fact he was acting in accordance with time-honoured British naval custom: a century before, in 1704, Admiral Sir George Rooke had been ordered to follow the Toulon fleet out of the Mediterranean if it eluded him, and Admiral John Byng had been given similar instructions in 1756.[50]

Moreover, Nelson's instinct was confirmed by the judgement of his most senior and experienced naval contemporary. Unbeknown to him, a change had just taken place at the Admiralty. Lord Melville had been ousted by his political opponents and was facing charges of corruption, and his place as First Lord had been taken by the veteran Admiral Sir Charles Middleton, now raised to the peerage as Lord Barham. On 2 May, Barham learned that the French fleet had escaped from the Mediterranean and was believed to be heading for the West Indies. Two days later, he issued orders to Admiral Lord Gardner, then in temporary command of the Channel fleet while Admiral William Cornwallis was absent on leave. Gardner was to detach a squadron under Vice-Admiral Cuthbert Collingwood, with orders to go to Madeira to discover whether Nelson had followed the French to the West Indies. If he found that Nelson had not passed, he was to go to the West Indies himself; if Nelson had already gone, Collingwood was to send two ships to reinforce him and then resume the blockade of Cádiz, where some Spanish battleships were still preparing to join the campaign. So, although they were separated by hundreds of miles, and were from different generations, Nelson and the new First Lord were nonetheless thinking exactly alike – both of them inheritors of a long and well-tried naval tradition.

As Nelson set off on his long voyage, on 11 May, Villeneuve was within three days of his landfall on the other side of the Atlantic, the French island of Martinique. With him he now had 17 battleships, 6 of them Spanish, and 5,262 troops, including 1,930 Spanish soldiers. His orders from Napoleon required that he should wait forty days for the Brest and Rochefort squadrons to join him, and that he should spend this time doing as much damage to British possessions and trade in the West Indies as possible. In fact, as he soon discovered, the Rochefort squadron had already returned to France. Having arrived on 20 February, Missiessy carried out a series of raids on key British islands before the news arrived of the failure of Villeneuve's January sortie. He therefore decided that it was not worth waiting any longer and so, even as Villeneuve dropped anchor at Fort de France in Martinique, Missiessy was already approaching Cape Ortegal, prior to making the run back into Rochefort. Lacking the reinforcement he had expected, and apparently mesmerised by the spectre of Nelson, whom he expected to be following him closely, Villeneuve remained virtually inactive, contenting himself merely with recapturing the Diamond Rock. This rock pinnacle, dominating the entrance to Fort de France, Martinique's main port, had been captured and fortified by the British, who were thus able to harass all shipping attempting to get in and out of the port.

Nelson, meanwhile, was driving his ships as fast as they would go. He now had with him only ten battleships, among them Keats's *Superb*, which was badly in need of a dockyard refit and very slow. Keats worked hard not to delay the fleet but Nelson, sensing that he would be fretting, wrote to him on 19 May: 'I am fearful that you may think that the Superb does not go so fast as I could wish. However that may be (for if we all went ten knots I should not think it fast enough) yet I would have you be assured that I know and feel that the Superb does all which is possible for a Ship to accomplish.'[51] He was already looking ahead to the battle that he confidently believed awaited him, and four days before, on 15 May, he had distributed the latest of his battle plans. Unable to summon his captains on board the *Victory* for a conference because the fleet was constantly under way, he apparently sent each one his own copy. They were distributed by an ingenious feat of seamanship. The copies were passed to the frigate *Amazon*, commanded by one of his protégés, William Parker. Parker manoeuvred the *Amazon* until she was on the weather bow of the leading battleship and then dropped a boat with an officer on board carrying the orders. The boat went alongside and delivered the letter, while Parker dropped back onto the battleship's lee quarter, where he picked up the boat again. He then repeated the manoeuvre with each successive battleship and so, as Parker later proudly remembered, 'the progress of the fleet was delayed as little as possible'.[52]

Sadly, this particular battle order has not survived. However, we can guess at its likely contents from comments that Nelson made to various people at around this time, and from the Order of Sailing and Battle which he issued at the same time.[53] It must be remembered that he expected to be considerably outnumbered by the enemy – certainly he was hoping to join with British reinforcements in the West Indies, although this would be offset by the reinforcements that Villeneuve was expected to have at his command. So, as in a similar situation in 1799 (see p. 47), he was prepared to sacrifice his fleet in the hope that, even if his smaller force was overwhelmed, he would still manage to inflict so much damage on the enemy's ships that they would not pose any further danger. However, he had now refined his plan of attack so as to give his initial blow the maximum force. The Order of Sailing and Battle shows his fleet arranged in two divisions, with one division, which he would lead, headed by his heaviest ships: *Canopus*, *Superb*, *Donegal* and *Victory*. In other words, he was planning to pack his punch – and, as we shall see, he was to develop and refine this idea in his last battle plan just before Trafalgar.

As Nelson had anticipated, the British fleet made a much faster passage than their opponents, gaining thirteen days on them. By 29 May they were close enough to Barbados for Nelson to send the *Amazon* on ahead, with Scott on board bearing a letter for Lord Seaforth announcing his imminent arrival: 'as the fleet will not anchor at Barbadoes I shall be much obliged . . . that you will give me all the information you know of the Enemys fleet and where I am likely to find Admiral Cochrane that I may get at the Enemy without one moments delay'.[54] Five days later they encountered two British merchantmen, and from them Nelson received at last the definite confirmation that he had been waiting for – the combined fleet was indeed in the West Indies. The following day, at 6 a.m., they sighted Barbados. In fact, by a quirk of the wind, the fleet arrived only five hours after the *Amazon* but, even so, they found the island already in arms and on the alert, as a result of earlier reports of Villeneuve's arrival. On 17 May, three days after the combined fleets reached Martinique, Seaforth had summoned a special meeting of the Barbados Assembly, 'to sanction such measures as may be indispensably necessary to save the Country'.[55] As a result, Seaforth had a force of 2,000 troops ready for action, under the command of

Lieutenant-General Sir William Myers. And he also had what he considered some excellent intelligence: Brigadier-General Robert Brereton, Commander of the British forces in St Lucia, had sent word that, on 28 May, the enemy fleet had been seen heading south for Trinidad. So when Nelson arrived he found Myers and Seaforth confidently expecting that he would embark the troops and sail for Trinidad.

Nelson was later to suggest that he allowed himself to be persuaded to go to Trinidad against his better judgement,[56] but there is no sign of such hesitation in his correspondence at the time – on the contrary, everything he wrote suggests that he believed that a battle was imminent. He at once set arrangements in motion for receiving the troops on board, instructing his captains that:

> as our Troops have been very much fatigued in marching on so short notice from the different out-posts for the purpose of embarking, consequently require every comfort which can be given them and as any distinction in victualling would under the present circumstances be very improper it is my intention . . . that they shall be victualled the same as the respective Ships' Companies.[57]

Orders also went to Captains Edmund Bettesworth of the sloop *Curieux* and William Henderson of the *Pheasant* to reconnoitre Tobago and Trinidad respectively. Henderson had not served with Nelson before and so, as usual, he received a full explanation of his new commander's requirements: 'You will duly appreciate the importance of this communication when I inform you that if you tell me the Enemy are not at Trinidad that I shall stand immediately for Grenada therefore I must not necessarily be carried to leeward.'[58] Finally, he wrote one of his customary 'eve of battle' letters to Emma. 'I have every reason to hope that the 6th of June will immortalise your own Nelson, your fond Nelson,' he told her, 'therefore only pray for my success and My laurels I shall with pleasure lay at your feet and a Sweet Kiss will be an ample reward for all your faithful Nelson's hard fag, for Ever and Ever I am your faithful ever faithful and affectionate, Nelson & Bronte.'[59] This does not sound like a man who doubts there is going to be a battle.

At first all the signs were that Brereton's information was correct. As the fleet – reinforced now by Cochrane's 74-gun flagship, HMS *Northumberland* and the *Spartiate*, another 74 and, like the *Canopus*, another French prize captured at the Nile – set course for Trinidad, Bettesworth returned to report that the Tobagan authorities had been told by an American that the French fleet had been seen heading south from St Vincent. As the fleet neared Trinidad it was mistaken for the French by the military posts there, who retired to their main defences, setting fire to their outlying blockhouses as they went, the smoke from which further reinforced the impression that the French and Spanish had landed. It was not until late on 7 June that Nelson finally learned the truth: the Bay of Paria, where he had expected to find the combined fleet at anchor, was empty and, the following day, a boat from Barbados joined him bringing news of the fall of Diamond Rock to the

French on 2 June. On the day that Nelson had arrived off Barbados, Villeneuve had still been at Martinique, and he had sailed northwards on the 5th. As Nelson later told Collingwood, if the British had gone north straight away, 'the battle would have been fought where Rodney fought his' – that is, off the Isles des Saintes between Dominica and Guadeloupe.

So Nelson headed back north again, assuring Seaforth 'every thing in my power shall be done to preserve the Colonies and to frustrate the intentions of the Enemy'.[60] In fact, although he did not know it, he had already achieved his objective – and by the mere force of his name and reputation. For, on 6 June, the combined fleet captured a convoy of fourteen British merchantmen off Antigua, and from the prisoners Villeneuve learned that his adversary had arrived. Abandoning all thoughts of waiting any longer for reinforcements from Europe, as Napoleon had ordered, he immediately began preparations for the return voyage. The captured merchantmen were put under the command of a single frigate; local troops gathered during their leisurely cruise through the islands were crammed into four other small ships to be transported back to their bases and, on 10 June, the combined fleet set sail eastwards. All they had to show for their time in the West Indies was the recapture of Diamond Rock and the taking of a small convoy. 'We have been masters of the sea for three weeks', commented one of Villeneuve's junior officers despairingly, 'with a landing force of 7,000 to 8,000 men and we have not been able to attack a single island.'[61]

Meanwhile, Nelson moved from island to island looking for traces of his quarry. Now it was Cochrane in whom he confided and with whom he consulted. 'I shall stand and communicate with Antigua,' he wrote on 11 June, 'farther I know not, nor can guess at our future movements.'[62] On 12 June they reached the wide anchorage at St John's, Antigua, with its guardian forts perched on the top of lushly wooded volcanic cones. There he received news that the French troops from Guadeloupe had returned to the island, and this convinced him that the combined fleet must be heading home. 'I hope to sail in the morning after them for the Strait's Mouth,' he told Marsden.[63] Myers and his troops were hurriedly landed and Cochrane in the *Northumberland* left behind, although Nelson took the *Spartiate* with him. Cochrane received a last note outlining some ideas for his future conduct, although 'circumstances and orders may very properly induce you not to attend to this suggestion. Wishing you My Dear Admiral every success which your zeal and activity so much merit, and thanking you most sincerely for your cordial co-operation.'[64]

As the fleet was getting under way on the 13th, the small schooner *Netley* found them. She had been the escort for the unfortunate convoy, and so her captain was able to give Nelson definite news of the enemy and of their likely course. Bettesworth was sent off post-haste in the *Curieux* with dispatches for the Admiralty warning that the French and Spanish were on their way, and another message went across to the senior officer in the River Tagus, telling him to let the admiral off Ferrol know what was happening, 'that he may be on

The Curieux *leaves Antigua, July 1805. The fast brig speeds on ahead of Nelson* to warn the Admiralty of the approach of the French and Spanish fleets.

his guard in case the Enemy are bound to Ferrol'.[65] Then, with every eventuality carefully covered, Nelson began the long return voyage, heading for the Straits.

The *Curieux* was also carrying the personal mail from the fleet – including a number of letters from Nelson. Reading those that have survived, it is clear that he was brooding on the missed battle. As he reflected on the events of the previous week, he began to shift the blame onto the shoulders of the unfortunate Robert Brereton. Copies of the General's 'information' were made and sent to many of his key contacts, exactly as, earlier in his career, Nelson had sent out accounts of his own actions. 'I am sure you will regret', he told Bickerton, 'that I missed the Enemy's fleet in the West Indies owing to information sent by General Brereton of which I send you a copy, otherwise June 6th: would have been a great day for Me and I hope a glorious one for our Country.'[66]

Similar letters went to the Duke of Clarence and Alexander Davison, both of whom could be relied on to pass the word around influential circles back in Britain. Others went to Ambassador Elliot at Naples, Commissioner Otway at Gibraltar, and Governor Ball and General Villettes in Malta to make sure that all his Mediterranean colleagues got the message. And he even made the same point to Marsden and Barham at the Admiralty. Needless to say, Emma got one too, and this is the most revealing in its exaggeration and choice of language: 'I have reason to hate the name of Brereton as long as I live and perhaps our Country for ever but it is vain to repine & fret myself ill. I know this too well but I cannot help it. The name and the circumstance absolutely haunts me.'[67]

This obsessive, relentless shifting of the blame to Brereton is completely out of character – as we have seen, on previous occasions, such as at Boulogne, Nelson had insisted on shouldering all the blame for any failure. This time, as he acknowledged to Emma, he was driving himself into a frenzy – which suggests strongly that the person he was trying most hard to convince was himself. Perhaps, subconsciously, he really did think that, on this occasion, he had made a major error of judgement.

All the same, even without a battle, he had achieved his main objective, having successfully driven the enemy fleet from the West Indies and effectively prevented them from doing much damage either to British possessions or to the all-important trade. He had with him a fleet at the peak of efficiency and in high morale. 'We are all half starved', wrote Robert Stopford of the *Spencer*, an old Mediterranean man, 'and otherwise inconvenienced by being so far away from a port but our recompense is that we are with Nelson.'[68] Moreover, he was driving before him a thoroughly demoralised opponent. As Henry Bayntun of the *Leviathan*, another long-serving Mediterranean captain, reassured him on 21 June, 'Your Lordship every night forms a part of his dreams.'[69] 'We shall yet get at the Enemy', replied Nelson, 'if they are bound for the Mediterranean . . . but I am not infallible.'[70]

He certainly was not infallible, and they were not bound for the Mediterranean. Villeneuve was actually heading for Cape Finisterre, in an attempt to carry out the main tenor of his orders and effect a junction with the Brest fleet. Luckily, however, Bettesworth in the *Curieux*, racing on ahead of Nelson, sighted the combined fleet and made careful note of their course. He then sailed on to Britain and delivered Nelson's dispatches, and his own observations, to Barham at the Admiralty on 8 July. His swift voyage gave Barham time to make dispositions to intercept Villeneuve, and on 9 July he ordered Cornwallis, by now in command once more of the Channel fleet, to detach a squadron under Vice Admiral Sir Robert Calder to cruise off Cape Finisterre. Calder reached his station on 17 July and so, in one of the most dramatic moments of the entire campaign, Villeneuve arrived off the Cape on 22 July, in full flight from one British fleet, only to find another one waiting for him in the mists. A scrambling, confused battle ensued, in which two Spanish battleships were captured and, on 31 July, the French and Spanish took refuge in the Spanish port of Vigo, moving to the more secure La Coruña on 2 August. Napoleon's ambitious plans to unite his fleets lay in tatters – his ships were still widely dispersed in Carthagena, Cádiz, La Coruña, Rochefort and Brest, and he was as far as ever from gaining control of the Channel. Ironically, on 3 August, he was at Boulogne, issuing orders as if the invasion of Britain was imminent. In effect, the invasion campaign was virtually over, and a completely new one was about to begin.

By the time Villeneuve reached La Coruña Nelson had been back in European waters for almost two weeks, having finally reached Gibraltar on 20 July. There he went ashore, noting in his journal, 'I went on shore for the first time since the 16ᵗʰ of June 1803 and from having my foot out the Victory two years, wanting ten days.'[71] Right until the last moment he had still been hoping that he would overtake the combined fleet but it was clear from all the information he received that they had not headed back for the Mediterranean. Off Cádiz he found Collingwood watching the remaining Spanish ships with a small squadron, and the two old friends exchanged letters, reflecting on the campaign. Collingwood had served most of his career in the Channel fleet and so, inevitably, his outlook was coloured by his previous experience, just as Nelson's tended to be coloured by his long service in the Mediterranean. As a result, on this occasion, Collingwood's judgement was more accurate than his friend's: 'I have considered the invasion of Ireland as the real mark and butt of all their operations . . . I think they will now collect their force at Ferrol, which Calder tells me are in motion – pick up those at Rochefort who I am told are equally ready and . . . proceed to Ireland.'[72]

This resolute opinion by a respected colleague was confirmed by news from the sloop *Termagant*, which had spotted the combined fleet off Finisterre on 19 July. So Nelson decided to follow the time-honoured practice and take his battlefleet north to join Cornwallis off the mouth of the Channel. 'I shall only hope', he told his friend, 'after all my long pursuit of <u>my</u> Enemy that I may arrive at the moment they are meeting you'.[73] However, before he left the area he made detailed dispositions for command in the Mediterranean while he was away. On arrival at Gibraltar he had discovered that Barham had replaced Melville and, in his first letter to the new First Lord, he set out his ideas, following his general thoughts with a long appreciation to Marsden, outlining the forces that would be required. Collingwood was to command from Cape St Vincent to Cape Spartel; Knight, based at Gibraltar, was to oversee the Straits; Bickerton was to return to the Mediterranean to watch over Naples, Sicily and Malta and protect the trade. Orders poured from the *Victory*'s Great Cabin putting all these arrangements in motion. 'All these matters I shall fully and clearly arrange,' he told Knight, 'and I hope to your satisfaction and the good of the Public Service.'[74]

On 25 July he sailed again, having first taken care to inform all his key colleagues of his intentions, and sending word ahead to the Admiralty. Yet again he encountered contrary winds, which forced him to make a long sweep to the west in order to catch the southerlies. He noted with his usual meticulousness in his journal, 'In summer time coming from the Mediterranean you must not expect to lose the Northerly wind until you get into the Longitude of 17° W.'[75] By being forced so far out into the Atlantic, he lost the final chance of falling in with Villeneuve – for the combined fleet was still at large and did not get into La Coruña until 3 August. But Collingwood and Nelson were completely in the dark, Calder having failed to inform them of

Letter from Nelson to Cornwallis, 15 August 1805. Nelson sends friendly greetings and gifts to his old friend at the end of the great chase.

what was going on to the north of them. Nothing highlights more starkly the difference between Nelson and his less imaginative contemporaries more starkly than this failure on the part of two admirals, Orde and then Calder, at critical moments in the campaign to share intelligence with their neighbouring colleagues. It was a mistake Nelson never made.

So, as 'My' Enemy slipped ignominiously from one port to another, watched ineffectually by a worthy but unimaginative admiral, Britain's most imaginative – but, for the moment, most unlucky – admiral fought his way home against foul winds, depressed and unhappy. He confided in his journal, 'I trust in Providence that it is all for the best but I a poor weak mortal suffer severely from the mortification of so apparently long a passage.' Finally, on 15 August, he sighted the Channel fleet off Ushant and, having left most of his ships with Cornwallis, continued towards Portsmouth accompanied only by Keats's *Superb* – now, at last, on her way home for her long overdue refit. Before he parted company, he wrote to his second-in-command, Thomas Louis, 'I have only a moment to beg that you will be so good as to express in the manner best calculated to do justice, the high sense I entertain of the merit of the Captains Officers and Ships' Companies lately composing the Squadron under my Command and assure their able and zealous commanders that their conduct has met my warmest approbation.'[76]

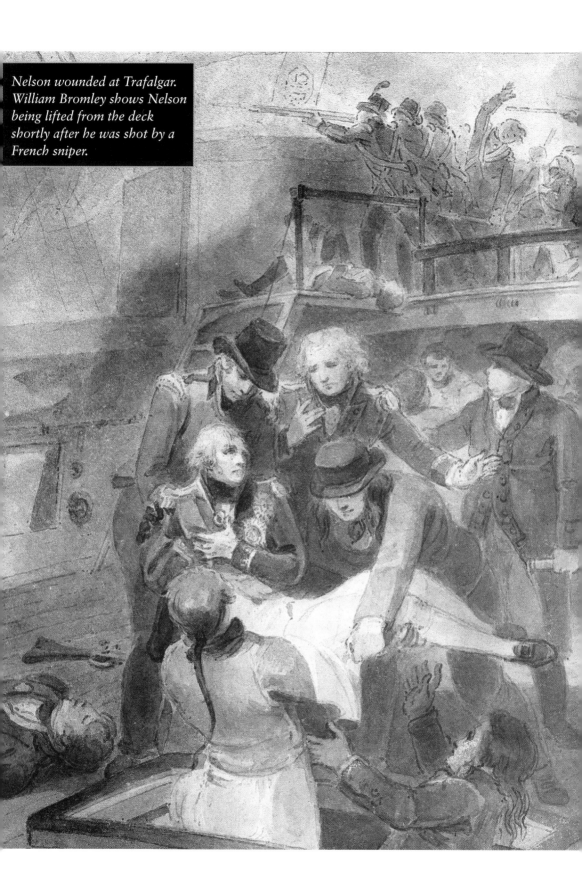

Nelson wounded at Trafalgar. William Bromley shows Nelson being lifted from the deck shortly after he was shot by a French sniper.

CHAPTER VII

The Battle of Trafalgar: September–October 1805

'I AM NOW SET UP FOR A *CONJURER*': NELSON IN ENGLAND, AUGUST–SEPTEMBER 1805

Nelson arrived in the *Victory* at Spithead on 18 August 1805 in a defensive mood. In his own eyes, he had failed: 'My enemy', as he called the combined fleet, was still at large, and he had not brought it to battle despite being close to doing so on at least three occasions. Moreover, on his way up the Channel he had seen the first newspaper reports of Calder's action and had learned that, as he told Thomas Fremantle, 'John Bull was not content, which I am sorry for. Who can, my dear Fremantle, command all the success which the Country may wish?'[1] He was also uncomfortable to discover that the papers were saying that he would have done better had he met the combined fleet; 'who can say that he will be more successful than another. I only wish to stand on my own merits and not by comparison.' General Brereton began to feature in his letters once again, a sign perhaps that he was worried that, when his superiors and the politicians began looking closely at his actions over the previous five months, he might find himself in the pillory alongside Calder.

He need not have worried. The story of his chase of a superior enemy force halfway across the world and back had captured the public imagination and, most important, he had saved the wealthy West Indies trade from any serious depredations. He quickly found that he was the hero of the hour. Cheering crowds greeted him when he finally went ashore at Portsmouth, and whenever he appeared in public in the days that followed, he was mobbed. 'I met Lord Nelson today in a mob in Piccadilly', Lord Minto told his wife, 'and got hold of his arm, so that I was mobbed too. It really is quite affecting to see the wonder and admiration, and love and respect, of the whole world . . . It is beyond anything represented in a play or a poem of fame.'[2] 'Thank God!' wrote Lord Radstock to him in delight. 'Thank God a thousand times that these Jack O'Lanterns are once more safely housed.' John Julius Angerstein of Lloyd's wrote, 'Your Grace has saved if not all many of the West India islands' and the West India merchants wrote asking him to accept a formal address of thanks for 'his bold and unwearied pursuit of the Combined French and Spanish squadrons'.[3]

Lord Barham, the new First Lord, at first remained aloof, confining himself to a formal request to see Nelson's journal; but having perused it he is supposed to have 'liberally declared [he] had not before sufficiently appreciated such extraordinary talents'.[4] The actual wording of that quotation probably owes more to William Nelson, who supplied many of Clarke and M'Arthur's anecdotes, than to Barham himself – but the fact remains that Barham did begin consulting Nelson closely and showed in a number of ways how much he trusted his judgement. The admiration was returned: 'You will find Lord Barham a wonderful man,' Nelson wrote to Bickerton some weeks later.[5]

Nelson's main reason for coming home was to rest and recover his health but, in fact, his private life in that all too short period of leave consisted of precious moments snatched from a busy round of public engagements. While he had been away at sea, Emma had carried out many improvements at Merton, which had turned it into a show house that was also a comfortable and attractive home. Now she had summoned many of his relatives to be with him, and the house was constantly full of guests. However, Nelson found time to go shopping for presents for Horatia – including a charming silver-gilt cup and a tiny knife, both engraved 'To my much loved Horatia' – to purchase new telescopes from Dollands and to replenish his own stock of clothes.[6] He even bought four sets of replacements for the facsimile stars that he wore on the breasts of his uniform coats. He also continued to take a close interest in the affairs of his protégés and friends and, as a

Horatia Nelson, c. 1805. Horatia as Nelson saw her during his brief leave in 1805 – four-and-a-half years old, and very bright.

result, his personal correspondence remained as taxing as ever. He was helped by John Scott, who rejoined him at Merton after a brief reunion with his own family and, so overwhelmed was Nelson with work, he had to take the step, unusual for him, of asking Scott to reply on his behalf to personal letters – for example, Dr Baird, who had treated Edward Parker in 1801, was told 'as His Lordship is particularly engaged with public business I am directed to return you his best thanks for your kind congratulations on his return to this Country'.

But there were still some letters that he wrote himself. Taking advantage of his regular meetings with Pitt, he wrote to ask the Prime Minister to make sure that Sir Thomas Thompson's wife would be looked after, should her husband die: 'I am sure from your liberal manner of acting that you will do what is proper for Sir Thomas. A more gallant active Zealous Officer was not in the Service.' Barham received a glowing testimonial to Dr John Snipe, formerly Physician of the Mediterranean fleet, who had died earlier that year: 'a better man in Private life nor a more able Man in His Profession I never met with.' He continued to fight to save William Layman's career, writing to Barham's secretary, J.D. Thompson: 'I consider Captain Layman a most zealous, able, active and gallant Officer . . . The loss of the services of men of such rare ability is to be lamented by the Country.' A young lad from Merton received a glowing testimonial in his patron's own handwriting: 'William Hasleham went out with me in the Victory a Boy and came Home with Me a Young Man. I believe him perfectly Sober & honest and he behaved very well while in my Service and left Me to please himself.' At some stage, probably in early September, Nelson went to a meeting with Sir Andrew Hammond, the Comptroller of the Navy, at the Navy Board's offices in Somerset House, carrying in his pocket some rough notes to remind him of the favours and appointments that he wanted to obtain for some of his 'followers': a 'timepiece' for William Bunce, carpenter of the *Victory*, and for Thomas Atkinson, the ship's Master, a post as a master attendant of a dockyard.[7] Clearly, even while on leave, he still remained as interested as ever in the careers of those who served him faithfully.

He was also still developing and refining his ideas for how he would fight his next battle. On the reverse side of his notes for the meeting at the Navy Board is a rough diagram, clearly drawn to accompany a verbal explanation of the tactics that he proposed to use (see box on p. 160), and we know that he gave a similar demonstration on at least two other occasions. The first was to Captain Richard Keats of HMS *Superb* who called on him at Merton. They went for a walk in the grounds, where Keats was treated to an enthusiastic exposition of how Nelson proposed to bring about what he called a 'pell-mell battle'. 'What do you think of it?' he asked. Keats hesitated, trying to find the words to express his excitement, and Nelson eagerly answered his own question: 'I'll tell you what I think of it. I think it will surprise and confound the enemy. They won't know what I am about.'[8] A few days later he called on his friend Henry Addington, now elevated to the peerage as Lord Sidmouth, at his house in Richmond Park. 'I shall be happy in taking you by the hand and to wish you a most perfect restoration to health,' said

THE 1805 BATTLE PLAN

The battle plan was discovered in the archive of the National Maritime Museum in the autumn of 2001 (Ref: BRP/6). It is on the reverse of a set of rough notes in Nelson's handwriting, the contents of which enable the document to be dated with some confidence to the autumn of 1805 when Nelson was briefly on leave in England.

The plan is in two halves. The top half, above the thin horizontal line, appears to show the British fleet crossing the head of the enemy line and then turning to take it between two fires.

The bottom half shows the enemy as a single thick diagonal line. To the left, the British can be seen forming up in three unequal lines. The top one then ranges alongside one part of the enemy line, while the other two break through the line cutting it into segments. It is even possible to catch an echo of the excitement with which Nelson has demonstrated the cutting of the line – his pen has dug deeply into the paper and the ink has flowed thickly.

For a full analysis of the diagrams and of the evidence for the provenance of the plan, see Colin White, 'Nelson's 1805 Battle Plan', *Journal of Maritime Research*, April 2002, www.jmr.nmm.ac.uk.

Nelson's 1805 battle plan.

his note confirming the appointment.[9] Sidmouth's descendants still preserve a small table on which Nelson demonstrated his tactics, using a finger dipped in wine.

While Nelson was enjoying his leave, another significant stage had been reached in the naval campaign. Having taken refuge in Ferrol, following his battle with Calder, Villeneuve had emerged again on 13 August. However, instead of sailing north, as ordered, to attempt to join with Ganteaume off Brest, he first headed west into the Atlantic and then vanished. On 20 August, the small British squadron under Collingwood, still patrolling off Cádiz, sighted a large fleet heading towards them. Collingwood withdrew his ships into the Straits of Gibraltar, watched from a distance as the French and Spanish battleships entered the port, and then proceeded to 'blockade' them with his tiny force, sending signals over the horizon to imaginary consorts. In the meantime, he sent Blackwood in the frigate *Euryalus* to report the enemy's position and to request reinforcements.

Collingwood's dispatches were addressed to the Admiralty and, strictly, Blackwood should have gone straight there with them. But he knew that Nelson would want to hear the news as soon as possible. So he made a brief diversion off the main road from Portsmouth to London in order to call in at Merton. He arrived at 5 a.m. on the morning of 2 September to find the Admiral already up and dressed, as was his custom. Nelson took one look at him and exclaimed, 'I am sure you bring me news of the French and Spanish fleets and I think I shall yet have to beat them.'

Blackwood continued on up the road to London and, shortly afterwards, Nelson followed him to the Admiralty, where he met once again with Barham. Now the combined fleet had been located, he knew he would be sent out to deal with it – but at that particular moment, there was no fleet for him to command. The ships of his old Mediterranean fleet had been absorbed into the Channel fleet, and Collingwood had only three battleships with him off Cádiz. So a new fleet had to be put together hurriedly. Sitting in the famous Board Room, the two men began to discuss the fleet's composition. According to Clarke and M'Arthur, Barham at this point handed Nelson a copy of the printed Navy List and invited him to choose his captains, upon which Nelson is supposed to have handed the booklet back with the words, 'Choose yourself my Lord. The same spirit actuates the whole profession; you cannot choose wrong.'

It is most unlikely that Nelson said any such thing. The speech – especially the use of the word 'actuates' – does not sound at all like him, and the sentiment, splendid though it sounds, is professional nonsense: Nelson knew as well as any that the captains list contained a number of duffers. In fact, we know that he made sure to hand-pick some key captains. He wrote to Captain Richard Keats of the *Superb*, 'Nothing, I do assure you, could give me more pleasure than to have you at all times near me.'[10] He promised Edward Berry that he would ask Barham to give him a ship. Philip Durham, of HMS *Defiance*, who had brought his ship home to repair the heavy damage she had sustained at Sir Robert Calder's action off Cape Finisterre, met Nelson at the Admiralty on 11 September. 'I am sorry your ship is not ready,' said Nelson. 'I should have been very glad to have you.'

'Ask Lord Barham to place me under your Lordship's orders,' replied Durham, 'and I will soon be ready.' The very next day, he received orders at Portsmouth written 'At the Admiralty Office' directing him 'to put yourself under my command'.[11] Even Sir Sidney Smith, the hero of Acre in 1799, was drawn into his new circle: Smith told his patron, William Windham, that Nelson had 'offer'd me command of the Inshore Squadron in the Mediterranean with full powers to act as circumstances might render practicable in attacking the enemy'.[12]

In fact, Nelson's approach to Smith was all part of a wider scheme being promoted by the Government, and especially by the new Minister at War, Lord Castlereagh, for the development of two new secret weapons: William Congreve's rockets mounted on 'double canoes', and 'torpedoes' (underwater explosive devices named after stinging fishes) devised by Robert Fulton. It had been decided that the weapons would be tried out, under Smith's overall control, on the French flotilla at Boulogne, in the early autumn. Then, if they proved successful, they would be used to mount a major attack on the combined fleet in Cádiz.[13] Nelson was sceptical, writing later to Castlereagh, 'I have always heard that where these things invented by Clever Men are practised that they very rarely answer.' But he was prepared to give them a fair trial: 'rely these gentlemen shall have every justice done to their plans.'[14]

There was another secret mission in the air – this time, a royal one. Colonel Hippisley, Secretary to the Prince of Wales, told Nelson that the Prince wished to meet him to arrange for him to carry home 'some Papers of much consequence which I obtained for Him from Italy'. It is not clear from the vague mentions of the mission in Nelson's correspondence exactly what these papers were; but they were obviously highly sensitive, since Hippisley felt it was 'not right to mention what they are other than "viva voce"', and Nelson was instructed to keep the package containing them safely on board until he returned, 'unless he has the opportunity of some safe and sure conveyance to send it Home'.[15] The meeting duly took place at the Prince's London residence, Carlton House, on 12 September, Nelson's last full day of leave. Previous accounts of this meeting have dismissed it as a crude attempt by the publicity-conscious George to bask in Nelson's reflected glory – but we now know that their meeting had a rather more serious purpose.

Everyone wanted to see Nelson. Louis wrote from the Channel fleet, to which the ships of his former squadron were now attached, 'Wou'd to God you were with us, believe me the loss of you has been much felt but we still have hopes of having you as our <u>Head</u>.' Pulteney Malcolm of HMS *Donegal* wrote in a similar vein: 'The Donegals feel most particularly flattered by your good opinion and it is their most anxious wish that they may serve again with you and our hopes are sanguine, for in such eventful times your Lordship will not be permitted to remain on shore and we believe that if in your power you will have your old friends with you again.'[16] William Beckford wrote to invite him to visit Fonthill. Hercules Ross, a friend from the early days in the West Indies, with whom he had kept up a regular correspondence, and his prize agent and friend, Alexander Davison, both summering in their respective northern homes, wrote to say they hoped to reach London in time to meet him. His old mentor, Lord Hood, wrote: 'I will call on you at any place & at any hour you will have the goodness to name.' And Lord Camden, with whom he had corresponded from the Mediterranean, called at his hotel in the hope of meeting him so that he could 'testify to that admiration that I feel, in common with the rest of the world, of the whole of your conduct after you heard of the Enemy having passed the Straits of Gibraltar'.[17]

Camden was not the only politician who wanted to meet Nelson. Senior ministers from Prime Minister William Pitt down asked him to call on them, and he found that he was being consulted not only on the current situation regarding the combined fleet and the invasion threat, but also on diplomatic affairs in the Mediterranean. It would seem that his carefully written and thoughtful reports during the previous two years had been noticed. He used his new-found influence to impress on them the importance of Sardinia. His efficient filing system now proved its worth: on 29 August, he wrote to the Prime Minister, 'I cannot rest until the importance of Sardinia in every point of view is taken into consideration. If my letters to the different Secretaries of State cannot be found I can bring them with me.' Even Lord Minto, although not a member of the Government, was drawn into this campaign. He was shown the letterbooks too, and it is clear that what he saw were the pressed-copy letterbooks, containing the sensitive material, rather than the official correspondence books.[18] So important had the diplomatic aspects of the Mediterranean commander's work become that it was decided a special team of diplomats should be attached to Nelson's staff. On 12 September, Alexander Scott and Lambton Este accompanied Nelson when he attended a meeting of key ministers in Downing Street. When the meeting broke up, Nelson came out to Este and said, 'I have just settled your business with Lord Liverpool. I am now going to the Admiralty and I shall order you a passage on board Captain Bolton's frigate. You will join me in six weeks.' Este was to head a team of six diplomats 'with commissions for the Foreign Office who were to assist with the arduous political negotiations which the Admiral had anticipated'.[19] This time Nelson would have a staff capable of dealing swiftly with the many demands of the Mediterranean station.

Despite all this attention from politicians and other members of the establishment, and despite the adulation of the ordinary people, who continued to mob him whenever he appeared in the streets, Nelson managed to keep a cool head. He was older and wiser than he had been in Naples in 1798. 'I am now set up for a conjurer', he told Richard Keats ruefully, 'and God knows they will very soon find out that I am far from being one . . . if I make one wrong guess the charm will be broken.'[20] Harriet, Lady Bessborough, who met him at a dinner, reported that:

> so far from appearing vain and full of himself as one had always heard, he was perfectly unassuming and natural. Emma wanted him to describe to the company how he had been mobbed in the streets but he gently stopped her.

'Why you like to be applauded, you cannot deny it.' He accepted that but added, 'no man ought to be too much elated by it . . . it may be my turn to see the tide set as strong against me as it ever did for me.'[21]

This judgement by a shrewd observer shows just how much Nelson had changed since the tense days in Palermo, when he had appeared unattractively vain and obsessed with his own achievements. It is as well to bear this in mind when looking at Nelson's most famous encounter during his leave – with Major-General Sir Arthur Wellesley, later the Duke of Wellington, in Lord Castlereagh's waiting-room on 12 September.

We have only Wellington's version of their meeting – and that was relayed many years after the event to the diarist John Wilson Croker. It is a very late, and second-hand, narrative – and so should be treated with rather more scepticism than some biographers have accorded it.[22] As Croker remembered, Wellington claimed that Nelson at first behaved in a very 'vain and silly' way, talking only of his own achievements – until, that is, he appeared to realise that he was talking to someone out of the ordinary, and went off to check who his companion was. He then returned transformed and proceeded to impress the young general with his statesmanlike judgements and knowledge of international affairs.

It would be fascinating to have Nelson's version of their encounter. Wellington could be chillingly aristocratic and superior when he wanted to be. Moreover, it is clear from his own account that he was rather put out to discover that Nelson did not appear to know who he was – which, since he had won a rare land victory at Assaye in India only two years before, must have been galling. It is fair to assume, therefore, that in the early part of their conversation, Wellington was stiff and distant – behaviour guaranteed to make Nelson feel insecure and defensive.

Whatever the reason for their initial failure to engage, the second part of their conversation was clearly much more successful. It would appear that Nelson recognised a kindred spirit – someone, like William Stewart, with whom he felt he could work – for he told Wellington that he hoped he would be appointed to command the troops destined for the occupation of Sardinia. Most important, he managed to break down the austere young patrician's reserve and to inspire, even to excite, him. As Wellington tellingly recalled, 'I don't know that I ever had a conversation that interested me more.' Even when relayed in this very one-sided account, the Nelson magic still shines through.

As a result of the delay while he and Wellesley waited for Castlereagh, Nelson returned to Merton later than expected that evening, to find an awkward situation awaiting him. Now that their parting was imminent, Emma was in great distress and, just when they needed to have some quiet time together, they found themselves having to entertain guests for dinner. Minto, who was there, reported disapprovingly and unsympathetically to his wife that Emma 'could not eat, and hardly drink, and near swooning and all at table'.[23] Later, Emma tried to create the impression that she had persuaded a reluctant Nelson that he had to go back to sea and she comforted herself with the idea that, having accepted her arguments, he had said, 'Brave Emma, good Emma; if there were more Emmas there would be more Nelsons.'[24] It is wholly understandable that she should have sought to assuage the pain of her loss in this way, but the story cannot be allowed to stand. It is certainly true that Nelson was reluctant to leave his happy home and beloved mistress and daughter; but in suggesting that her lover had to be persuaded to do his duty, Emma wronged him. All his correspondence at the time bears witness to a resigned acceptance of his destiny: 'I hold myself ready to go forth whenever I am desired although God knows I want rest but self is entirely out of the question,' he told George Rose. Emma had to learn, as Frances had before her, that for Nelson 'Duty is the great business of a Sea Officer, all private considerations must give way to it, however painful it is.'[25]

He was, however, more sensitive to Emma's worries and fears than he had ever been to those of his wife, and he did what he could to allay them. Marriage was of course impossible so long as Frances lived but, at some stage during the last days, possibly on Wednesday 11 September, he went through a strange little ceremony with Emma that was clearly designed to reassure her of his commitment to their relationship – in personal affairs, as in public, he recognised the value of the symbolic gesture. The exact details are uncertain, but it would appear that he went with her and a few friends to the nearby parish church (see picture on p. 166) and there, having received communion privately, they exchanged rings.[26] He then took her by the hand and said publicly, 'Emma, I have taken the sacrament with you this day to prove to the world that our friendship is most pure and innocent and of this I call God to witness.'[27] The living proof that their relationship was anything but 'pure' in the sense that he meant it was asleep in her nursery when, eventually, Nelson left Merton at about 10.30 p.m. on Friday 13 September. We are told that Horatia's father prayed by her bedside and returned at least three times to watch her sleeping before he could tear himself away and climb into the post chaise that was to take him to Portsmouth. He left behind him a household almost in mourning: 'Cou'd you see us all My dear Mr Scott, how wretched we are you wou'd pity us,' wrote Emma to John Scott the following day. 'Poor little Horatia cried at breakfast for godpapa.'[28]

Driving through the night, Nelson reached Portsmouth at about 6 a.m. on the 14th. Waiting for him at the George Hotel in the High Street was the Rector of Merton, the Revd Henry Lancaster, with his young son, who was joining the *Victory* as a midshipman. Mr Lancaster returned to Merton bearing the first of a steady stream of notes to 'My dearest and most beloved of women, Nelson's Emma', telling her of his safe arrival. 'God protect you and Horatia.' Then Nelson walked across to the dockyard to meet with the Commissioner, Sir Charles Saxton, to discuss the ships that were even then being hurriedly fitted out to join his growing fleet off Cádiz and to issue a string of his characteristic 'utmost expedition' orders. He also took the opportunity to view the new Blockmills, where blocks for ships' rigging were being produced using the country's first steam-powered production line. Back at the George before noon, he found waiting for him two members of the Government who had come to wish him God-speed:

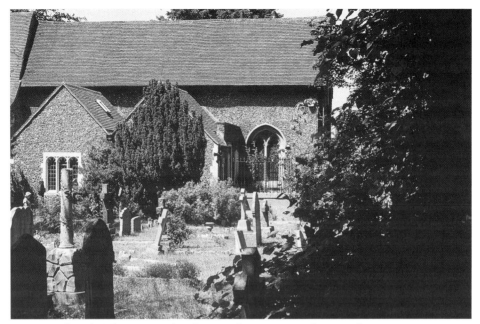

*Merton Church. The scene of Nelson and Emma's exchange of rings on
11 September 1805.*

George Rose, the Vice-President of the Board of Trade and a close associate of
Pitt, and the Treasurer to the Navy, George Canning. Off went another note to
Emma, telling her, 'I have been overwhelmed with business from the moment of
my arrival but you are never for one moment absent from my thoughts.'[29] He also
told her that Rose and Canning were going to come with him to the *Victory* to
'eat my scrambling dinner', a phrase that vividly conjures up the sense of busy
purpose he was exuding. Both the Scotts were with him, and it would seem that he
was writing and dictating letters and orders virtually on the move – almost as if he
was talking on a mobile phone. For example, George Murray, who was too ill to
rejoin him as Captain of the Fleet, received a short note to thank him for the gift
of a haunch of venison: 'I am this moment getting in the Boat.'[30]

Finally, he was ready to go on board the *Victory*, which was lying some
three miles away at the anchorage at St Helen's, at the eastern end of the Isle of
Wight. By now, word of his arrival had spread around Portsmouth and a large
crowd had gathered in the narrow streets outside the hotel. The usual place of
embarkation for officers was at the Sally Port, just a few hundred yards away, at
the seaward end of the High Street. But the crowd was now so dense that it would
be extremely difficult for him to make his way through them, and so he chose an
alternative route. Accompanied by the two politicians and the two Scotts, he left
the George by a back door and, emerging into a sidestreet, headed for the beach,
where his barge had been ordered to meet him. However, the crowd heard what

he was doing and poured after him. The Revd Thomas Socket, tutor to the sons of Lord Egremont, had brought his pupils over from Petworth to see Nelson depart, and they got caught up in all the excitement: 'people crowded after him in all directions to get a sight of him. I was amused by the eagerness of a common sailor I met, who was running with all his might and who, on being asked by another if he had seen him, replied, "No but d—n the old b—r I should like to see him once more" and away he posted at full speed.'[31]

He was heading for a small tunnel through the fortifications leading to a drawbridge that crossed the moat to an outlying battery, known as the Spur Redoubt. From there, a small door opened directly onto the beach.[32] Behind him the crowds pushed their way past the guarding sentries onto the King's Bastion, a large battery overlooking the beach. Among them was an American tourist, Benjamin Silliman, who had been caught up in the surge, and he saw Nelson actually embark:

> by the time he had arrived on the beach some hundreds of people had gathered in his train, pressing all around and pushing to get a little before him to obtain a sight of his face. I stood on one of the batteries near which he passed and had a full view of his person. As the barge in which he was embarked pushed away from the shore the people gave three cheers, which his Lordship returned by waving his hat.[33]

As he settled back into his seat, with its commander-in-chief's green cushions, and as the well-practised crew picked up their stroke, Nelson turned to Captain Hardy, who had come to collect him, and said, 'I had their huzzas before; I have their hearts now.' He had learned to appreciate the difference between simple (and ephemeral) popularity and genuine (and lasting) admiration and love. Characteristically, he recorded his mood in a prayer, written in his journal either during his brief stay in Portsmouth or when he got on board the *Victory* at St Helen's – characteristically, too, he made sure it was preserved for posterity by making a copy. Much less famous than his morning-of-battle prayer at Trafalgar, it deserves to be better known, for it is a perfect expression of the feelings of those who put their lives in harm's way for the sake of others:

> May the Great God whom I adore enable me to fulfil the expectations of my Country, and if it is His good pleasure that I should return, my thanks will never cease being offered up to the Throne of His Mercy. If it is his good providence to cut short my days upon earth I bow with the greatest submission, relying that He will protect those so dear to me that I may leave behind. His will be done. Amen, amen, amen.

So he returned to the Great Cabin of the *Victory* after an absence of only twenty-five days, and the familiar smell of tar and hemp, and unwashed male bodies, enveloped him again – accompanied by the smell of fresh paint, since his cabin had been redecorated during the ship's brief stay in the dockyard. He had even been given one of the new-fangled water cisterns in his lavatory.

'WE ARE ONE AND I HOPE EVER SHALL BE': NELSON OFF CÁDIZ

The following day, the wind came to the east, and Nelson was off down the Channel, with the familiar lift and roll of his flagship under his feet once more – and the usual mountain of paperwork to occupy him. Although the combined fleet at Cádiz was currently his main concern, he still had all the business of the Mediterranean to deal with. The Viceroy of Sardinia was assured:

> even during my short stay in England I did not neglect to represent to His Majesty's Minister the exact state of the Island of Sardinia and of the great distress your Royal Highness was in from want of pecuniary assistance. And I have the satisfaction of assuring your R H that the necessity of succouring His Sardinian Majesty, to enable him to prevent Sardinia from falling into the hands of the French, is sensibly felt, and proper measures will speedily be taken for that purpose.

Meeting Bickerton coming north on sick leave, he wrote to bring him up to date and to 'hope you will have a much longer spell on shore than I have had'. And messages went ahead to Collingwood, still commanding off Cádiz, and to the Governor of Gibraltar urging them to do all they could to prevent the news of his arrival reaching Cádiz. He noted in his journal on 25 September that he had been told by the captain of HMS *Constance* that the enemy were still in Cádiz, 'therefore I yet hope they will await my arrival'.[34] He finally arrived, after a slow passage, on 28 September. The following day, his forty-seventh birthday, the signal was made to the fleet to 'Close round the admiral', and according to the *Victory*'s log, 'Vice Admiral Collingwood came on board, Sir Robert Calder and the respective captains.'

It is one of the most famous scenes in Nelson's story – the dinner with his captains on the eve of battle, when he shared with them the 'Nelson touch' that had reduced Keats to silence in the Merton garden and which he had sketched rapidly for another colleague on the back of his meeting notes. But the details of the occasion have become obscured in the constant retelling, and a couple of misconceptions have arisen. The first concerns those who were actually present. It is, for example, now clear that very few of his former Mediterranean colleagues were there: most of them were serving in a squadron under Rear Admiral Louis stationed close inshore at Cádiz, and a newly discovered letter from Nelson to Louis shows that they remained there, rather than gathering around the *Victory* with the rest of the fleet. 'I was truly glad to see you and my old friends again yesterday,' he wrote on the 29th, and then went on to tell Louis to stay where he was until 'I call You and Your Squadron to me'.[35] Moreover, a number of the captains who later fought at Trafalgar had not yet arrived – Berry, for example,

'Some shed tears; all approved'. Nelson explains his battle plan to his excited captains after dinner in the Victory. *Seated next to him is his second-in-command, Vice-Admiral Cuthbert Collingwood.*

who came out some weeks later in the *Agamemnon*, Conn, who brought the newly refitted *Royal Sovereign* out to be Collingwood's flagship and then changed from her into the *Dreadnought*, and Durham, who was still on his way out with the *Defiance*. And some of those who were present at the dinner did not take part in the battle because, by 21 October, they had been sent on detached duty or had gone home.

Another common misconception is that there was one big dinner party. In fact Nelson could seat no more than eighteen to twenty people at once around his dining table, and so the captains were entertained in two batches – the seniors on the 29th and the juniors the next day. Thomas Fremantle, in command of the 98-gun *Neptune*, who dined on the second day, noted in his journal, 'The juniors and I never passed a pleasanter day,' and two of those 'juniors' confirmed this impression. George Duff of the *Mars* told his wife, 'I dined with His Lordship yesterday and had a very merry dinner. He certainly is the pleasantest admiral I ever served under.' Edward Codrington of the *Orion* wrote home of 'the superiority of Lord Nelson in all these social arrangements which bind his captains to their admiral'. He had a particular reason to be grateful to his new commander – in a typically thoughtful gesture, Nelson had handed him a letter from his wife, saying, 'As it was entrusted to me by a lady I make a point of delivering it myself.'[36]

Most important, the famous birthday dinner was not a one-off event – it was the first of many such social occasions. Having won his captains' hearts and inspired them as a group, Nelson then, as was his custom, continued to meet with them in twos and threes for dinner and a walk on the quarterdeck, getting to know them as individuals. So, for example, the third-in-command, Rear Admiral Lord Northesk, with whom he had not served before, received two further invitations to dinner, on 3 October and again on the 15th: 'It is likely to be a very fine day therefore will you do me the favour of dining on board the Victory, your Captain I shall of course expect with you.'[37]

The team of captains that eventually fought at Trafalgar was the least homogeneous that Nelson ever commanded in a major battle. Even at Copenhagen, most of the captains of the hurriedly raised fleet had served together before in the Channel or North Sea fleets, and at the Nile, as we have seen, Nelson not only inherited a team that had worked together for years, but he also had nearly two months in which to stamp his own style upon it. By contrast, the Trafalgar fleet was hurriedly created, almost from scratch. Ships were drawn from various sources: some summoned from the Mediterranean, others detached from the Channel; yet others rushed out of the English dockyards. Even when the fleet began to assemble off Cádiz, its composition was never static. Some ships were sent off to pick up stores and water, and others arrived from England – the last to join, on 14 October, was the 64-gun *Africa*, commanded by Captain Henry Digby. As a result, of the twenty-seven commanders of battleships who eventually took their ships into action on 21 October, only ten had previously served with Nelson, either in the Mediterranean campaign of 1803–5 or earlier. Indeed, only six captains in the entire fleet had commanded battleships in a fleet action before. So Nelson had to work fast to mould his disparate, and relatively inexperienced, colleagues into a fighting unit.[38]

It is clear that most of the captains responded enthusiastically. Nelson famously told Emma that the effect of his briefing at the birthday dinner 'was like an electric shock. Some shed tears all approved', and it would appear that their excitement was shared by all ranks in the fleet. Able Seaman James Martin of the *Neptune* wrote home, 'it is Imposeble to Discribe the Heartfelt Satisfaction of the whole fleet upon this occasion and the Confidance of Success with which we were inspired'.[39] Collingwood, now Nelson's second-in-command, was treated in the same open, frank, consultative manner that he had employed with Graves and Bickerton. Notes passed between them daily, discussing all aspects of their work, from the minute details of fleet administration to the wider strategic situation. In this case, given the shortness of the time available, Nelson was fortunate that he had as his second a man with whom he had served so often before and to whom he was so personally close. 'Telegraph upon all occasions without ceremony,' he told 'My dear Coll', 'We are one and I hope ever shall be.'[40]

As well as entertaining his captains, Nelson also issued them with a string of orders, each couched in his trademark urgent, emphatic language, and designed to galvanise the whole fleet and get it working quickly in his way. There was the usual attention to humane detail: men sent to hospital were to have a statement of their case sent with them. His long-accumulated weatherlore was put to good use: ships were to shorten sail and get their topgallant masts down each night, 'as gales of wind increase so suddenly in this Country'. A common identity was established by the order that, in battle, all ships were to wear the white ensign[41] and to suspend a Union flag from the fore topgallant stay. And, as usual, he demanded alertness and prompt execution of orders: 'When the Signal to Wear is made in the Night it is expected by the time the Third in Command shall have repeated the signal that the Sternmost and Leewardmost ships are before the Wind.'[42] The words 'by the time' were inserted in Nelson's own handwriting. Although his Public Order Book for this period has, sadly, not survived, it is clear he was using one and, as with the previous examples we have examined, he was taking a personal interest in their contents and using them as a way of continuing his dialogues with his captains. Fremantle summed up his methods neatly: 'the energy and activity on board the *Victory* will make those who are slack keep a much better look out and preserve better discipline.'[43]

As in the Mediterranean in 1803–5 Nelson's energy and activity are vividly captured in the pages of his letterbooks – especially the pressed-copy versions, which he and his staff continued to maintain, as well as the official letter and order books. These show that his correspondence was as voluminous and wide-ranging as ever. There was the routine business of the fleet: he found that a number of ships in his hastily composed force were low on water and stores, and so he devised a system for sending them into Gibraltar and Tétouan in rotation to re-stock. First to go, on 3 October, was Louis and the former Mediterranean squadron, sent on their way with a classic Nelsonian *envoi*: 'I rely with Confidence upon your Judgment, Zeal and expedition in forwarding the Service.' Louis protested that they might miss the battle that everyone believed was imminent, but Nelson assured him that he was being sent first so as to give him a good chance of being back in time. In fact, Louis's premonition was correct, and so he, Hallowell, Malcolm and Stopford all missed Trafalgar. Rear Admiral John Knight, now serving under Nelson's command based at Gibraltar, was reminded of the importance of keeping the Emperor of Morocco happy: 'upon no account whatever must we risk being cut off from Supplies from Barbary . . . in short the health of the fleet depends upon the Moors being kept in good humour.'[44]

The long letter to Knight also contained details of the new disposition of the Mediterranean fleet. While the battleships remained concentrated off Cádiz as long as the combined fleet was there, the ordinary service of the station was continued by the smaller ships. On 8 October Barham was reminded of Nelson's urgent need for frigates, 'for I must send up to watch Toulon & Genoa, where an Embarkation of Troops is reported to be prepared'. As always, he was much concerned with patronage: Sam Sutton was being invalided home, taking with him a letter to Barham recommending him in the warmest terms: 'He is a most Excellent Officer and whenever his health may permit no Ship in His Majestys Service will be more ably commanded than the one He may be appointed to.' This meant the *Amphion* was vacant, and so Nelson took the opportunity to give this 'plum' to William Hoste, who had rejoined his patron after a long separation. Hoste was also given a special mission – to carry presents from King George III to the Dey of Algiers to put the final seal on the returning amity after the protracted negotiations started by Keats back in 1804. He filled the vacancy in Hoste's *Eurydice* by moving up his nephew by marriage, Thomas Bolton. 'I think some arraingement will soon take place for your advantage at least no opportunity will be missed by your faithful friend,' he had promised him ten days earlier, and he was as good as his word.[45]

A less pleasant aspect of Nelson's business at this time was the matter of Sir Robert Calder. Realising that his victory on 22 July was not well regarded at home, Calder had demanded a court of enquiry, and on 13 October he began his return voyage, taking with him Nelson's friendly good wishes for 'a quick passage and a most happy termination to your enquiry'. Earlier, Nelson had refused to join in the chorus of condemnation of Calder, and he now permitted him to go home in his flagship, the 98-gun second rate *Prince of Wales*, thus depriving himself of a major unit at a most critical moment. 'I trust', he told Barham, anticipating official criticism, 'that I shall be considered to have done right as a man and to a Brother Officer in affliction – my heart could not stand it and so the thing must rest.'[46]

Intelligence reports began to flow once again – for example, an excellent batch of information about the combined fleets in Cádiz from Henry Bayntun of the *Leviathan*, who knew well from his previous experience under Nelson the sort of detail that his chief liked: 'There are 39 Sail of the Line & 6 frigates ready and fitting, much jealousy between the two nations – Villeneuve spoken ill of – the Minister Ducré [i.e. Decrès] expected at Cádiz to take the chief Command . . . the ships in general are badly manned . . . He says L'Aigle is famously manned and all stout fellows.' It was certainly true that Napoleon had decided to supersede Villeneuve – but his replacement was Admiral Rosily, not Decrès, who remained the Minister of Marine. Nonetheless, Bayntun's intelligence was remarkably accurate. For example, *L'Aigle* did indeed turn out to be 'famously manned' and her 'stout fellows' later put up a splendid fight against HMS *Bellerophon*. Finally, diplomatic contacts also continued. Ambassador Elliot at Naples received an assurance that a battleship would be kept there and an apology that the letter was not longer: 'With the business of such a fleet I am not very idle therefore I only write what is most interesting for you to know. You must forgive the other kind of writing.' Emma, too, was told on 13 October not to expect long letters: 'I am working like a horse in a mill but never the nearer finishing my task, which I find difficulty enough in getting and keeping clear from confusion but I never allow it to accumulate.'[47]

Although he was still able to lift his eyes to the wider horizons of his command, his main attention was focused on the fleet sheltering in Cádiz. As always, he kept the main body of his force out of sight over the horizon; but he was determined that, this time, they should not escape him. So he placed a squadron of frigates to watch the port under the command of Henry Blackwood, who had returned in company with him in HMS *Euryalus*. 'I am confident you will not let these gentry slip through our fingers,' he told him on 4 October. Between this scouting force and the main fleet he positioned some of his faster battleships in a chain, thus enabling him to keep in close touch with Blackwood by signals – a task made considerably easier by Popham's telegraphic system of signals, copies of which had been circulated. Blackwood was amazed by the innovation. 'I am now *talking* with Lord Nelson,' he told his wife.[48]

'NOTHING IS SURE IN A SEAFIGHT': NELSON'S BATTLE PLAN

On 9 October, Nelson issued a tactical memorandum outlining some of his ideas for the battle that they were now expecting almost daily – what he called, in a letter to Emma, 'The Nelson Touch'. Because it is the last plan he wrote, the temptation to see it as his final statement on the subject of tactics is very strong, and it has often been treated as such – in 1913, for example, the Admiralty even went so far as to appoint a special committee to examine the memorandum and to decide to what extent Nelson actually succeeded in carrying out his plan on 21 October. Such reverence is inappropriate. It is more helpful to see the plan, first, as part of a continuing process – a snapshot of Nelson's thinking at the time, rather than a culmination – and, second, as an essentially ephemeral document designed for a specific situation, and for specific forces. There are timeless elements to it of course but, as we shall see, they are in the general tenor and the underlying ethos of the plan, rather than in its tactical detail.

Like its predecessors in 1798 and again in 1804, the memorandum (see p. 208) repeatedly emphasises Nelson's overall objective – annihilation. He wants 'to make the business decisive' and for him this means continuing the fight 'until they are captured or destroyed'. The document bristles with aggressive words: 'follow up the blow', 'over-power', 'cut through'. Reading it aloud gives a vivid sense of Nelson's speaking manner, and so it probably reflects the sort of things he said at the briefing in the *Victory*'s Great Cabin.

To achieve this decisive result, he is going to divide his fleet into three divisions: two larger ones commanded by himself and Collingwood, and a smaller advanced squadron of 'the fastest sailing Two-decked ships'. As we have seen, this idea of separately operating divisions goes right back to his 1798 plan and is a running theme through most of his subsequent plans for fleet actions. What sets the 1805 plan apart is that each division now has a distinctive function: Collingwood is to take on the enemy's rear; Nelson will ensure that his movements are 'as little interrupted as possible' and the advanced squadron is to make 'every effort' to capture the enemy commander-in-chief. He hopes that fragmenting the enemy line in this way will bring about what he called in his conversation with Keats at Merton 'a pell-mell battle' – in other words, a confused maelstrom, in which the superior gunnery and seamanship of his individual ships will have the maximum advantage over their floundering, less well-trained opponents. And he anticipates that by the time the van of the enemy can get round to help their comrades, the

British fleet will have already won its victory and will be in a position to fight off any counter-attack.

However, Nelson is still concerned about the amount of time required to form the fleet up in Order of Battle, as happened in Hotham's actions in 1795, and to avoid this he repeats a device which he has already used in earlier plans, 'the Order of Sailing is to be the Order of Battle'. He reinforces this by issuing an Order of Sailing and Battle with the memorandum: again, as already noted, he had done this on most previous occasions. He also insists that he wants the attack to be made as speedily as possible – ships are 'to set all their sails, even steering [studding] sails in order to get as quickly as possible to the Enemy's line'. This is partly because he wants to wrong-foot his opponent, as at the Nile – but it is also because he is introducing another element into his plan that makes the approach highly risky for the British.

He says that he wants Collingwood to 'lead through' the enemy line about the twelfth ship from their rear, while he does the same 'about their Centre'. In other words, he is attacking the enemy line head on – cutting through their line at right angles. This particular idea first made its appearance in his 1804 plan, and it is clear that he got the idea from Rodney's victory at the Battle of the Saintes in 1782 (where the British had cut through the French line in two places) and from the tactical works of John Clerk of Eldin. In May 1806, Hardy wrote to Lord Barham's secretary, J.D. Thompson:

> Our departed friend Lord Nelson read Mr Clerk's works with great attention and frequently expressed his approbation of them in the fullest manner; he also recommended all the captains to read them and said that many hints might be taken from them. He most approved of the attack from to-windward and considered that breaking through the enemy's line [was] absolutely necessary to obtain a great victory.[49]

However, the problem with a head-on attack such as this was that it exposed the bows of the leading ships to the concentrated fire of the enemy. Nelson's insistence on setting all sail, contrary to all contemporary practice, was designed to reduce the time his ships would take to get through the danger zone. He also sought to lessen the risk by using a method he had begun to consider both in the Mediterranean plan and in the one issued during the great chase: his Order of Battle and Sailing shows quite clearly that, once again, he was packing his punch, by placing all his heaviest ships at the head of his divisions. Not only would they be better able to stand the punishment they would receive – but they would also be able to deliver a very heavy first blow as they broke through the line.

So, to sum up: he is planning to sail into action in three divisions, each with a specific task. The divisions are each to take on part of the enemy line, breaking through at various points, creating maximum confusion and then overpowering the fragmented enemy with superior force. To minimise the risk of the head-on approach, he is going into action with all speed possible and with his biggest and most powerful units to the fore. He expects that by landing a swift and overwhelming blow like this, he will be able to defeat most of the enemy line before their excluded van can do anything to help their comrades.

So much for the tactics. None of the individual elements were particularly new or revolutionary. Attack in divisions; cutting through the line; containing part of the enemy line; even the 'pell-mell' battle: all these had been tried and tested in earlier battles. But the memorandum is also much concerned with matters of command – and it is here, above all, that its timeless elements are to be found. First, Nelson devolves control of the divisions to the subordinate commanders – just as he had done in 1798. Second, echoing his 1804 memorandum, he remarks that 'nothing is sure in a Sea Fight beyond all others', and so he devolves responsibility even further – to the individual captains: 'in case Signals can neither be seen or perfectly understood, no captain can do very wrong if he places his ship alongside that of an Enemy.'

There is also the matter of how the plan was actually communicated. First, Nelson had formed the plan weeks in advance – the 9 October memorandum is close in its essentials to the plan outlined verbally to Captain Keats in the garden at Merton over a month before and also to the one Nelson scribbled on the back of his notes at the Navy Board Office. Second, he had taken the trouble personally to explain the plan, both orally and in writing, to all his captains, so each of them understood both the plan itself and his own part in it. And third, he was prepared to trust his captains to act wisely on their own initiative – even though most of them were unknown to him. Nelson told Emma that some of the captains assembled on board the *Victory* wept with excitement when the plan was explained to them – and it is likely that it was his wonderful trust that moved them to tears, rather than the details of his tactics.

THE 'NELSON TOUCH'

With his characteristic gift for the telling phrase, Nelson dubbed his battle plan 'The Nelson Touch', and the phrase has perplexed historians ever since. There are a number of theories of how he came by it; but the most plausible would seem to be that it is derived from a speech in his favourite Shakespeare play, *Henry V*. One of the play's choruses describes the warrior king's sensitive way of dealing with his frightened men on the eve of battle as 'a little touch of Harry in the night'. We know that Emma occasionally used the name 'Henry' for Nelson in poetry in lieu of 'Horatio', which was less easy to scan. Writing to Emma Hamilton just before his arrival with the fleet off Cádiz, Nelson reminded her about the Nelson Touch, 'which, *we* say, is warranted never to fail'.

Seen in this context, it seems most likely that the famous phrase originated as a lovers' sexual joke.

'WHAT A BEAUTIFUL DAY!': THE APPROACH TO BATTLE

On 19 October, Nelson penned one of his regular notes to Collingwood: 'What a beautiful day. Will you be tempted out of your ship? If you will hoist the assent and the Victory's pendants.' Collingwood later wrote on this last note from his friend, 'Before the answer to this letter had got to the Victory the signal was made that the Enemy's fleet was coming out of Cádiz and we chased immediately.' So immediately, indeed, that they reached the mouth of the Straits of Gibraltar before the combined fleet had completed its sortie – it was not until 2 p.m. on the 20th that all the French and Spanish ships were clear of harbour and formed in two columns on a south-easterly course. For this was not the beginning of an attempt to renew the threat of invasion. Villeneuve's orders were to take the troops he still had on board to Naples, there to begin a new front in the developing campaign against Austria. Naples was a close ally of Austria's, and Napoleon hoped that an attack on her would force the Austrians to divert troops from the main front. So the combined fleet was heading south, towards the Straits of Gibraltar.

This time, however, there was no likelihood that Nelson would lose them. His frigate and fast battleship 'chain' worked superbly under Blackwood's direction, keeping him informed of the enemy's exact course and position – as Nelson noted in his journal, 'The Frigates and lookout ships kept sight of the enemy most admirably all night and told me by signals which tack they were upon.'[50] Alerted by Blackwood to the slowness with which the enemy were deploying, he returned northwards, keeping well to the west of them, until at dawn on the 21st he was in an ideal position to launch his attack from the windward. After all the frustrations and near-misses of the earlier campaign, this time his careful plans worked like clockwork and delivered the combined fleet into his arms exactly as he had hoped.

The growing light revealed a spectacular sight: on the eastern horizon, etched against the sunrise, was a fleet of thirty-three battleships, stretched out in a straggling, irregular line some 5 miles long. George Hewson, in the 98-gun *Dreadnought*, commanded by John Conn, described the scene for his family: 'The human mind cannot form a grander or more noble sight. The morning was remarkably fine, the sea perfectly smooth and the lightness of the wind allowed every sail to be spread. One fleet resolutely awaited the approach, the other moved Majestically slow to the encounter.'[51] So 'majestically slow' indeed was the British approach, because of the lightness of the wind, that it took them almost 5 hours to get within range, even though they set all possible sail, including studding sails. At 6.40 a.m., in accordance with Nelson's plan, the *Victory* signalled the fleet to form Order of Sailing in two columns and to clear for action. Ten minutes later the order went to bear up to eastward, and the attack began. Because of the detachments he had made, Nelson had only twenty-seven ships with him, and so he had to abandon his plan for a third, 'containing' division. But, as we shall see, he had worked out another way to keep part of the enemy's force held down.[52]

Nelson began the day, as he always did, with prayer. This was, however, not a private petition: he wrote it out in full in his personal journal and then, presumably to make sure it survived, made an exact copy. Discovered after his death, it was published and quickly became part of the Nelson Legend – indeed it is still read out every Trafalgar Day in the official naval ceremony on the quarterdeck of HMS *Victory*:

> May the Great God whom I worship Grant to my Country and for the benefit of Europe in General a great and Glorious Victory and may no misconduct in anyone tarnish it, and may humanity after Victory be the predominant feature in the British Fleet. For myself individually I commit my life to Him who made me, and may his blessing light upon my endeavours for serving My Country faithfully, to Him I resign myself and the Just cause which is entrusted to me to defend. Amen. Amen. Amen.[53]

It is a wonderful summing up of his personal and professional ethos. The victory for which he prays is to be 'for the benefit of Europe in General' and not just for Britain – no little-Englander he! The petition for 'humanity after Victory' is wholly Nelsonian (and particularly applicable today), as is his conviction that he is defending a 'Just cause'. But it is the phrase 'I commit my life to Him who made me, and may his blessing light upon my endeavours for serving My Country faithfully' that comes closest to the beating heart of the man. Over thirty years later he was still, deep down, the boy who, in the glow of his 'golden orb', had vowed to be a hero and serve his King and Country.

He had already committed his thoughts to paper for Emma and Horatia. Emma was told, 'I will take care that my Name shall ever be most dear to you and Horatia both of whom I love as much as my own life.' With Horatia, he abandoned all pretence about her parentage: 'Receive my dearest Horatia the affectionate Parental blessing of your Father.' He also, famously, wrote a codicil to

---

WHEN WAS THE PRAYER WRITTEN?

In the account of the battle he gave to Sir Nicholas Harris Nicolas (Nicolas, vol. 7, p. 150), Lieutenant John Pasco noted that he visited the Great Cabin at about 11 a.m., intending to discuss a personal matter with Nelson. Finding him on his knees writing, he supposed that Nelson was 'then penning that beautiful Prayer', and so subsequent biographers have placed the writing of the prayer at this time.

However, this cannot be right, since in the journal entry that immediately precedes the prayer, Nelson makes it clear he wrote it at about 7 a.m.

There are two possible explanations. First, it is possible that, when Pasco saw him, Nelson was making the copy of the prayer that has also survived. Second, it is possible that he was not writing a prayer at all but the famous 'codicil' which, shortly afterwards, he asked Blackwood and Hardy to witness. He may only have been kneeling because it was the easiest way for him to write, most of his furniture having been removed to the hold.

his will in which he left them both as 'a legacy to my King & Country' and asked that they should be provided for: 'These are the only favours I ask of my King & Country at the moment when I am going to fight their Battle.' Notoriously, and dishonourably, his King and Country failed to honour this last request.[54]

His personal preparations complete, Nelson now set to work to prepare his men. Some of his captains were even then addressing their assembled ship's companies on their quarterdecks, and some of their speeches have been recorded. In the *Minotaur*, for example, Captain Mansfield said: 'I shall say nothing to you of courage, our country never produced a coward, for my own part I pledge myself to the Officers & Ships Company never to quit the ship I may get alongside of, till either she strikes, or sinks, or I sink. I have only to recommend silence & a strict attention to the order of your officers.'[55]

But such distant formality was not Nelson's way. Instead of summoning his men to him, he went to meet them himself, visiting the *Victory*'s gun decks and stopping to chat to each gun's crew as they waited at their action stations. Able Seaman John Brown remembered his words: 'My noble lads this will be a glorious day for England whoever lives to see it. I shan't be satisfied with twelve ships this day as I took at the Nile.' Nelson had also realised that Popham's new signalling system offered him the opportunity of 'speaking' to all the men of his fleet – the first time that an admiral had ever done so. Arriving eventually on the poop of the *Victory*, he called the Signal Lieutenant, John Pasco, over and said, 'Mr Pasco, I wish to say to the fleet, "England confides that every man will do his duty". You must be quick for I have another signal to make which is for close action.' Picking up on the word 'quick', Pasco suggested that he should substitute 'expects', which was in Popham's codebook, for 'confides', which was not and would therefore have to be spelled out letter by letter. Nelson agreed, and so the reworded signal was sent. Although Pasco's change was understandable in practical terms, it was nonetheless regrettable. 'Confides', with its sense of trust and of personal confidence, is much more 'Nelsonian' in its tone and sentiment than the harsher, more mandatory, 'expects'.[56]

In fact the signal received a rather mixed reception. It would appear from their logs that the majority of the battleships did not take it in – although nearly all of them recorded the standard signal No. 16 for 'Close Action', which immediately followed it.[57] This suggests that Popham's codebook had not reached every ship in the fleet. Even in those that did receive it, the message was often garbled by the time it reached the men: in the *Minotaur* it was recorded as 'the Victory made a general telligraph the purport of which was I hope every man will do his duty like an Englishman'.[58] In the *Polyphemus*, Henry Blackburn thought the message was 'Hope Every English man would beheave with his usual heroism and exert every means to destroy the Enemies of there Country'. Only a few ships both received the signal and passed its message on to the men, as Nelson had clearly intended, and significantly these ships were commanded by captains who had served with Nelson before. In John Conn's *Dreadnought*, for example, George Hewson remembered: 'on the purport of this [signal] being explained to the ships company it was received

Hoisting 'England Expects'. Standing on the Victory's *poop deck, Nelson talks to Hardy and Blackwood as 'England Expects' is hoisted. Pasco, the Signal Lieutenant, is in the background, left, holding a speaking trumpet. In the foreground, secretary John Scott checks the wording of the signal.*

ENGLAND EXPECTS

Nelson's famous signal has been much misquoted – indeed the misquotation started almost at once. Some of the British ships recorded the wording in their logs as 'England expects every man *to* do his duty' and this version has proved remarkably persistent – it even appears on the base of the Nelson column in Trafalgar Square. Then, in 1811, the tenor John Braham and poet Samuel Arnold composed a song, 'The Death of Nelson', which was an instant 'hit' and was performed all over the British Empire throughout the nineteenth century. The signal formed part of the song's refrain and, to make the words fit the metre, Arnold altered them to 'England expects that every man *this day* will do his duty'. Once again, this version has proved very persistent and still crops up today.

Confusion even surrounds Nelson's original wording of the signal. Pasco (who should have known) was clear that the wording Nelson originally ordered was 'England confides', but there is also a theory that he originally intended to say '*Nelson* confides' but was persuaded against it. However, close examination of the accounts of those who actually witnessed the ordering and hoisting of the signal suggests that this is unlikely.

with a burst of applause and every individual seemed animated with a determination to conquer'.[59] Perhaps the most telling reaction came from the man in the fleet who knew Nelson best, Cuthbert Collingwood. Seeing the repeated hoists of flags on board the *Victory* as the signal was made,[60] he remarked crossly, 'I do wish Nelson would stop signalling. We all know what we have to do.' However, when the actual words of the signal were reported to him, and he realised it was not another operational signal as he had supposed, he 'expressed delight and admiration and made it known to his officers and ship's company'.[61]

'We all know what we have to do.' That phrase neatly sums up Nelson's pre-battle achievement. Thanks to his briefings, his dinners and the memorandum, all his immediate subordinates were clear about his intentions and their role in the battle. It would appear, too, that in at least some of the ships the plan reached the more junior officers as well. For example, in the *Bellerophon*, John Cooke showed the memorandum to his First Lieutenant, William Cumby, in case he was killed, and Conn had obviously made it known to his officers in the *Dreadnought*, for George Hewson later wrote: 'Lord Nelson had so well foreseen the likely position of the enemy that he planned the manner in which every ship was to be brought into action and sent written direction to the Captains of the fleet so that there was no occasion for signals.'

This is not to say, however, that Nelson had completely relinquished control of the fleet as the slow approach developed. Hewson was wrong in thinking that no signals were made. Nelson in fact made a number, including direct orders to ships in Collingwood's division – which may account for Collingwood's initial annoyance when he saw 'England Expects' being hoisted. Most important, not long before the first shots were fired Nelson signalled, 'Prepare to anchor at close of day', which shows that, weatherwise as ever, he was reading the signs in the sky and in the long, rolling swell sweeping in from the west underneath his ships, and planning ahead for the storm that he could tell was on its way. Moreover, as at Copenhagen, he sent verbal orders to individual captains, using Blackwood, who had come on board the flagship at the start of the day, as his messenger. Fremantle was told that Nelson intended 'to cut through the enemy's line about their 13th or 14th ship and then to make sail upon the Larboard tack for their Van'. Later, Blackwood was sent to the rearmost battleships in Nelson's line 'to tell their Captains that he depended on their exertions and that if by the mode of attack prescribed they found it impracticable to get into Action immediately, they might adopt whatever means they thought best, provided that it led them quickly and closely alongside an Enemy.'[62] Right up to the very last moment he was still underlining his ethos, consciously echoing the most important passage in the memorandum: 'no captain can do very wrong if he places his ship alongside that of an enemy'.

The cheers that greeted 'England Expects' were indicative of the festive, almost celebratory, spirit in which the British were sailing into battle. Midshipman William Badcock of HMS *Neptune* remembered that 'One would have thought that the people were preparing for a Festival rather than a combat; the bands playing God save the King, Rule Britannia, Britons Strike Home, the crews stationed on the forecastles of the various ships cheering the ship ahead of them.' In the *Ajax*, Lieutenant, Royal Marines Samuel Ellis remembered that 'three or four as if in mere bravado were dancing a hornpipe'.[63]

On board the *Victory* concern for Nelson's personal safety was now mounting. Far from seeking to escape, as had been expected, the French and Spanish were accepting battle. At about 7 a.m., they had worn, so as to get their heads to the northwards and the bolt-hole of Cádiz under their lee, and were now awaiting the British attack with great determination. At the same time, the wind was very light and so, even with all sails set – including studding sails – the British ships were moving at little more than a walking pace, which meant it would take them at least half an hour to get through the danger zone before they could fire their guns in reply. Sailing in full sight at the head of her line, the *Victory* presented a magnificent target, and everyone in the combined fleet knew that it was Nelson's flag flying at her foremast. Various attempts were made to reduce the danger. At one stage, for example, Blackwood thought he had persuaded Nelson to let the next astern, the *Temeraire*, overtake the *Victory* and lead the line, and he rushed off in his boat to give the necessary orders to Captain Eliab Harvey. But when he returned to the flagship, he found Nelson was refusing to slow down – indeed, when Lieutenant John Yule, on his own initiative, ordered a badly set studding sail to be taken in and reset, he found an angry Nelson at his side berating him for shortening sail. Eventually, the *Temeraire* began to surge up on the flagship's starboard quarter; but then her captain found himself on the receiving end of Nelson's ire. 'I'll thank you, Captain Harvey,' came a shout from the *Victory*'s quartergallery, 'to keep your proper station, which is *astern* of the *Victory*!' Fremantle in the *Neptune*, who was ranging on the flagship's other quarter, was sharply desired 'not to keep quite so close'.[64] Even attempts to make Nelson change his coat, or at least to cover up his stars, received similar short shrift: 'This is no time to be shifting a coat,' he said sharply. A 'performance leader' to the end, he realised that to change out of the coat his men had seen him wearing daily for the previous two years would send them completely the wrong message.

Nelson's insistence on staying at the head of his line has been written off as simple recklessness by some biographers, and even that most distinguished of naval historians, Julian Corbett, has portrayed this stage of the battle as a simple 'race' between the two old comrades, Nelson and Collingwood.[65] Undoubtedly there was an element of contest in their joint, headlong rush into battle. But Nelson also had a much more important reason for staying where he was. It is now clear that he wanted to use his line to carry out the task of his missing third division, namely that of 'containing' the enemy van, and the best way he could do so was by leading it himself.

Further down Nelson's line, Edward Codrington in HMS *Orion* now noticed that the *Victory* suddenly hauled out to port for a while, her bows pointing towards the ships in the combined fleet's van. 'How beautifully the admiral is carrying into effect his intentions!' he called out to his First Lieutenant, John

THE TRAFALGAR COAT

A common myth still persists that Nelson was clothed in a full dress coat or a highly decorated one at Trafalgar. In fact he wore on the day of battle the same, rather threadbare, 'undress' uniform coat that he had worn every day in the preceding months. It was plain and unadorned, apart from the facsimiles of his stars of knighthood which, as was the custom at that time, he wore sewn on his left breast.

After his death, the coat was given by Hardy to Emma Hamilton, who later gave it to one of her creditors in settlement of a debt. Eventually, in 1845, it was purchased for the nation by Prince Albert and placed on public display at Greenwich, where it has remained ever since. It is now in the National Maritime Museum.

Croft. Nelson was acting in accordance with a special memorandum he had issued to his captains at about the same time as his 9 October battle plan. This introduced a new signal ordering his ships to 'pass thro' the Enemy line as quick as possible and at the same time'. He then went on, '[t]he Admiral will probably advance his fleet to the van of theirs before he makes the Signal in order to deceive the Enemy by inducing them to suppose it is his intention to attack their Van'. The move was noticed by the French and Spanish as well. In a letter written shortly after the battle, Rear Admiral Dumanoir commanding the van said, 'The left column, having Admiral Nelson at its head, bore at first at the French vanguard.' And a recently discovered Spanish plan of the battle in the Houghton Library at Harvard, drawn by someone serving in the van, clearly shows the *Victory* heading towards the foremost enemy ships.[66]

By now the *Victory* and her immediate supporters were almost within range of the enemy's guns, while to the south Collingwood's *Royal Sovereign* was already coming under heavy fire. When the *Victory* was about a mile and a half away from the enemy line a ranging shot was fired, but it fell short. A few moments later, another fell alongside, followed by a third which went over the ship and a fourth which went straight through the main topgallant sail. There was a brief pause, and then suddenly the van opened a tremendous fire, battering the *Victory* with round shot and dismantling shot from more than 200 guns. Some impression of the hail-storm of iron through which she passed can be gained from her surviving fore topsail, which is riddled with holes like a collander. As these first shots started to hit home, Nelson sent Blackwood back to his frigate with the fateful words, 'God bless you, Blackwood, I shall never speak to you again.'

Now the huge risk that Nelson had taken in making his head-on approach revealed itself, as the flagship began to suffer serious damage and to take casualties. Among them was John Scott, cut in two on the quarterdeck; while a doubleheaded shot fired at the flagship's rigging killed eight marines in one go. But, at the same time, Nelson's countermeasure of placing his heavy ships at the head of his line was also paying off – Villeneuve later told Blackwood how impressed he had been by the inexorable approach of the great three-deckers.

'ENGAGE THE ENEMY MORE CLOSELY!': THE BATTLE

Having convinced Dumanoir that he was about to attack the van, it was now time for Nelson to head for his real target, the centre. So, in a move that has been missed in many accounts of the battle, and never depicted in any of the great paintings of it, he now ordered the *Victory* to be turned to starboard and, followed by his two consorts, sailed down the enemy line, searching for a weak point at which to break through. The course alteration was so sudden that Harvey in the *Temeraire* was forced to 'immediately put our helm a-port to steer clear of the *Victory*'. As the two great ships made their turn, their arcs of fire opened and both let fly with the first broadsides from their port guns. This image of the *Victory* feinting and sidestepping like a light-footed rugby-player, disguising until the last moment the place for which she was actually aiming, is most telling. Right to the end of his life, Nelson was still handling his battleships like frigates.

And he was still uttering his personal battle-cry – the one he had learned from William Locker in the *Lowestoffe*. For the *Victory* was now flying the last signal he had ordered from Pasco: 'Engage the Enemy More Closely.' As he had done at the Nile and again at Copenhagen, he left it flying throughout the battle to remind his captains what he expected of them.

Slowly the *Victory* sailed past the ships of the allied centre on an opposite course, probing for a gap. Desperately, the French and Spanish ships closed up together, trying to prevent him from forcing his way through. Eventually, Hardy pointed out to Nelson that he could not avoid getting entangled with at least one of the enemy ships and was told to push through nonetheless. So, finally, Hardy turned to port again and literally thrust his way through the enemy line astern of Villeneuve's *Bucentaure*, pouring a devastating broadside into her stern as he did so (see picture on p. 184). Captain Jean Lucas, commanding the *Bucentaure*'s next astern, the *Redoutable*, gallantly edged his ship close up in an attempt to assist his admiral but he was pushed aside by the *Victory*'s forward motion. The two ships became entangled and drifted to leeward, opening up a large gap in the enemy line through which the following ships of Nelson's division poured. The battle had only just begun and already he had achieved his aim of separating the enemy van and centre from its rear.

Further to the south, the ships of Collingwood's division were also coming into action – some distance astern of their Admiral, who had broken through the enemy line astern of the *Santa Anna* at about 12.30 p.m. Their approach was very different from that of Nelson's division. As they headed towards the enemy line, they fanned out into a rough line of bearing, or echelon formation, rather than a line ahead. So instead of pouring through a single gap and bringing overwhelming force to bear on a small group of enemy ships, as Nelson's ships were doing, they hit the French and Spanish line in a number of different places and began a series of individual ship-to-ship contests. Moreover, Collingwood began this enveloping movement by attacking the eighteenth ship in the enemy line, the *Santa Anna*, flagship of Vice Admiral Ignacio de Alava, which meant that his fourteen ships

The Victory *at Trafalgar. Nicholas Pocock captures the moment when the* Victory *broke through the Franco-Spanish line, just astern of Villeneuve's* Bucentaure.

were taking on a total of sixteen enemy ships. So he did not have the superiority in numbers that Nelson had envisaged and, as a result, some of the ships in his division, such as *Belleisle* and *Bellerophon*, had a very hard time indeed.

Meanwhile, in the *Victory* Nelson and his men were now engaged in a deadly, close-quarters struggle with Lucas's *Redoutable*. It had not been Nelson's intention to get tied down in this way – as he had told Fremantle, he planned, having broken through the line, to turn and move northwards to lead an attack on the enemy van from leeward. But Lucas's gallant move to support the *Bucentaure* had thwarted this, and now the British flagship was immobilised. She was also taking heavy casualties from the sharpshooters that Lucas had specially trained and stationed in the *Redoutable*'s rigging, hoping for just such a close-quarters encounter.

For now, therefore, Nelson could do very little to contribute to the development of the battle apart from setting an example to his men – which he and Hardy proceeded to do. As the bullets and grenades rained down, and as the *Victory*'s upper deck became a slaughterhouse, they continued calmly to pace up and down the narrow space between the 12-pounder cannon on the quarterdeck, turning at one end in front of the remains of the ship's wheel, shattered by round shot during the long approach, and at the other just before the hatchway leading down to the upper gun deck. As they walked, the *Redoutable*'s sharpshooters would have been clearly visible through gaps in the swirling gunsmoke – close enough, indeed, for them to distinguish individual features. The raw physical courage of that slow, calm walk can stand alongside any of the more dramatic acts of bravery in Nelson's career.

At about 1.15 p.m. Nelson felt a sharp blow high on his left shoulder, followed by a distinct snap as his backbone was broken. As his legs buckled under the force of the blow and he fell to his knees in the pool of blood left behind by John Scott's grisly demise, he tried to support himself with his left arm, but this was now useless, and he fell onto his left side. By the time Hardy reached him, he had already realised that he had taken a death wound, 'Ah Hardy, they have done it at last,' he said almost ruefully, and when Hardy tried to protest, he added firmly, 'My backbone is shot through.'[67] As he was carried below, we are told that he covered up his stars with a handkerchief – his leader's instincts still working, he did not want to discourage his men with the news of his wounding at such a critical moment in their close-fought contest with a gallant and determined foe.

It is highly unlikely that the bullet was deliberately aimed at him. The muskets of the *Redoutable*'s sharpshooters simply were not accurate enough for such a shot. From about 30 feet above him and some 15 yards away laterally, the Frenchmen's view would have been obscured by swirling smoke and the complex rigging of the two ships, both of which would have been rolling in the swell.

In the cockpit, below the waterline, where the wounded were treated in comparative safety, Nelson was stripped of his clothes and laid on an improvised bed against the ship's port side. In an attempt to spare him unnecessary discomfort, they cut his tight-fitting breeches off him but, even so, the pain caused by all this handling must have been excruciating. The *Victory*'s surgeon, Dr William Beatty, soon established that Nelson's self-diagnosis had been correct and that nothing could be done for him.[68] At first he thought that death was imminent and breathlessly gave orders regarding his own personal affairs, with loving messages to Emma and Horatia. When he realised that he still had some time left, he became calmer and began to think again about the battle that was still raging above his head. He wanted news of what was going on; but the only man who could tell him with any authority was Hardy, and he was preoccupied with the deadly struggle with the *Redoutable*. He sent his aide, Midshipman Richard Bulkeley, son of one of Nelson's friends and a protégé, to explain the delay and, recognising the youngster's voice, Nelson sent remembrances to the father. Then, despite the mounting agony as his chest cavity filled with blood, he clung on to life, waiting for news. At one stage he was asked about the pain; he replied that it was so great he wished he were dead but added, 'Yet one would like to live a little longer.' During this time, Chaplain Scott was constantly at his side, rubbing his chest to try to relieve the pain, giving him sips of lemonade and fanning him. He later remembered that they also recited scraps of prayers together, but Nelson was so breathless that he could not string together a complete sentence and was forced to speak in short, gasping phrases.

Meanwhile, the battle for which he had prepared so carefully and so long was unfolding very much as he had planned – although not quite so smoothly and evenly as some of the older accounts suggest. The risk he had taken with his headlong attack had paid off, but the heavy damage suffered by his leading ships showed just how great that risk had been. Also, once the battle settled down into

a series of ship-to-ship contests, it soon became clear that some of the enemy vessels were well-prepared for the type of fighting that was emerging. Lucas had not been alone in training his men for close-quarters action and, in a number of cases, the very close range at which the battle was fought evened the odds between the combined fleet and the British. For example, *L'Algesiras*, flying the flag of Rear Admiral Charles Magon, gave Charles Tyler's *Tonnant* a very hard time, with a combination of accurate gunnery and a hail of bullets from sharpshooters in the rigging, and was only captured after a long and bloody fight in the course of which Magon himself was killed with a bullet in the chest. A similar close contest was fought by *L'Aigle* and the *Bellerophon*, while Collingwood's *Royal Sovereign* took over two hours to subdue the gallantly defended *Santa Anna*.

Additionally, despite all the time and care that Nelson had spent in briefing and inspiring his captains, not all of them performed equally well on the actual day of battle. Some – especially Edward Codrington in *Orion*, Israel Pellew in *Conqueror*, Charles Tyler in *Tonnant* and Henry Bayntun in *Leviathan* – were highly effective and mobile. They ranged among the enemy ships, assisting British comrades who were in difficulty and, as Nelson had intended, combining with other British ships to bring overwhelming force to bear on isolated opponents. So, for example, Pellew first forced *Bucentaure* to surrender after her long battering by successive British ships passing under her stern, and then assisted in the defeat of the *Santissima Trinidad*, before finally helping to reduce *L'Intrepide*, another most gallantly defended French ship, to a wreck. It is interesting to note that with the exception of Codrington – who was in any case exceptional as an officer – all those who performed most imaginatively at Trafalgar had served with Nelson over a long period.

Other captains, like William Hargood of the *Belleisle*, John Cooke of the *Bellerophon*, George Duff of the *Mars* and Richard Moorsom of the *Revenge* – all of them in Collingwood's outnumbered division – found themselves fighting lone battles against superior odds. Duff and Cooke paid for their gallantry with their

The Battle of Trafalgar, c. 2 p.m. W.L. Wyllie's great panorama shows the battle at its height. The Victory *is in the centre, in the middle of the huge gap that has opened up in the Franco-Spanish line; to the left Collingwood's* Royal Sovereign *engages the* Santa Anna. *To the right the masts of the* Santissima Trinidad *are falling. On the extreme right, the Franco-Spanish van is still struggling to get back into the battle.*

lives, and Moorsom, who was severely wounded, later went so far as to remark, 'I am not certain that our mode of attack was the best' – which is perhaps understandable in the light of the ordeal he and his ship's company suffered. Having arrived early in the midst of the fighting, not far astern of Collingwood, he found himself surrounded by three enemy ships, with which he fought a bloody duel for over half an hour, suffering almost eighty casualties, before Philip Durham in the *Defiance* came to his rescue.

A few of the captains either did not understand Nelson's intentions or did not feel inclined to follow them. Neither Robert Redmill in the *Polyphemus*, nor Richard Grindall in the *Prince* appears to have made very strenuous efforts to get their ships into action, and Collingwood's Flag Captain, Edward Rotheram, later said of Grindall that 'he behaved very ill at the Trafalgar action'.

Despite the great gallantry and skill displayed by many of the French and Spanish crews, by 2.30 p.m. the battle was clearly going the British way and, having finally overwhelmed the gallant *Redoutable*, with the timely assistance of the *Temeraire*, Hardy felt able to leave the quarterdeck and pay a short visit to the cockpit. He told Nelson that twelve or fourteen of the enemy were already in British hands, but that the van had at last begun the expected counter-attack, adding 'I have therefore called two or three of our fresh ships round us and have no doubt of giving them a drubbing'. So Nelson's plan was still working well – he had of course foreseen this move in his memorandum and had said that 'I look with confidence to a Victory before the Van of the Enemy could succour their Rear'. Hardy returned to the deck to coordinate the defence, leaving Nelson still struggling to keep death at bay. By now he had lost all sensation in his lower body, and his thoughts were flitting between the battle and Emma. 'What would become of poor Lady Hamilton if she knew of my situation?' he asked Scott. About 50 minutes later Hardy returned and, taking Nelson's hand, congratulated him on a brilliant victory, which he said, 'was complete though he did not know how many of the enemy were captured, as it was not possible to perceive every ship distinctly'. But he was sure that fourteen or fifteen ships had surrendered. 'That is well,' Nelson replied, 'but I bargained for twenty.' He then gave his last operational order, 'Anchor, Hardy, anchor.' Clearly taken aback at such an order, when the battle was still raging, Hardy suggested that perhaps Collingwood should now take charge of affairs. The effect of this remark was striking. Nelson struggled to sit up, and gathering all his strength replied, 'Not while I live, I hope,' and then emphasised his order with a classic Norfolkism, 'No, do *you* anchor, Hardy' – 'do you' in this case being a command, not a question. 'Shall we make the signal, sir?' asked Hardy, making sure that he had understood Nelson's intention. 'Yes,' came the reply, 'for if I live, I'll anchor.'[69]

So, almost to his dying moment, Nelson remained the admiral. It can be seen in his instinctive covering of his stars as he was carried below; his friendly message to his young protégé Bulkeley; his thirst for accurate news about the progress of the battle; his insistence that he wanted twenty prizes; and now, finally, in his refusal to relinquish command. Accounts of his death in the standard biographies tend, rightly and understandably, to emphasise the human and personal aspects of the famous death scene. But it is important to remember, too, that he retained his professional faculties right to the end. Indeed, it would seem that he fought to stay alive as long as possible, despite appalling pain, so that he could make sure that his professional task was complete.

Now, however, he began to sink fast – almost as if the effort to assert his authority had finally exhausted the remarkable strength and stamina he had summoned for his struggle with death. Reverting to personal matters once more, he asked Hardy not to throw him overboard and to take care of 'dear Lady Hamilton'. And then he asked him to kiss him. Hardy knelt and kissed his cheek. 'Now I am satisfied,' said Nelson, 'Thank God I have done my duty.' Standing up, Hardy looked down for a few moments at his friend and patron, and then knelt again and kissed his forehead. Nelson could no longer see clearly. 'Who is that?' he asked. 'It is Hardy.' 'God bless you, Hardy.'

It is one of the most affecting and poignant farewells of history – and yet, sadly, it has been the subject of ridiculous evasions by those who find it embarrassing that our greatest national hero asked another man for a kiss. The ludicrous fiction has even been invented that Nelson actually spoke in Turkish, 'Kismet [fate], Hardy,' and that Hardy misheard him. But three eyewitnesses, all of whom were within a few feet of Nelson when he spoke, record the request,[70] and so there can be no doubt that the kiss was both asked for and given. Significantly, no one who has actually been in combat, and who has experienced the special, and very close, bond that forms between those who share danger together, has any difficulty in accepting this last act of comradely tenderness in the life of a man who led by tenderness and affection.

But the final scene was not yet quite complete. For, as Nelson began to slip away – his voice now so faint that Scott, bending close, could scarcely hear the last words, 'God and my country' – Henry Blackwood arrived in the *Victory*'s

Death of Nelson. *J.M.W. Turner's brilliant evocation of the moment that Nelson fell. It gives a far better impression of the swirl and confusion of battle than most of the other, more formal, posed paintings of the same scene.*

cockpit. Hearing the news from Collingwood, who had been informed by Hardy of Nelson's wound some time before, he leapt into his boat and rushed through the dying battle to the flagship – as he later told his wife, he found Nelson 'at the gasp of death'.[71] Shortly after Surgeon Beatty had pronounced Nelson dead, Edward Berry came on board having, like Blackwood, been rowed through the carnage. So, most appropriately, two key members of the Band of Brothers were there right at the end: Blackwood, representing the new generation, and Berry, one of the original comrades from Cape St Vincent and the Nile.

Berry returned to the *Agamemnon*, where Midshipman Joseph Woolnough noted that tears were pouring down his captain's face as, without speaking to anyone, he went straight down below. By now rumours were spreading, since Berry's barge crew had been told by their friends in the *Victory* that the Admiral had been wounded, so eventually the First Lieutenant, Hugh Cook, decided to ask the Captain for definite news. Moments later he returned with the tidings they had been dreading and, as Woolnough later remembered, 'A stranger might have supposed from the gloom that spread among us that we had been beaten instead of being the conquerors.' A similar reaction was seen throughout the fleet. As Lieutenant Andrew Green of the *Neptune* noted: 'The melancholy Account which we at this time [sunset] received of the loss of our Much beloved Honoured &

Respected Commander-in-Chief threw a damp on our Spirits which we were by no means prepared for after so decisive a Victory.' George Hewson of the *Dreadnought* wrote:

> Lord Nelson lived to hear that the Victory was gained he said he died happy recommended the fleet to be anchored embraced Captain Hardy (whom he loved as his son) and gave up the ghost. His death is greatly lamented by every person in the fleet, he had endeared himself to the seamen and officers by his humanity and conciliatory manners and in him his country has lost the greatest Admiral of the age.

In passing, it is interesting to note that Hewson's account shows that the famous kiss – and Nelson's final order to anchor – were known about in the fleet within days of the battle.[72]

The end of the story can be quickly told. As Berry and Blackwood paid their respects to their dead friend, the battle was fading out. The threatened counter-attack by the van had been parried by Hardy's swift concentration of the fresh British ships, and four French ships under Dumanoir had made off to the south, leaving *L'Intrepide* in British hands. The rear, under the Spanish commander-in-chief Frederico Gravina, was making its way back into Cádiz. Behind them, they left seventeen allied ships in British hands, while *L'Achille* was a blazing torch. Nelson's fleet had won his longed-for victory of annihilation.

'HE NOW BEGINS HIS IMMORTAL CAREER'

In 1897, Alfred Mahan ended his great *Life of Nelson* with a celebration of the aptness of the timing and manner of Nelson's death: 'His duty was done and its fruit perfected. Other men have died in the hour of victory but for no other has a victory so singular and so signal graced the fulfilment and ending of a life's work. "Finis coronat opus" has of no man been more true of Nelson . . . his part was done when Trafalgar was fought.' The idea that Nelson died with his work complete was very prevalent in the nineteenth century, and indeed it persists to this day. There is also a sense that, by dying so gloriously, he secured his own immortality. As Lady Londonderry wrote, on hearing of the news: 'He now begins his immortal career having nothing left to achieve upon the earth and bequeathing to the English fleet a legacy which they alone are able to improve. Had I been his wife or mother, I would [rather] have wept him dead than see him languish on a less splendid day. In such a death there is no sting, and in such a grave an everlasting victory.'[73]

Nelson's legacy is certainly still potent for the Royal Navy – and, indeed, for some foreign navies as well. And it is certainly arguable that he would not have achieved such immortality, nor have been such an inspiring example to future generations, if he had not died at Trafalgar. But it is also possible to argue that the country lost more than it gained by his premature death. As we have seen, his natural talent, carefully nurtured by his various mentors and continually honed by experience, had flowered superbly in the long and taxing campaign in the Mediterranean in 1803–5, as well as in the more dramatic and action-packed months of the Trafalgar Campaign. He was, in terms of both talent and experience, by far the most effective of all Britain's war leaders in 1805. It is true that, after his death, the war at sea fragmented and there were no other great campaigns or major battles – but who can say what might have happened if he had lived? In the past, judgements about what he might have done post-Trafalgar have been made without a full appreciation of the scale of his achievements in 1803–5. Thanks to all the new material, we now have a better understanding of his abilities as an administrator, diplomat and intelligence officer, and so it is possible to speculate that there could well have been a role for him in the new style of the war. Indeed, it is not too far-fetched to contemplate him as a potential First Lord of the Admiralty.

In the end, though, despite his excellence, as a practical sailor, as a tactician and as an administrator, it was his human qualities that made him so successful as a leader. Thomas Byam Martin spoke of his 'most happy way of gaining the affectionate respect of all who had the happiness to serve under his command. I never conversed with any officer who had served under Nelson without hearing the most hearty expressions of attachment and admiration of his frank and conciliating manner to all who showed themselves zealous in the execution of their duties.' And Jane Austen's brother Francis, who served with him in the Mediterranean, summed him up in words that deserve to be better known. Writing just days after Trafalgar to his fiancée Mary Gibson, he said: 'I never heard his equal, nor do I expect again to see such a man. To the soundest judgement he united prompt decision and speedy execution of plans; and he possessed in a superior degree the happy talent of making every class of persons pleased with their situation and eager to exert themselves in forwarding the public service.'[74]

'His body is buried in peace'.
The Dean of St Paul's (centre)
leads the final prayers at the
state funeral, as Nelson's
friends and colleagues gather
round his coffin.

St Paul's Cathedral, 9 January 1806

At about 5 p.m. on 9 January 1806, the organist of St Paul's Cathedral, Thomas Attwood, began to play his 'Grand Funeral Dirge'. As the sombre notes echoed around the packed building, a long and complicated procession began to form up in the choir of the cathedral. An hour or so before, the body of Vice Admiral Lord Nelson, encased in a splendid, gilded coffin, had been placed in front of the high altar while the service of Evensong was performed. Now the procession was to escort the coffin out into the vast space beneath the great dome, where the last act of the elaborate ceremonial would take place – the burial.

The procession was so long that it took fully 15 minutes to reach its destination, even though it had to cover only a few yards. But Attwood had anticipated this and had composed the piece so that it could be repeated constantly, until he received a signal that everyone was in place. Slowly, as the heavy, grief-laden notes increased in intensity, and as each member of the stately, black-swathed crocodile reached the special dais in the middle of a great circular amphitheatre of seats, a pattern began to emerge. By the time the coffin arrived and was lifted onto the high catafalque, in sight of all, the key players in the ceremonial were waiting in their appointed places.

Each had an official title – from the Chief Mourner to the bearers of the various pieces of regalia, such as the 'Banner of Emblems'. But each was also a friend or naval colleague of the deceased and so, as Nelson lay there amid all this melancholy splendour, he was surrounded by men who represented every stage of his long naval career.

Appropriately, the Chief Mourner was Admiral of the Fleet Sir Peter Parker, who had given him his crucial early promotions in the West Indies. He was supported by another mentor, Samuel, Lord Hood, and by William, Lord Radstock, who had been Nelson's next ahead at the Battle of Cape St Vincent.

Parker's train was borne by Henry Blackwood, Captain of the *Euryalus* at Trafalgar, who had witnessed Nelson's dying gasp. The four pall-bearers included Eliab Harvey, who had commanded the *Temeraire* at Trafalgar, and Sir John Orde, whom Nelson had always regarded as a rival, even an enemy. The supporters of the heavy tasselled canopy included William Domett, Nelson's Captain of the Fleet in the Baltic, and nearby were lieutenants from the *Victory* carrying the 'bannerols of family lineage', including John Pasco, who had supervised the hoisting of 'England Expects'. The faithful Thomas Hardy was carrying the Banner of Emblems, and other Trafalgar captains were carrying various items of heraldic regalia – Francis Laforey of the *Spartiate* bore the Standard, and Nelson's banner as a Knight of the Bath was borne by Robert Moorsom of the *Revenge*. Even the coffin-bearers themselves were sailors from the *Victory*, supported by others who were carrying the ship's vast, shot-torn colours flown during the battle.

This was a marvellous cross-section of Nelson's naval colleagues – but, as in December 1797, there was one notable absentee. Once again, Lord St Vincent was not present – now in his seventies, he had asked to be excused on the grounds of ill-health. Some historians have questioned whether the illness was genuine and have suggested that his absence signified continued disapproval of his former protégé. But a recently discovered letter to his sister shows that he was indeed very ill, while another to a friend, written some weeks before, expresses his willingness 'to contribute in every way to pay the most liberal, and respectful, Tribute to the eminent Services, and rever'd memory of my late gallant friend Lord Nelson'.

As we have seen, long before 1805 St Vincent had come to admire Nelson's qualities not just as a fighter but as a man of business and as a statesman. He also disliked humbug and flummery intensely and so, for him, the promise of posthumous glory and immortality for his 'gallant friend' was very little comfort: 'I was prepared for anything great from Nelson,' he wrote when he first heard the news of his victory and death, 'but not for his loss.'

He knew, better than anyone, how much was still left to be done.

APPENDIX I

Nelson's Battle Plans

1. THE NILE CAMPAIGN: JUNE 1798

General Order

Vanguard at Sea 18th: June 1798

As it is very possible that the Enemy may not be formed in regular Order of battle on the approach of the Squadron under my Command, I may in that case deem it most expedient to attack them by separate Divisions, in which case the Commanders of the Divisions are enjoined to keep their ships in the **Closest Order** possible and on no account <u>whatever</u> to risk the separation of one of their ships.

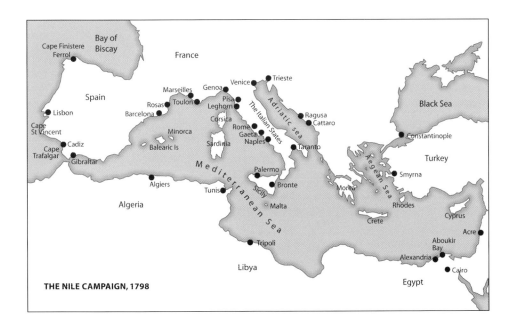

THE NILE CAMPAIGN, 1798

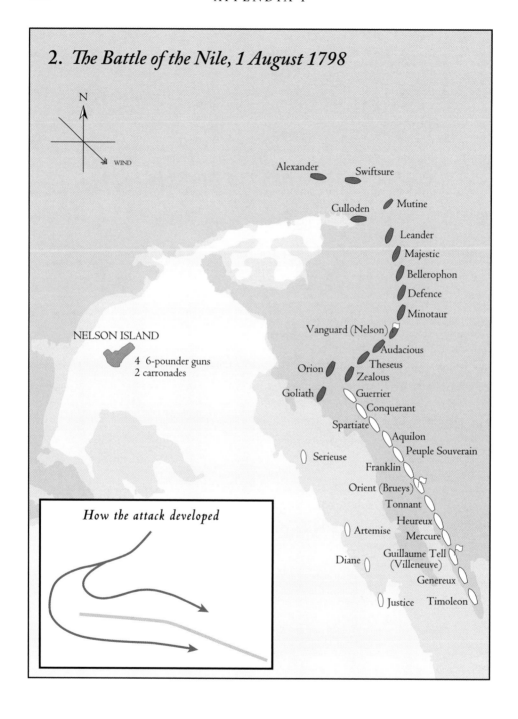

2. *The Battle of the Nile, 1 August 1798*

N

WIND

Alexander

Swiftsure

Culloden

Mutine

Leander

Majestic

Bellerophon

Defence

Minotaur

Vanguard (Nelson)

Audacious

NELSON ISLAND

Theseus

Orion

Zealous

4 6-pounder guns
2 carronades

Goliath

Guerrier

Conquerant

Spartiate

Aquilon

Serieuse

Peuple Souverain

Franklin

Orient (Brueys)

Tonnant

Heureux

Artemise

Mercure

Diane

Guillaume Tell
(Villeneuve)

Genereux

Justice

Timoleon

How the attack developed

The captains of the Ships will see the necessity of strictly attending to **Close Order** and should they compel any of the Enemys ships to strike their Colours they are at liberty to judge and Act accordingly, whether or not it may be advisable to cut away their Mast and Bowsprit, with this special observance, Namely that **The Destruction of the Enemys Armament is the Sole Object**.

The Ships of the Enemy are therefore to be taken possession of by an Officer and <u>one</u> Boats Crew <u>only</u> in order that the British Ships may be enabled to continue the attack and preserve their stations.

The Commanders of the Divisions are to observe that no considerations are to induce them to separate from pursuing the Enemy, unless by Signal from me, so as to be unable to form a speedy junction with Me, and the Ships are to be kept in that Order that the whole Squadron may act as a single ship.

When I make the Signal No 16 the Commanders of the Squadrons are to lead their separate Squadrons and they are to accompany the signals they may think proper to make with the appropriate Triangular Flag. Viz Sir James Saumarez will hoist the Triangular flag white with a Red Stripe, significant of the Van Squadron under the Commander in the Second Post. Captain Troubridge will hoist the Triangular Blue flag significant of the Rear Squadron under the Commander in the third Post. And when I mean to address the centre Squadron only I shall accompany the Signal with the Triangular Red Flag significant of the Centre Squadron under the Commander in Chief.

Horatio Nelson

1st Division	2d Division	3d Division
Vanguard	Orion	Culloden
Minotaur	Goliath	Theseus
Leander	Majestic	Alexander
Audacious	Bellerophon	Swiftsure
Defence		
Zealous		

Source: BL: 30260 ff. 5–6

2. THE BATTLE OF COPENHAGEN: 2 APRIL 1801

As Vice-Admiral Lord Nelson cannot with precision mark the situation of the different descriptions of the Enemy's Floating Batteries and smaller Vessels, lying between their two-decked Ships and Hulks, the Ships which are to be opposed to the Floating Batteries, &c., &c., will find their stations by observing the stations of the Ships to be opposed to the two-decked Ships and Hulks.

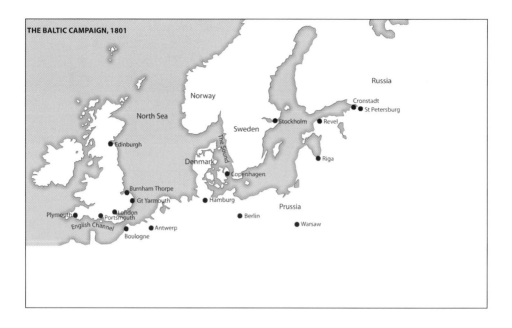

THE BALTIC CAMPAIGN, 1801

LINE OF BATTLE

	(Edgar	)	
These Ships are to	(Ardent	)	
fire in passing on	(Glatton	)	Are to lead in succession
to their stations	(Isis	)	
	(Agamemnon*	)	

The Edgar to anchor abreast of No. 5, (a sixty-four gun Ship, Hulk.) The Ardent to pass the Edgar, and anchor abreast of Nos. 6 and 7. The Glatton to pass the Ardent, and anchor abreast of No. 9, (a sixty-four gun Ship, Hulk.) The Isis to anchor abreast of No. 2, (a sixty-four gun Ship, Hulk.) The Agamemnon to anchor abreast of No.1.

Bellona,*	)	
Elephant,	)	
Ganges,	)	To take their station and anchor,
Monarch,	)	as is prescribed by the following
Defiance,	)	arrangement
Russell,*	)	
Polyphemus,	)	

Memorandum. No. 1 begins with the Enemy's first Ship to the southward.

No.	Rate.	Supposed Number of guns mounted on one side.	Station of the Line as they are to anchor and engage.
			(Agamemnon
1	74	28	(Desiree is to follow
			(Agamemnon, and rake No.2.
2	64	26	Isis
			(It is hoped the Desiree's
			(fire will not only rake
3	(Low Floating Batteries,)		(these two Floating Batteries.
	(Ship-rigged, rather lay)		(Capt. Rose is to
4	(within the Line)	10	(place the six Gun Brigs
			(to as to rake them also.
5	64	27	Edgar
6)	Pontoon	10)	
7)	Frigate Hulk	12)	Ardent
8)	Small – no guns visible,	)	
9)	64	20)	Glatton
10)	Ship, Gun-boat of 22 guns	11)	Bellona, to give her
11)	Pontoons, or . .	12)	attention to support the
12)	Floating Batteries . .	12)	Glatton.
13	74`	36	Elephant
14)	Pontoons, or . .	12)	
15)	Floating Batteries . .	12)	Ganges
16	64 . . .	30	Monarch
17	64 . . .	30	Defiance
18	64 . . .	30	Russell
19	74 . . .	30	Polyphemus
20	(A small Ship, supposed a)		
	(Bomb,)	11	

The six Gun-boats, Captain Rose is to place with the Jamaica, to make a raking fire upon No. 1. The Gun-boats, it is presumed, may get far enough astern of No. 1, to rake Nos. 3 and 4; and Captain Rose is to advance with the Ship and Vessels under his orders, to the Northward, as he may perceive the British fire to cease where he is first stationed.

Nos. 1, 2, 3, and 4, being subdued, which is expected to happen at an early period, the Isis and Agamemnon are to cut their cables, and immediately make sail and take their station ahead of the Polyphemus, in order to support that part of the Line. One Flat Boat manned and armed, is to remain upon the off side of each Line of Battle Ship. The remaining Flat Boats, with the Boats for boarding, which will be sent by Admiral Sir Hyde Parker under the command of the First Lieutenant of the London, are to keep as near to the Elephant as possible, but out of the line of fire, and to be ready to receive the directions of Lord Nelson.

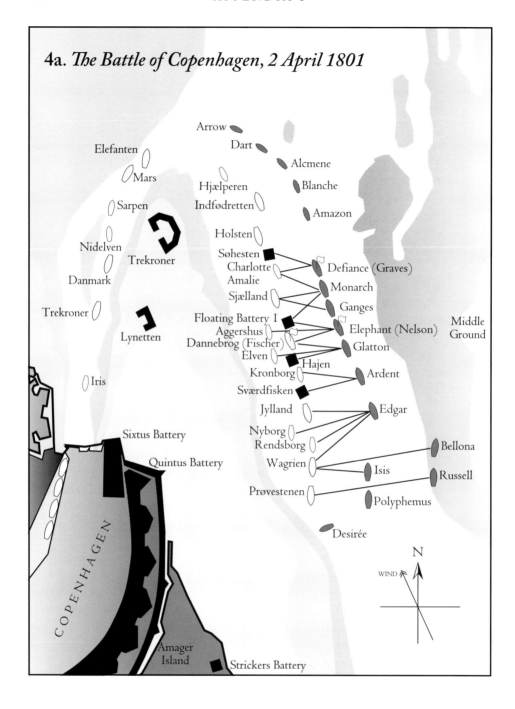

4a. *The Battle of Copenhagen, 2 April 1801*

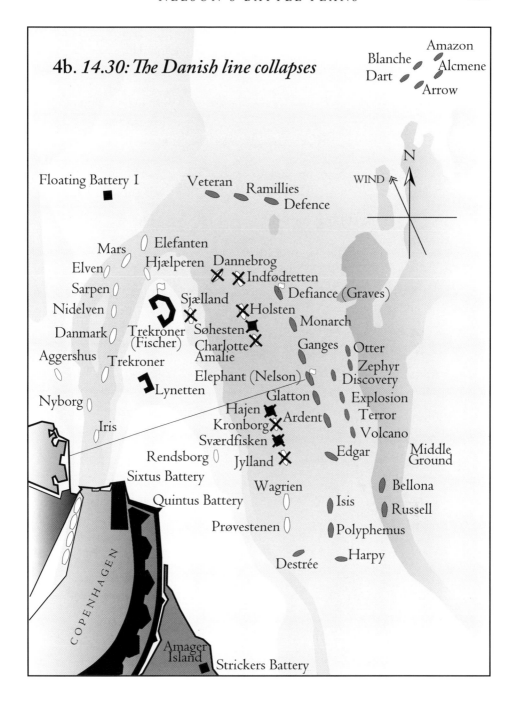

4b. 14.30: The Danish line collapses

Blanche
Dart
Amazon
Alcmene
Arrow

Floating Battery I

Veteran
Ramillies
Defence

N
WIND

Mars
Elven
Sarpen
Nidelven
Danmark
Aggershus
Trekroner

Elefanten
Hjælperen
Sjælland
Trekroner
(Fischer)
Søhesten
Charlotte
Amalie
Elephant (Nelson)
Lynetten

Dannebrog
Indfødretten
Defiance (Graves)
Holsten
Monarch
Ganges
Otter
Zephyr
Discovery
Explosion
Terror
Volcano

Nyborg
Iris
Rendsborg
Hajen
Kronborg
Sværdfisken
Jylland
Glatton
Ardent
Edgar
Middle
Ground

Sixtus Battery
Quintus Battery
Wagrien
Bellona
Isis
Russell
Polyphemus

Prøvestenen
Destrée
Harpy

COPENHAGEN

Amager
Island
Strickers Battery

The four Launches with anchors and cables, which will be sent by Admiral Sir Hyde Parker, under the command of a Lieutenant of the London, to be as near to the Elephant as Possible, out of the line of fire, ready to receive orders from Vice-Admiral Lord Nelson.

The Alcmene, Blanche, Arrow, Dart, Zephyr, and Otter, Fire-Ships, are to proceed under the orders of Captain Riou, of the Amazon, to perform such service as he is directed by Lord Nelson.

Source: Nicolas, *Letters*, vol. 6, pp. 304–7

3. THE ATTACK ON BOULOGNE: 15 AUGUST 1801

On board the Medusa, off Boulogne, 15th August, 1801

Eight Flat Boats, with 8-inch howitzers, with a Lieutenant in each, and fourteen men, to be under the direction of Captain Conn. Artillery to be in them, as arranged by Captain Brome.

Six Flat Boats, with 24-pounder carronades, with a Lieutenant in each, besides Seamen, and eight Marines, with the number of boats hereafter specified, to be under the command of Captains Somerville, Cotgrave, Jones and Parker.

This force, under the direction of the four Captains before-mentioned, is to be divided into four Squadrons, consisting of 13–15 Boats each; and two Boats of each of those Divisions to be particularly allotted and prepared for the purpose of cutting the Enemy's cable and sternfast, and to be furnished with stout hook-ropes, to be the more ready to take them in tow. The others are to attack the opponent Divisions, which is to be done at last quarter-flood, at the Pier-head. When any Boats have taken one Vessel, the business is not to be considered as finished; but a sufficient number being left to guard the Prize, the others are immediately to pursue the object, by proceeding on to the next, and so on, until the whole of the Flotilla be either taken, or totally annihilated; for there must not be the smallest cessation until their destruction is completely finished.

The Boats from the Ships are to be armed with pikes, cutlasses, and tomahawks, except the Marines, who, as usual, are to have their muskets, bayonets, and cartouch-boxes filled with ammunition. Every Boat is to have a broad-axe well sharpened, and likewise a carcase, or other combustibles, with a match, ready to set the Enemy's Vessels on fire, should it be found impracticable to bring them off; but if it is possible they are to be brought off.

The First Division is to be under the direction of Captain Somerville, who is to attack the Enemy's Vessels at the Eastern end, and to consist of the following Boats:

Flat Boats	. .	2	)
Leyden	. .	4 Boats	)
Eugenia	. .	1	)
Jamaica	. .	2	) To assemble on board the Leyden
Nile	. .	1	)
Argus	. .	1	)
Queen	. .	1	)
Antelope	. .	1	) Total, 13
		—	)
		13	)

Second Division, to be under Captain Parker, and to attack next to Captain Somerville:

Flat Boats	. .	2	)
Medusa	. .	4	)
Snipe	. .	1	)
Eclipse	. .	1	)
Venus (1)	. .	1	)
Queenborough	. .	1	) To assemble on board the Medusa
Hecla	. .	1	)
Hunter	. .	1	)
Hind	. .	1	)
Greyhound	. .	1	)
Minx	. .	1	)
		—	) Total, 15
		15	)

Third Division, under Captain Cotgrave, to attack the Enemy with the following Boats, next to Captain Parker:

Flat Boats	. .	2	)
York	. .	4	)
Gannet	. .	1	)
Explosion	. .	1	)
Ferret	. .	1	) To assemble on board the York
Lively	. .	1	)
Bruiser	. .	1	)
Providence	. .	1	)
Express	. .	1	)
Ranger	. .	1	)
Lively	. .	1	)
		—	) Total, 15
		15	)

Fourth Division, under Captain Jones, to attack the Enemy with the following Boats, at their Westernmost part:

Flat Boat	. .	1	)	
Isis	. .	4	)	
Diligence	. .	1	)	
Plumper	. .	1	)	
Cygnet	. .	1	)	
Dolphin	. .	1	)	
Sulphur	. .	1	)	
Renown	. .	1	)	
King George	. .	1	)	
Active	. .	1	)	
Stag	. .	1	)	
		—	)	Total, 14
		14	)	

All the Boats remaining are to be in readiness, manned and armed, on board the different Ships and Vessels, to put off the moment the firing begins, that they may afford all the assistance in their power.

The Revenue, Hired, and other fast-sailing Cutters, after the firing has commenced, are to keep close in shore, to be ready to tow the Enemy's Vessels out, as they are captured.

Captain Conn, who commands the Division of Howitzer Boats, which are to assemble on board the Discovery as soon after sunset as possible, is directed to put off the same time the signal is given for other Boats, and to row as near as possible in the centre of the Pier-head, and when the attack is begun by us, or by the Enemy, he is to open his fire from the howitzers upon the batteries and camp.

It is directed that each Division of Boats be formed into two Sub-divisions, and to be made fast to one another as close as possible. The Captain commanding the Division is to lead one, and any Lieutenant he pleases to appoint, the other.

The Boats are on no account to cut, or separate from one another, until they are close on board the Enemy.

The Captains commanding the Divisions have permission to make any additional arrangements in the mode of attack they may think will more easily facilitate it, and the subordinate Officers are strictly directed to carry into execution, with the utmost alacrity and attention, all such orders as they may receive. The greatest silence is to be observed by all the people in the Boats, and the oars to be muffled.

The Commander-in-Chief relies with the most perfect confidence on the unanimous exertions of the Officers and Men under his command, for the complete success of the enterprise.

It is recommended that, at half-past ten, the Boats shall be manned, and at eleven o'clock by the watch, that the Divisions of Boats shall, by the signal of six lanterns,

hung over the guns of the Medusa, put off, and row in the order prescribed under
the Medusa's stern, from whence they will start as soon as all are arrived.

Watchword	.	.	Nelson
The Answer	.	.	Bronte

Nelson & Bronte

Source: Nicolas, *Letters*, vol. 6, pp. 460–3

4. THE MEDITERRANEAN PLAN: 1804

The business of an English Commander-in-Chief being first to bring an Enemy's
Fleet to Battle, in the most advantageous terms to himself, (I mean that of laying
his Ships close on board the Enemy, as expeditiously as possible) and, secondly, to
continue them there, without separating, until the business is decided; I am
sensible beyond this object it is not necessary that I should say a word, being fully
assured that the Admirals and Captains of the Fleet I have the honour to
command, will, knowing my precise object, that of a close and decisive Battle,
supply any deficiency in my not making signals; which may, if extended beyond
these objects, either be misunderstood, or, if waited for, very probably, from
various causes, be impossible for the Commander-in-Chief to make: therefore, it
will only be requisite for me to state, in as few words as possible, the various
modes in which it may be necessary for me to obtain my object, on which
depends, not only the honour and glory of our Country, but possibly its safety,
and with it that of all Europe, from French tyranny and oppression.

 If the two Fleets are both willing to fight, but little manoeuvring is necessary;
the less the better; – a day is soon lost in that business: therefore I will only
suppose that the Enemy's Fleet being to leeward, standing close upon a wind on
the starboard tack, and that I am nearly ahead of them, standing on the larboard
tack, of course I should weather them. The weather must be supposed to be
moderate; for if it be a gale of wind, the manoeuvring of both Fleets is but of little
avail, and probably no decisive action would take place with the whole Fleet. Two
modes present themselves: one to stand on, just out of gun-shot, until the Van-
Ship of the Line would be about the centre Ship of the Enemy, then make the
signal to wear together, then bear up, engage with all our force the six or five Van-
Ships of the Enemy, passing certainly, if opportunity offered, through their Line.
This would prevent their bearing up, and the Action, from the known bravery and
conduct of the Admirals and Captains, would certainly be decisive: the second or
third Rear-Ships of the Enemy would act as they please, and our Ships would give
a good account of them, should they persist in mixing with our Ships. The other
mode would be to stand under an easy but commanding sail, directly for their
headmost Ship, so as to prevent the Enemy from knowing whether I should pass
to leeward or windward of him. In that situation, I would make the signal to

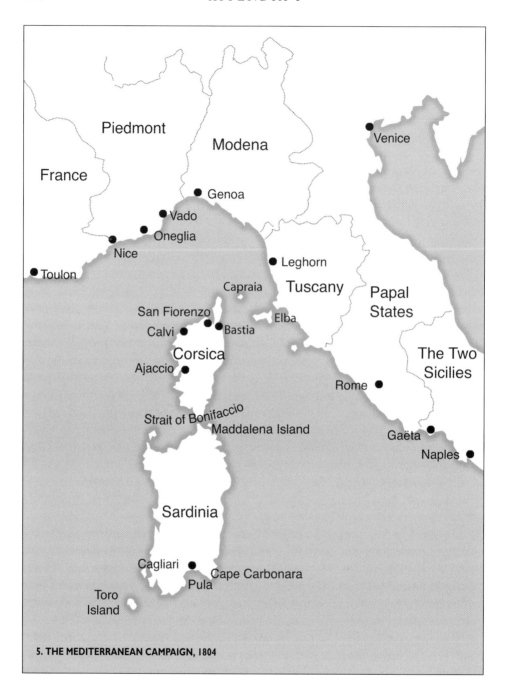

5. THE MEDITERRANEAN CAMPAIGN, 1804

engage the Enemy to leeward, and to cut through their Fleet about the sixth Ship
from the Van, passing very close; they being on a wind, and you going large, could
cut their Line when you please. The Van-Ships and the Enemy would, by the time
our Rear came abreast of the Van-Ship, be severely cut up, and our Van could not
expect to escape damage. I would then have our *Rear* Ship, and every Ship in
succession, wear, continue the Action with either the Van-Ship, or second Ship, as
it might appear most eligible from her crippled state; and this mode pursued, I see
nothing to prevent the capture of the five or six Ships of the Enemy's Van. The
two or three Ships of the Enemy's Rear must either bear up or wear; and, in either
case, although they would be in a better plight probably than our two Van-Ships
(now the Rear) yet they would be separated, and at a distance to leeward, so as to
give our Ships time to refit; and by that time, I believe, the Battle would, from the
judgment of the Admiral and Captains, be over with the rest of them. Signals from
these moments are useless, when every man is disposed to do his duty.

The great object is for us to support each other, and to keep close to the Enemy,
and to leeward of him.

If the Enemy are running away, then the only signals necessary will be, to
engage the Enemy as arriving up with them; and the other Ships to pass on for the
second, third, &c giving, if possible, a close fire into the Enemy in passing, taking
care to give our Ships engaged, notice of your intentions.

Source: Nicolas, *Letters,* vol. 6, pp. 443–5

5. THE GOURGEAN BAY PLAN: APRIL 1804

Victory, at Sea, 28th April, 1804

Memorandum

As it is my determination to attack the French Fleet in any place where there is a
reasonable prospect of getting fairly alongside of them, and as I think that in
Hieres Bay, Gourjean Bay, Port Especia, Leghorn Roads, Ajaccio, and many other
places, opportunities may offer of attacking them, I therefore recommend that
every Captain will make himself, by inquiries, as fully acquainted with the above-
mentioned places as possible – viz, for Hieres Bay, the Petite Passe, Grande Passe,
and Passage from the Eastward; Gourjean Bay, (of which I send a Chart from the
latest surveys made,) Port Especia, and, in particular, the Northern Passage into
Leghorn Roads, from which side it is only, in my opinion, possible to attack an
Enemy's Fleet to advantage; and with the Gulf of Ajaccio.

In going into attack an Enemy's Fleet, it is recommended, if possible, to have
the Launch out, and hawsers and stream-anchors within her; and, with any other
Boats, to lay out of gunshot, ready to act as circumstances may require. Ships, in
bringing up, will anchor as the Captains may think best, from circumstances of
wind and weather, and the position of the Enemy; but I would recommend

strongly having the *four* large anchors clear for letting go; because I know, from experience, the great difficulty, with crippled masts and yards, getting an anchor over the side; and it is probable that it may be necessary to remove the Ship after an Action, and to leave some of her anchors behind. The Ship will anchor in such a manner as to give each other mutual support for the destruction of the Enemy.

Nelson & Bronte

A chart of Gourjean Bay to be delivered to each Line-of-Battle Ship

Source: Nicolas, *Letters*, vol. 6, p. 519

6. THE 'TRAFALGAR' PLAN: OCTOBER 1805

(Secret) Victory, off Cádiz, 9th October, 1805

Memorandum.

Thinking it almost impossible to bring a Fleet of forty Sail of the Line into a Line of Battle in variable winds, thick weather, and other circumstances which must occur, without such a loss of time that the opportunity would probably be lost of bringing the Enemy to Battle in such a manner as to make the business decisive, I have therefore made up my mind to keep the Fleet in that position of sailing (with the exception of the First and Second in Command) that the Order of Sailing is to be the Order of Battle, placing the Fleet in two Lines of sixteen Ships each, with an Advance Squadron of eight of the fastest sailing Two-decked Ships, which will always make, if wanted, a Line of twenty-four Sail, on whichever Line the Commander-in-Chief may direct.

The Second in Command will, after my intentions are made known to him, have the entire direction of his Line to make the attack upon the Enemy, and to follow up the blow until they are captured or destroyed.

If the Enemy's Fleet should be seen to windward in Line of Battle, and that the two Lines and the Advanced Squadron can fetch them, they will probably be so extended that their Van could not succour their Rear.

I should therefore probably make the Second in Command's signal to lead through, about their twelfth Ship from their Rear, (or wherever he could fetch, if not able to get so far advanced); my Line would lead through about their Centre, and the Advanced Squadron to cut two or three or four Ships a-head of their Centre, so as to ensure getting at their Commander-in-Chief, on whom every effort must be made to capture.

The whole impression of the British Fleet must be to over-power from two or three Ships a-head of their Commander-in-Chief, supposed to be in the Centre, to the Rear of their Fleet. I will suppose twenty Sail of the Enemy's Line to be untouched, it must be some time before they could perform a manoeuvre to bring their force compact to attack any part of the British Fleet engaged, or to succour their own Ships, which indeed would be impossible without mixing with the Ships engaged.

Something must be left to chance; nothing is sure in a Sea Fight beyond all others. Shot will carry away the masts and yards of friends as well as foes; but I look with confidence to a Victory before the Van of the Enemy could succour their Rear, and than that the British Fleet would most of them be ready to receive their twenty Sail of the Line, or to pursue them, should they endeavour to make off.

If the Van of the Enemy tacks, the Captured Ships must run to leeward of the British Fleet; if the Enemy wears, the British must place themselves between the Enemy and the Captured, and disabled British Ships; and should the Enemy close, I have no fears as to the result.

The Second in Command will in all possible things direct the movements of his Line, by keeping them as compact as the nature of the circumstances will admit. Captains are to look to their particular Line as their rallying point. But, in case Signals can neither be seen or perfectly understood, no Captain can do very wrong if he places his Ship alongside that of an Enemy.

Of the intended attack from to windward, the Enemy in Line of Battle ready to receive an attack,

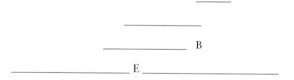

The divisions of the British Fleet will be brought nearly within gun shot of the Enemy's Centre. The signal will most probably then be made for the Lee Line to bear up together, to set all their sails, even steering sails, in order to get as quickly as possible to the Enemy's Line, and to cut through, beginning from the 12 Ship from the Enemy's Rear. Some Ships may not get through their exact place, but they will always be at hand to assist their friends; and if any are thrown round the Rear of the Enemy, they will effectually complete the business of twelve Sail of the Enemy.

Should the Enemy wear together, or bear up and sail large, still the twelve Ships composing, in the first position, the Enemy's Rear, are to be *the* object of attack of the Lee Line, unless otherwise directed from the Commander-in-Chief, which is scarcely to be expected, as the entire management of the Lee Line, after the intentions of the Commander-in-Chief, is [are] signified, is intended to be left to the judgment of the Admiral commanding that Line.

The remainder of the Enemy's Fleet, 34 Sail, are to be left to the management of the Commander-in-Chief, who will endeavour to take care that the movements of the Second in Command are as little interrupted as is possible.

Nelson and Bronte

Source: Nicolas, *Letters,* vol. 7, pp. 89–92

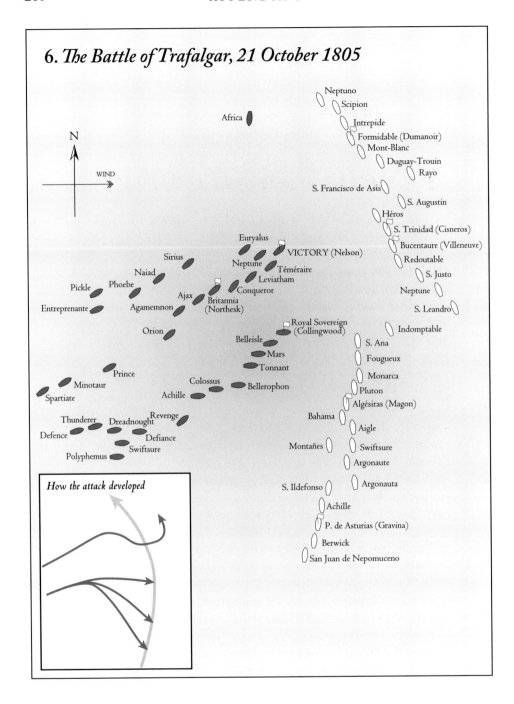

6. *The Battle of Trafalgar, 21 October 1805*

Neptuno

Scipion

Intrepide

Formidable (Dumanoir)

Mont-Blanc

Duguay-Trouin

Rayo

Africa

N

WIND

S. Francisco de Asis

S. Augustin

Héros

S. Trinidad (Cisneros)

Euryalus

VICTORY (Nelson)

Bucentaure (Villeneuve)

Sirius

Neptune

Redoutable

Naíad

Téméraire

Leviatham

S. Justo

Pickle

Phoebe

Conqueror

Neptune

Ajax

Entreprenante

Agamemnon

Britannia
(Northesk)

S. Leandro

Orion

Royal Sovereign
(Collingwood)

Indomptable

Belleisle

S. Ana

Mars

Fougueux

Tonnant

Monarca

Prince

Pluton

Minotaur

Colossus

Bellerophon

Algésiras (Magon)

Spartiate

Achille

Bahama

Aigle

Revenge

Thunderer

Dreadnought

Montañes

Swiftsure

Defence

Defiance

Argonaute

Swiftsure

Polyphemus

Argonauta

S. Ildefonso

Achille

P. de Asturias (Gravina)

Berwick

San Juan de Nepomuceno

How the attack developed

A Nelson Chronology

1758   29 September, Horatio Nelson born at Burnham Thorpe, Norfolk.

1767   26 December, Catherine Nelson, Nelson's mother, dies.

1771   Joins HMS *Raisonable* as a midshipman.

      August, sails to the West Indies in the *Mary Anne*, a merchant ship.

1773   June to September, joins Arctic expedition.

      Joins HMS *Seahorse* and sails to East Indies.

1775   Invalided from his ship suffering from malaria. Returns to England.

      War of American Independence begins.

1777   April, passes examination for lieutenant.

      Appointed to HMS *Lowestoffe* for service in the West Indies.

1778   September, appointed first lieutenant of HMS *Bristol*.

      December, appointed commander of HMS *Badger*.

1779   June, promoted to post captain, appointed to command HMS *Hinchinbrook*.

1780   Takes part in the Nicaraguan expedition (Capture of Fort San Juan).

      Falls ill and returns home to England.

1781   Appointed to command HMS *Albemarle*. Convoy service in Baltic and Channel.

1782   Joins North American Squadron. Visits Quebec and New York.

1783   War of American Independence ends. Returns home. Visits France.

1784   Appointed to command HMS *Boreas*. Sails for West Indies.

1785   May, meets Frances Nisbet.

1786   Appointed ADC to Prince William Henry.

1787   11 March, marries Frances Nisbet at Nevis.

      Returns to England. Placed on half-pay. Lives at Burnham Thorpe with his wife.

1793   Beginning of the French Revolutionary War.

      26 January, appointed to command HMS *Agamemnon*.

      June, sails for the Mediterranean.

      September, visits Naples. Meets Sir William and Lady Hamilton.

1794   January to August, Corsican campaign.
       12 July, right eye injured at Calvi.
1795   14 March, Hotham's Action. HMS *Agamemnon* in action with the *Ça Ira*.
       April, appointed commodore in command of a squadron operating off the
       NW coast of Italy.
1796   Continues to operate off NW coast of Italy.
       10 July, captures the island of Elba.
       19 September, captures island of Capraia.
       Transfers to HMS *Captain*.
1797   14 February, BATTLE OF CAPE ST VINCENT. Created Knight of Bath.
       Promoted to rear admiral. Hoists flag in HMS *Theseus*.
       25 July, failure of attack on Santa Cruz, Tenerife. Loses right arm.
       Returns home and goes to Bath to recover.
1798   March. Hoists flag in HMS *Vanguard* and joins fleet off Cádiz.
       May, enters Mediterranean in command of a detached squadron.
       July, in pursuit of the French Toulon fleet with Napoleon on board.
       1 August, destroys the French fleet at Aboukir Bay, BATTLE OF THE NILE,
       badly wounded in the head.
       Created Baron Nelson of the Nile.
       22 September, arrives at Naples.
       29–31 November, captures Leghorn.
       23–26 December, rescues Neapolitan Royal Family from advancing French
       army and takes them to Palermo.
1799   23 January, the French capture Naples.
       8 June, transfers his flag to HMS *Foudroyant*.
       June, assists in the recapture of Naples. Orders the trial of Commodore
       Carracciolo.
       Created Duke of Bronte by King of Naples.
       Begins relationship with Emma Hamilton.
       September–December, acting commander-in-chief.
1800   January, Lord Keith becomes commander-in-chief.
       February–March, takes part in the blockade and siege of Malta.
       June, recalled home. Returns overland with the Hamiltons.
       August and September, in Vienna.
       6 November, arrives at Great Yarmouth.
1801   1 January, promoted to vice admiral.
       Separates from his wife.
       18 January, hoists flag in HMS *San Josef*.
       Late January, Emma Hamilton gives birth to her first daughter (by Nelson),
       Horatia.
       12 March, sails, with Admiral Sir Hyde Parker, to the Baltic.
       2 April, THE BATTLE OF COPENHAGEN. Flies flag in HMS *Elephant*.
       Created viscount.
       6 May, succeeds Parker as commander-in-chief.

June, returns home.

July, appointed to command anti-invasion forces in the Channel.

Hoists flag in HMS *Medusa*.

15 August, failure of attack on Boulogne.

1 October, armistice signed between Britain and France.

22 October, returns home to Merton, which he shares with Sir William and Emma Hamilton.

1802 25 March, Treaty of Amiens (end of the French Revolutionary War).

1803 16 May, Napoleonic war begins. Appointed C-in-C Mediterranean.

18 May, hoists flag in HMS *Victory*.

8 July, joins the fleet off Toulon.

1804 January, prevents French invasion of Sardinia.

May and June, skirmishes with the French fleet off Toulon.

1805 January – First French sortie.

April–July, Second French sortie. Chases combined French and Spanish fleet to West Indies and back.

18 August, arrives in England. To Merton on leave.

14 September, rejoins the *Victory* at Portsmouth.

28 September, takes command of the fleet off Cádiz.

21 October, THE BATTLE OF TRAFALGAR.

6 November, news of Trafalgar arrives in England.

4 December, *Victory* arrives at Portsmouth with Nelson's body on board.

1806 8 January, funeral procession on the River Thames.

9 January, funeral service in St Paul's Cathedral.

Glossary

beam: the width of a ship; also a heavy timber running between the ship's sides to support the decks

beat (to): to move to windward by a succession of tacks (q.v.)

breech: the rear of a gun

bower anchor: the main anchors in a ship, stowed in the bows

bring to: to slow down a ship by pointing her head into the wind

cable-length: an expression of distance at sea. One cable = 200 yards (183 metres); ten cables = 1 nautical mile

capstan: a vertical revolving cylinder, turned by poles pushed by sailors, used for hauling in heavy ropes, especially anchor cables

carronade: a short gun, firing heavy shot for short-range action

carcass: a hollow shell, filled with inflammable material

close hauled: when sailing into the wind, the head of the ship is pointed as close to the wind as possible while still keeping the sails filled

close reefed: reduce the area of the topsails exposed to the wind by tying the reefs as tightly as possible

commodore: at this time, a temporary rank, given to a senior captain in command of a squadron or division of the fleet

convoy: a group of merchant ships under armed escort

coxswain: a petty officer in charge of a ship's boat

double: to attack an enemy on both sides

doubleshotted: to load a cannon with two shot, or balls

The Downs: the anchorage off Deal sheltered from winds from the east by the Goodwin sands

draught: the depth of water needed to float a ship

frigate: a smaller, fast warship with one gundeck, and between about 28 and 44 guns

knot: the nautical measure of speed – i.e. one nautical mile an hour

langridge: anti-personnel projectile – loose pieces of metal stuffed into a container

muzzle: the mouth of a gun

nautical mile: 6,075.6 feet. 60 nautical miles make up 1 degree of latitude

The Nore: a sheltered anchorage in the mouth of the Thames, close to Sheerness

orlop: the lowest deck of a ship, immediately above the hold and below the waterline

port: holes cut in the side of a warship, through which the guns are pointed

post captain: a naval rank, given to officers commanding sixth rate ships or anything larger (known as 'post ships')

pratique: a certificate allowing a ship to enter harbour having confirmed that her crew is healthy

prize money: the proceeds of the sale of a captured vessel (and, where appropriate its cargo) that was distributed among the crew of the ship(s) that had made the capture

rate: larger British warships were divided into six 'rates' ranging from first rates (such as Nelson's *Victory*) with 100 or more guns to sixth rates (such as the *Boreas*) with 28 guns

reef: reduce the area of the sails exposed to the wind by hoisting up part of the sail and tying it to the yard. Most sails had two rows of reef points

Royal mast: a light spar added above the topgallant (q.v.) in lighter winds

scurvy: an illness caused by lack of Vitamin C. Symptoms including bleeding gums and general debility – and in extreme cases could result in death

Sea Fencibles: a force of mariners allowed exemption for service in the Royal Navy on condition that they volunteered for service in times of emergency

shot: a generic term for all types of projectile fired by guns. Included round shot; 'dismantling' shot for tearing down rigging, such as bar- or chain-shot and anti-personnel shot, such as grapeshot

sloop: a small warship, one rank down from a frigate, with its guns on the upper deck

Spithead: the large sheltered anchorage between Portsmouth and the Isle of Wight

spring: a special rope attached to the anchor rope, or a mooring line, that could be hauled on to turn a ship's head

studding sails: lighter sails, suspended from special booms attached to the end of the yards, used to increase a ship's speed in light winds

tack: to change a ship's direction by turning its head through the wind

taken aback: when a ship's sails are filled from the wrong side, thus stopping her forward movement

topgallant: the upper section of a mast

topmast: the middle section of a mast

van: the foremost section of a fleet

warp: to move a ship out of harbour, or against the wind, by attaching ropes to buoys, or special fixings onshore, and hauling in on the capstan

wear: to change a ship's direction by turning its stern through the wind

yard: horizontal beam hung from the masts, from which the sails were hung

Notes

Chapter I, The Making of an Admiral

1. Clarke and M'Arthur, *Life*, vol. 1, p. 24.
2. Naish, *Letters*, pp. 138–9.
3. Nelson to Gaskin, 9 September 1803, BL: 34953 f. 185.
4. See White, *Encyclopaedia*, p. 16 and *Letters*, pp. 130–1.
5. Nelson to Wilson, 23 December 1802, BL: 30114 ff. 1–2.
6. Nelson to Cockburn, 15 May 1796, Library of Congress: Cockburn Papers vol. 13.
7. Dann, *Journal*, p. 207.
8. For a highly detailed examination of Nelson's early career, based very largely on the newly discovered material, see Sugden, *Nelson*. See also Roger Knight's brilliantly insightful new biography.
9. Nelson's 'Sketch of my life', Nicolas, *Letters*, vol. 1, p. 2.
10. Quoted in Sugden, *Nelson*, p. 84.
11. Nicolas, *Letters*, vol. 5, p. 520.
12. For the best modern account of Nelson's time in the West Indies in 1784–7, see Knight, *Pursuit*.
13. Nelson to Hood, 5 May 1793, NA: Pitt MS 30/8 ff. 40–1.
14. Nelson to John Udney, 24 February 1794, NMM: AGC/18/3.
15. Nelson to Frances Nelson, 17 February 1796, Naish, *Letters*, p. 284.
16. Nelson to Jervis, Nicolas, *Letters*, vol. 2, pp. 271–2. For a full account of the capture of Capraia, see White, *1797*, pp. 10–11.
17. Spencer to Nelson, 26 April 1796, NMM: CRK/11.
18. Nelson to Drake, 10 September 1796, Clive Richards Collection: CRC/10.
19. The best accounts of these battles are still those in Mahan. See his *Life*, vol. 1, pp. 162–82.
20. Nelson to Hoste, 2 April 1795, Clive Richards Collection, CRC/8.
21. Nelson to Frances Nelson, 9 July 1795, Naish, *Letters*, p. 216.
22. Nelson to Clarence, 15 July 1795, NMM: AGC/27. Nelson wrote over seventy letters to Clarence between 1787 and 1805, only about half of which have been published. They provide a fascinating insight into his professional opinions, expressed frankly to a close friend. For full transcripts, see White, *Letters*.
23. Nelson to Hamilton, 1 October 1796, Monmouth: E431.
24. For a full description see White, *1797*, pp. 16–20.
25. Much of this new material was revealed at the *St Vincent 200* Conference at Portsmouth on 15 February 1997. See Howarth, *St Vincent*. For a full account, based on all this new material, see White, *1797*, pp. 41–85.
26. Nelson's account, Nicolas, *Letters*, vol. 2, p. 341.
27. Nelson to the Duke of Clarence, 26 May 1797, NMM: AGC/27/24. Only parts of this letter have been published. For full transcription, see White, *Letters*, pp. 194–6.
28. Enclosure in a letter from Nelson to Clarence, 15 June 1797, NMM: AGC/27/25. Nelson also sent a transcription of the note to Frances, and this has featured in most biographies since. However, it is now clear that the wording in this recently discovered version is the original, and the

version sent to Frances was 'edited' by Nelson. See White, *Letters*, p. 189.

29. For a full account, based on all the latest research in both British and Spanish sources, see White, *1797*, pp. 103–31.

30. Frances Nelson's son by her first marriage.

31. Nelson to Sir John Jervis, 16 August 1797, Nicolas, *Letters*, vol. 2, p. 435.

32. Nelson to the Revd Weatherhead, 31 October 1797, Nicolas, *Letters*, vol. 2, p. 451.

33. Nelson to Jervis, 6 October 1797, Nicolas, *Letters*, vol. 2, p. 448.

34. Nelson to Fellowes, 2 October 1797, HL: HM34017.

Chapter II, The Battle of the Nile and the Mediterranean

1. Nelson to Lady Collier, March 1798, Nicolas, *Letters*, vol. 2, p. 5; Nelson to Campbell 16 March, PML: MA321.

2. Berry to Nelson, 8 March 1798, BL: 34966.

3. Nelson to Frances Nelson, 5 April 1798, Naish, *Letters*, p. 390.

4. Nelson to Frances Nelson, 3 April 1798; Frances Nelson to Nelson, 5 April 1798, *ibid.*, p. 423.

5. St Vincent to Spencer, *Spencer Papers* II, p. 144.

6. St Vincent to Nelson, 2 May 1798, Nicolas, *Letters*, vol. 3, p. 12.

7. Nelson to St Vincent, 8 May 1798. Nicolas prints a brief extract from this letter in *Letters*, vol. 3, p. 15 in which the passage about slow movements has been edited out. This restored version is taken from a copy in the Clive Richards Collection: CRC/85. 'Europa' is Europa Point, the southernmost tip of Gibraltar.

8. 1798–9, BL: 30260; 1801 (Copenhagen and Baltic), SAD: D/173; 1801 (Channel), RNM: (Admiralty Library) MS200.

9. Nelson to Captains, 8 May 1798, BL: 30260 f. 1.

10. Nelson's report to St Vincent, Nicolas, *Letters*, vol. 3, pp. 15–16.

11. Ross, vol. 1, p. 195.

12. Nelson to Frances Nelson, 24 May 1798, Naish, *Letters*, p. 396.

13. Hardy first caught Nelson's eye while serving in the frigate *La Minereve* in the Mediterranean in 1796–7 and distinguished

himself during the action with the *Santa Sabinia*.

14. St Vincent to Nelson, 11 May 1798, Nicolas, *Letters*, vol. 3, p. 15.

15. Nelson to Troubridge, 20 October 1803, BL: 34954 ff. 49–52.

16. Nelson's Public Order Book, BL: 30260 ff. 3–4.

17. Berry's *Narrative*, Nicolas, *Letters*, vol. 3, p. 49.

18. Lavery, *Nile*, p. 156; Vincent, *Nelson*, p. 256.

19. The details of the ships and the quotation from the anonymous French officer come from Battesti: unpublished paper, given at the *Nile 200* Conference, 1998.

20. For an excellent analysis of the intelligence operations during the campaign, see Duffy, 'British Naval Intelligence', pp. 278–88.

21. Hamilton to Nelson, 30 June 1798, Lavery, *Nile*, p. 125.

22. Willyams, p. 16.

23. NMM: CRK/14. Printed in Naish, *Letters*, pp. 407–8.

24. Ball to Nelson, Nicolas, *Letters*, vol. 3, p. 41.

25. Nelson to St Vincent, 29 June 1798, *ibid.*; Nelson to Hamilton, 20 July 1798, *ibid.*, p. 44.

26. The French aspects of the battle and the preparations for it come from the excellent book by Michelle Battesti and from her unpublished paper presented to the *Nile 200* Conference at Portsmouth in 1998.

27. Battesti, from unpublished paper given at the *Nile 200* conference in 1998.

28. Battesti, *La Bataille*, p. 88.

29. Memo by Webley, Sturges Jackson, *Logs*, vol. 2, p. 26.

30. Battesti, *La Bataille*, p. 94.

31. Lavery, *Nile*, p. 178.

32. Sturges Jackson, *Logs*, vol. 2, p. 7.

33. Nelson to all captains, 23 February 1804, BL: 34970 f. 79.

34. I am indebted to Frank Goddio and his team for sharing their findings with me – including the insights given here about the process of *L'Orient*'s destruction – during a memorable visit to the battle site in 1999. For superb illustrations of the wreck and debris, see Foreman and Phillips, pp. 185–209.

35. Nelson to Howe, 9 January 1799, Nicolas, *Letters*, vol. 3, p. 230; Lachadenède, Battesti, *La Bataille*, pp. 113–14.

36. *Ibid.*, p. 191.

37. Nelson to St Vincent, 3 August 1798, Nicolas, *Letters*, vol. 3, p. 57.

38. Nelson to Curtis, 29 September 1798, HL: HM34203.

39. Nelson to Captains, 2 August 1798, Nicolas, *Letters*, vol. 3, p. 61.

40. Alexander Davison, a friend from his days as a frigate captain in North America who, following his appointment as prize agent for the Nile, became a close friend of Nelson's and virtually his banker.

41. Nelson to Darby, 3 August 1798, private collection; Nelson to Maurice Nelson, 12 August 1798, BL: Eg2240 f. 5; Nelson to Maurice Nelson, 2 February 1799, Monmouth: E604; Nelson to Lord Mayor, 8 August 1798, Nicolas, *Letters*, vol. 3, p. 95.

42. The sword is still in the collections of the City of London, now housed in the Museum of London, and makes occasional appearances at appropriate banquets in the Guildhall.

43. Nelson to Hood, 11 August 1798, NMM HOO/4 (464); Nelson to Hamilton, 8 August 1798, Nicolas, *Letters*, vol. 3, p. 93; Hamilton to Nelson, 8 September 1798, Morrison, p. 334.

44. Nelson to Curtis, 29 September 1798, HL: HM 34203; Nelson to St Vincent, Nicolas, *Letters*, vol. 3, p. 144.

45. Fuller details of this little-known operation are now available following the discovery of Nelson's very detailed report, written for the Hamiltons, on which the brief outline given here is based. Nelson's report, 1 December 1798, WCL: Hubert Smith Collection, vol. I. For the full report, see White, *Letters*, pp. 219–20.

46. King to Spencer, 3 October 1798, BL: 75817.

47. For the full story of this extraordinary incident, see Coleman, 'Nelson, the King and his Ministers', pp. 6–12.

48. Nelson to the Tsar, undated, NMM: CRK/14/31.

49. Nelson to Acton, 21 December 1798, US Naval Academy: Zabrieski Collection.

50. His four periods ashore were: 26 December 1798–19 May 1799 (*five months*);

13 August–4 October 1799 (*six weeks*); 22 October 1799–16 January 1800 (*three months*); and 16 March–24 April 1800 (*five weeks*).

51. J. Maurice (ed.), *The Diary of Sir John Moore*, I, p. 367.

52. Knight, *Cornelia*, I, p. 146.

53. See especially David Constantine's excellent new biography, *Fields of Fire*.

54. The account is contained in a letter from Lock to General Thomas Graham, NLS: Lynedoch Papers, 35599 f. 50. For the full text, and analysis, of the fascinating account of this hitherto-unknown incident, see White, 'A Public Argument', *Trafalgar Chronicle* 13 (2003).

55. Coleman, *Nelson*, p. 1.

56. Nelson to Curtis, 17 January 1799, HL: HM34020; Nelson to Frances, 17 January 1799, Naish, *Letters*, p. 480; Nelson to Lady Parker, 1 February 1799, Nicolas, *Letters*, vol. 3, p. 248.

57. Nelson to Clarence, 11 April 1799, *ibid.*, p. 324.

58. Nelson to Ball, 12 May 1799, *ibid.*, p. 353; Nelson to Troubridge, 17 May 1799, *ibid.*, p. 357; Nelson to Emma Hamilton, 19 May 1799, *ibid.*, p. 381; the prayer book is preserved in the Royal Naval Museum: 1991/267.

59. Order of Battle and Sailing, Nicolas, *Letters*, vol. 3, p. 362; Nelson to St Vincent, 23 May 1799, *ibid.*, p. 365.

60. Nelson to Hardy, 3 June 1799, NLS: 5308 f. 1817.

61. Nelson to Gibbs, 11 August 1803, Nicolas, *Letters*, vol. 5, p. 160.

Chapter III, The Battle of Copenhagen and the Baltic

1. St Vincent to Nepean, November 1800, Laughton, *Miscellany*, vol. 1, p. 329.

2. For a full examination of the breakdown of their marriage, see White, 'The Wife's Tale'.

3. Nelson to Spencer, 19 July 1799, BL: 75832 f. 40.

4. Nelson to St Vincent, 20 January 1801, Nicolas, *Letters*, vol. 4, p. 275.

5. Nelson to Emma Hamilton, Morrison, *Autograph Letters*, p. 532.

6. Nelson to Frances Nelson, 17 February 1801, NMM: DAV/2/50.

7. St Vincent to Nepean, 11 January 1801, Bonner-Smith, *Letters*, vol. 1, p. 13.

8. Parker to Spencer, 14 January 1801, Corbett, *Spencer*, vol. II, pp. 275–6.

9. Nelson to Spencer, 17 January 1801, Nicolas, *Letters*, vol. 3, p. 274.

10. Order Book, 20 February 1801, SAD D/173 f. 1.

11. Nelson to Troubridge, 26 February 1801, PML.

12. Nicolas, *Letters*, vol. 4, p. 299.

13. Nelson to Tyler, 27 February 1801, NMM TYL/1/69; Nelson to Nepean, 28 February 1801, NA: ADM 1/4 Ha4.

14. Nelson to Troubridge, 4 March 1801, Laughton, *Miscellany*, p. 415.

15. St Vincent to Nelson, 2 March 1801, Bonner-Smith, *Letters*, vol. 1, p. 83.

16. Nelson to Troubridge, 8 March 1801, Laughton, *Miscellany*, p. 417.

17. St Vincent to Parker, 11 March 1801, Bonner-Smith, *Letters*, vol. 1, p. 86.

18. Nelson to Troubridge, 13 March 1801, Laughton, *Miscellany*, p. 420.

19. Parker to Nelson, 14 March 1801, NMM CRK/19.

20. Nelson to Davison, 16 March 1801, Nicolas, *Letters*, vol. 4, p. 294.

21. Nelson to Troubridge, 2 March 1801, Laughton, *Miscellany*, p. 422.

22. Parker to Admiralty, 23 March 1801, NA: ADM1/4 f. 215–16.

23. Nelson to Troubridge, 23 March 1801, Laughton, *Miscellany*, p. 424.

24. *Naval Chronicle*, vol. 37, p. 3446.

25. Nelson to Parker, 24 March 1801, Nicolas, *Letters*, vol. 4, pp. 295–8.

26. Parker to Nelson, 24 March 1801, NMM CRK/9; Nelson's Journal, 23 March 1801, NMM: CRK/14.

27. Nelson's Journal, 26 March 1801, NMM: CRK/14.

28. Nelson to Emma Hamilton, 6 March 1801, Pettigrew, *Memoirs*, vol. 1, p. 449.

29. Nelson's Journal, 26 March 1801, NMM: CRK/14.

30. All these orders are dated 26 March 1801 and are to be found in SAD D/173 f. 4.

31. Nelson to Emma Hamilton, 26 March 1801, Pettigrew, *Memoirs*, vol. 1, p. 449.

32. Nelson to Murray, *c.* 29 March 1801, Nicolas, *Letters*, vol. 4, p. 298.

33. Nelson to Troubridge, 30 March 1801, Laughton, *Miscellany*, p. 425.

34. Nelson to Emma Hamilton, 31 March 1801, Morrison, *Autograph Letters*, vol. 2, p. 132.

35. *Ibid.*, p. 132.

36. The following account of the battle is based on the new material presented at the *Copenhagen 200* conference in Portsmouth. For conference papers, see Howarth (ed.), *Copenhagen*. I am also indebted to my colleague Ole Feldbaek's superb account based on Danish sources, now available in English. Finally, I am indebted to my colleagues at the Naval Museum of Denmark for arranging a site visit for me, which greatly increased my understanding of the battle from the Danish point of view.

37. Nelson's Journal, 31 March 1801, NMM: CRK/14.

38. The details of the Danish line of defence are taken from Feldbæk, *Copenhagen*.

39. Nelson's Battle Orders, Nicolas, *Letters*, vol. 4, pp. 304–7.

40. *Ibid.*, p. 306.

41. Colonel Stewart's account of the battle is in *ibid.*, pp. 307–13.

42. Nelson to the Duke of Clarence, 4 April 1801, BL: Add Mss 46356 f. 37.

43. Nicolas, *Letters*, vol. 4, p. 307.

44. As always, the timings given in the various ships' logs differ widely. In preparing this account of the battle, the timings have been standardised as much as possible, using Hyde Parker's signal No. 39, 'Discontinue the action', as the baseline.

45. Nicolas, *Letters*, vol. 4, p. 315.

46. W.S. Millard, 'A Midshipman at Copenhagen', *Macmillans Magazine*, June 1895.

47. Harrison, *Life*, vol. 2, p. 295.

48. Stewart to William Clinton, 6 April 1801, NMM: AGC/14/27.

49. Nicolas, *Letters*, vol. 1, p. 2.

50. Fremantle, *The Wynne Diaries*, vol. 2, p. 41.

51. Stewart to Clinton, see note 48.

52. Notebook of Robinson Kittoe, private collection.

53. Clarke and M'Arthur, *Life*, vol. 2, p. 40.

54. Stewart to Clinton, see note 48.

55. Beckwith to Andrew Strahan, 4 April 1801. Tushingham and Mansfield, *Nelson's Flagship*, p. 155.

56. Southey, *Life*, p. 226.
57. Harrison, *Life*, vol. 2, p. 295.
58. A notable exception being Terry Coleman, who believes the whole incident with the telescope to be an invention of Stewart's. See *Nelson*, pp. 258–9.
59. Sturges-Jackson, *Logs*, vol. 2, p. 103.
60. *Ibid.*, p. 103.
61. All three orders – none of which have been noticed before in any account of the battle – are in SAD/D173 f. 9.
62. Transcribed from a photograph of the original, which is now in the Danish Royal Archive.
63. Stewart's account, Nicolas, *Letters*, vol. 4, p. 310.
64. *The Edinburgh Advertiser*, 24 April 1801. Taken from a facsimile in *The Trafalgar Chronicle* 10, The 1805 Club, 2001.
65. Fremantle, *Wynne Diaries*, p. 41.
66. Pettigrew, *Memoirs*, vol. 2, p. 18.
67. Sturges-Jackson, *Logs*, vol. 2, p. 102.
68. Nelson to the Duke of Clarence, 3 April 1801. See note 10.
69. Sturges-Jackson, *Logs*, vol. 2, p. 102.
70. Tushingham and Mansfield, *Nelson's Flagship*, p. 155.
71. Stewart to Clinton, see note 48.
72. The Queen of Denmark, mother of the Crown Prince, was King George III's sister, Princess Caroline Matilda.
73. Nelson to Clarence, 4 April 1801, BL 46356 f. 37.
74. Nelson to Lindholm, 4 April 1801, WCL: HSC Book A.
75. Nelson's Journal, 7 April 1801, NMM: CRK/14.
76. Nelson to St Vincent, 5 April 1801, Nicolas, *Letters*, vol. 4, p. 336.
77. Gatty, *Scott*, p. 73.
78. Nelson's Journal, 9 April 1801, NMM: CRK/14.
79. Nelson to Clarence, 10 April 1801, BL: 46356 f. 40.
80. Nelson to Troubridge, 12 April 1801, Laughton, *Miscellany*, pp. 427–8.
81. Thompson to the Revd James Daubeny, 25 April 1801, Sturges-Jackson, *Logs*, vol. 2, p. 109.
82. Nelson to Thompson, 12 April 1801, BL: 46119, f. 115.
83. *The Naval Review*, 1951, p. 243.

84. Nicolas, *Letters*, vol. 4, pp. 343–4.
85. Parker to Nelson, 21 April 1801, NMM: CRK/9.
86. Nelson to Fremantle, private collection; Nelson to Tyler, NMM: TYL/1/71; Parker to Nelson, NMM: CRK/14; Scott's diary: Gatty, p. 76.
87. St Vincent to Nelson, 17 April 1801, Bonner-Smith, *Letters*, p. 91.
88. Nelson to Troubridge, 28 April 1801, Laughton, *Miscellany*, p. 431.
89. Bonner-Smith, *Letters*, p. 69.
90. Nelson to Nepean, 5 May 1801, NA: ADM 1/4 Ha74.
91. Nelson to Totty, 5 May 1801, SAD: D/173 f. 13.
92. Nelson to Murray, 8 May 1801, SAD: D/173 ff. 17–18.
93. Nelson to the Swedish Admiral, 8 May 1801, Nicolas, *Letters*, vol. 4, p. 363.
94. Nelson to Clarence, 10 May 1801, BL: 46356 f. 44.
95. Nelson to the Governor, 11 May 1801, NA: ADM 1/4 Ha83.
96. Nelson to St Vincent, 22 May 1801, Nicolas, *Letters*, vol. 4, p. 380.
97. Pahlen to Nelson, 13 May 1801, *ibid.*, pp. 371–2.
98. Nelson to Pahlen, 16 May 1801, *ibid.*, p. 373.
99. Nelson to Murray, 19 May 1801, SAD D/173 ff. 24–5.
100. Crauford to Nelson, 10 May 1801, WCL: Volume A.
101. Nelson to Crauford, 8 June 1801. Private collection of Mr Zvi Meitar. The whole letter is printed in White, *Letters*.
102. St Vincent to Nelson, 31 May 1801, Bonner-Smith, *Letters*, pp. 100–1.
103. Lambert, *Nelson*, p. 212.
104. Parker to Emma Hamilton, 14 June 1801, private collection.
105. Nicolas, *Letters*, vol. 4, p. 386.
106. Nelson to Berry, 2 June 1801, NMM: BER/6/13.
107. Nelson to Clarence, 15 June 1801, BL: 46356 f. 49.
108. Details of ceremony and Nelson's speech: *Naval Chronicle* 5, p. 552; Parker to Emma Hamilton, 14 June 1801, private collection.
109. Nelson to Emma, 1 July 1801, private collection.

Chapter IV, The Channel Command

1. *The Naval Chronicle*, vol. 6, p. 73.
2. Monarque, 'Latouche-Tréville'.
3. *Ibid.*, p. 275.
4. Bonner-Smith, *Letters*, vol. 1, p. 125.
5. *The Naval Chronicle*, vol. 6, p. 100.
6. Returns of the Squadron, BL: 34918 ff. 292–7.
7. For a full list of Nelson's fleet in early August 1801, see White, 'Public Order Book'.
8. Memorandum by Lord Nelson, 25 July 1801, Nicolas, *Letters*, vol. 4, pp. 425–8.
9. Morrison, vol. 2, pp. 157–9.
10. RNM (Admiralty Library) MS200. For a full transcription of the contents of the book, see White, 'The Public Order Book'.
11. Nicolas, *Letters*, vol. 4, p. 432.
12. Parker to Emma, 30 July 1801, Pettigrew, *Memoirs*, vol. 2, p. 135.
13. Nelson to Victualling Office, 31 July 1801, Monmouth: E990 f. 90.
14. Nelson to Berry, 28 July 1801, SAD: D/173 f. 51.
15. Nelson to Senior Officers, 29 July 1801, SAD: D/173 f. 57.
16. Parker to Emma, 30 July 1801, Pettigrew, *Memoirs*, vol. 2, p. 135.
17. Nelson to Emma, 12 August 1801, *ibid.*, p. 149.
18. Parker to the commanders of the gun brigs, 3 August 1801, RNM: MS200.
19. Nelson to Emma Hamilton, Pettigrew, *Memoirs*, vol. 2, p. 139.
20. Charnock, *Biographical Memoirs*, p. 335.
21. Nowell to Nelson, 7 August 1801, NMM: CRK9.
22. Nelson to Clarence, 5 August 1801, Nicolas, *Letters*, vol. 4, p. 441.
23. Nelson to Lutwidge, 3 August 1801, *ibid.*, p. 436.
24. Laughton, *Miscellany*, p. 292.
25. Schomberg to Nelson, 26 July 1801, BL: 34918 f. 83.
26. Nelson to captains, SAD: D/173, f. 70.
27. Nelson to all captains, 10 August 1801, RNM (AL): MS200.
28. Nelson to Captain Burchall, 10 August 1801, SAD: D/173, f. 74.
29. Nelson to St Vincent, 10 August 1801, Nicolas, *Letters*, vol. 4, p. 450.
30. St Vincent to Nelson, 11 August 1801, Bonner-Smith, *Letters*, vol. 1, p. 134.
31. Nelson to Emma Hamilton, 11 August 1801, Pettigrew, *Memoirs*, vol. 2, p. 149.
32. Parker to Davison, 9 August 1801, private collection.
33. The details of Hawkins's report and Nelson's resulting comments, all come from the same letter from Nelson to St Vincent: Nicolas, *Letters*, vol. 4, pp. 456–7.
34. All these orders are transcribed in White, 'Public Order Book', pp. 236–9.
35. This exposition of Nelson's plan and the subsequent account of what happened have been constructed from his orders in Nicolas, *Letters*, vol. 4, pp. 460–3; papers in his in-letters for August 1801, BL 34918; and the reports of the captains in Charnock, *Biographical Memoirs*, pp. 290–335.
36. For example, see Hibbert, *Nelson*, p. 81; Vincent, *Nelson*, pp. 449–50.
37. Monarque, 'Latouche-Tréville', pp. 278–9.
38. The timings for the attack are taken from the log of the *Medusa*. NA: ADM 51/1437/7. They differ from those given in the various reports but, as always, timings given by different participants rarely synchronise.
39. Nelson to St Vincent, 17 August 1801, Nicolas, *Letters*, vol. 4, p. 470.
40. Nelson to Emma Hamilton, 15 August 1801, Pettigrew, *Memoirs*, vol. 2, p. 154.
41. Faye, *Echec*, p. 18.
42. Nelson to St Vincent, 16 August 1801, Nicolas, *Letters*, vol. 4, p. 465.
43. Nelson to St Vincent, 16 August 1801, *ibid.*, p. 465; St Vincent to Nelson, 17 August 1801, Bonner-Smith, *Letters*, vol. 1, p. 137; Nelson to the fleet, Nicolas, *Letters*, vol. 4, p. 472.
44. Nelson to Emma Hamilton, 19 August 1801, Pettigrew, *Memoirs*, vol. 2, p. 162.
45. Parker to Emma Hamilton, 21 August 1801, *ibid.*, p. 169.
46. Nelson to Emma Hamilton, 28 September 1801, *ibid.*, p. 192.
47. Captain Owen's reports to Nelson are in BL 34918. Nelson to Lutwidge, 23 August 1801, Nicolas, *Letters*, vol. 4, p. 478.
48. Nelson to anon, 21 August 1801, Library of Congress, USA.
49. Nelson to Emma Hamilton, 31 August 1801, Pettigrew, *Memoirs*, vol. 2, p. 173.

50. Nelson to Nepean, September 1801, NMM: CRK/15.

51. St Vincent to Nelson, 8 August 1801, Bonner-Smith, *Letters*, vol. 1, p. 133.

52. Nelson to Emma Hamilton, 31 August 1801, Pettigrew, *Memoirs*, vol. 2, p. 173.

53. Nelson to Emma Hamilton, 20 September 1801, Morrison.

54. Both letters, together with many others in a similar vein, are in BL: 34918.

55. Nelson to Davison, 9 October 1801, Nicolas, *Letters*, vol. 4, p. 506; Nelson to St Vincent, 29 September 1801, *ibid.*, p. 500; Nelson to Keith, 14 September 1801, NMM: KEI 18/4 (46).

56. See, for example, Nelson to St Vincent, 24 September 1801, Nicolas, *Letters*, vol. 4, pp. 484–5.

57. Owen to Nelson, 26 September 1801, NMM: CRK/9.

58. Nelson to St Vincent, 3 October 1801, Nicolas, *Letters*, vol. 4, p. 504; St Vincent to Nelson, 5 October 1801, Bonner-Smith, *Letters*, vol. 1, p. 146.

59. Nelson to all captains, 19 October 1801, RNM (AL): MS200.

Chapter V, The Mediterranean Campaign

1. Nelson to Addington, 25 October 1801, DRO: 152M/C1802/ON8. For a full transcription, see White, *Letters*, pp. 309–11. For an examination of the 'Hot Press', see Lavery, *Trafalgar*.

2. Nelson to Bishop of London, 6 April 1804, BL: 34954 ff. 263–9.

3. Nelson to Patterson, 15 April 1803, HL: HM 3418.

4. Nelson to Addington, 20 May 1803, DRO: 152M/C1803/ON37.

5. Crockett to Nepean, 31 May 1803, BL: 34919 f. 94.

6. Nelson to Emma Hamilton, 30 May 1803, Pettigrew, vol. 2, p. 302.

7. Nelson to Pownall, 3 June 1803, Nicolas, *Letters*, vol. 5, p. 78.

8. Nelson to Addington, 23 May 1803, DRO: 152M/C1803/ON28.

9. Those in company when the *Amphion* joined them off Toulon were: battleships *Kent* (74 guns), *Donegal* (74), *Superb* (74), *Belleisle* (74), *Triumph* (74), *Renown* (74), *Agincourt* (64), *Monmouth* (64); frigates and sloops: *Medusa*, *Weazle*, *Termagant*, *Camelion*.

10. Nelson to Emma Hamilton, 8 July 1803, Pettigrew, *Memoirs*, vol. 2, p. 514.

11. Nelson to St Vincent, 8 July 1803, Nicolas, *Letters*, vol. 5, p. 123.

12. Nelson to Hobart, 8 July 1803, Bucks Records Office: D/MH/H/WarC/90.

13. Nelson to Troubridge, 20 October 1803, BL: 34854 49 f. 52.

14. Nelson to Clarence, 14 April 1803, BL: 46356 ff. 88–9.

15. Nelson to Strachan, 6 October 1803, Susan Lucas Collection.

16. Nelson to Cork, 15 July 1787, Nicolas, *Letters*, vol. 1, p. 247.

17. Nelson to Boyle, *Naval Chronicle* 30, p. 34.

18. Nelson to Bickerton, 19 October 1803, *Monmouth*: E451.

19. Nelson to Spiridion Foresti, 14 June 1804, BL: Add Mss 34956 ff. 126–9.

20. St Vincent to Nelson, 21 August 1803, Bonner-Smith, *Letters*, vol. 2, p. 320.

21. Nelson to Troubridge, 20 October 1803, BL: 34954 ff. 49–52.

22. For a number of examples of his routine correspondence on this subject, see White, *Letters*, pp. 333–49.

23. Nelson to Otway, 15 January 1805, HL: HM34192.

24. Nelson to Moseley, 11 March 1804, BL: 34958. Nicolas prints an edited version of this letter in *Letters*, vol. 5, p. 437. Nelson's original wording has been used here.

25. Nelson to Clark, 23 September 1803, NMM: AGC/18/11.

26. The records of Nelson's extraordinary achievement in maintaining the supplies of his fleet are to be found in the Western Manuscripts of the Wellcombe Trust MS 3679. This hitherto under-used resource has recently formed the basis for a brilliant study of this subject, *Feeding Nelson's Navy* by Janet Macdonald.

27. Macdonald, *Feeding Nelson's Navy*, p. 164.

28. Nelson to Baird, 30 May 1804, Nicolas, *Letters*, vol. 6, p. 41.

29. Nelson to Fremantle, January 1804, private collection.

30. Gwyther, 'Turin', pp. 47–74.

31. *Ibid.*, p. 53.

32. *Ibid.*, p. 69.

33. Nelson to the priest of La Maddalena, 18 October 1804, BL: Add Mss: 34957. The original letter is displayed in the church at La Maddalena, along with the silver, which has recently been restored with the assistance of The 1805 Club.

34. This was most probably one of the medals struck by Nelson's friend and prize agent, Alexander Davison, and presented to all those who fought in the battle. We know that Nelson kept a small stock of the medals with him, which he used as special presentation items, as on this occasion.

35. Pietro Magnon to Scott, RNM: Scott Papers. The original is in French (CSW's translation).

36. Nelson to Lieutenant Hamilton, 2 August 1804, USNA Zabrieski Collection.

37. St Vincent to Nelson, Bonner-Smith, *Letters*, vol. 2, p. 328.

38. Nelson to Admiralty, 11 October 1804, NA: ADM 1/408 N149.

39. i.e. Napoleon Bonaparte.

40. Nelson to Grand Vizier, *c.* 14 June 1803, private collection.

41. Drummond to Nelson, 22 July 1803, NMM: CRK/4.

42. Nelson to Foresti, 4 October 1804, BL: Add Mss 34957 f. 125.

43. Nelson to Frere, 10 April 1804, US Naval Academy: Zabrieski Collection.

44. Nelson to Acton, 18 March 1804, US Naval Academy: Zabrieski Collection.

45. Nelson to Acton, 23 March 1804, US Naval Academy: Zabrieski Collection.

46. Nelson to Queen of Naples, 7 October 1804, Clive Richards Collection: CRC/52.

47. Queen Maria Carolina was of course an Austrian by birth, a daughter of the Empress Maria Theresa.

48. Nelson to Queen of Naples, 7 October 1804, Clive Richards Collection: CRC/52.

49. Nelson to Acton, 28 March 1805, US Naval Academy: Zabrieski Collection.

50. C. White, 'Commerce, Consuls and Clergymen, Nelson's Intelligence Service in the Mediterranean, 1803–5'. Unpublished paper presented to the British Commission for Maritime History.

51. Nelson to Duff, 4 October 1803, BL: Add Mss 34953 ff. 161–2.

52. Blanckley to Nelson, 1 August 1803, BL: 34919 f. 349.

53. Gayner to Nelson, CRK/14.

54. Gayner to Nelson, 16 January 1804, NMM: CRK/14.

55. Macdonald, *Feeding Nelson's Navy*, p. 69.

56. Layman to Nelson, 27 July 1803, BL: 34919 f. 173.

57. Woodman's report to Nelson, 8 October 1804, NAS: GD/51/2/1082/25.

58. Nelson to Bickerton, 15 January 1804, HL: HM 34189.

59. Nelson to Merry, 11 February 1804, BL: Add Mss 34955 ff. 89–90.

60. Nelson to Trigge, 13 January 1804, Houghton: 196.5/36.

61. Campbell to Nelson, 23 February 1804, private collection.

62. Nelson to Sotheron, 28 March 1805, NMM: MON/2.

63. The *Victory* of course survives in the Historic Dockyard at Portsmouth – now splendidly restored to her 1805 condition, and Nelson's quarters have been painstakingly reconstructed, based on meticulous research. Much of the furniture mentioned here has survived – most of it is now displayed in the Royal Naval Museum alongside the ship.

64. *Naval Chronicle*, 18, pp. 188–90.

65. Murray had been promoted to Rear Admiral of the Blue in May 1804.

66. Nelson to Keats, 30 March 1805, Nicolas, *Letters*, vol. 6, p. 386.

67. Gatty, p. 129.

68. *Ibid.*, p. 121.

69. White, *Letters*, p. xx.

70. Nelson's workload has been reconstructed from routine orders in the Official Order Books at Monmouth, orders in Nicolas (vol. 6), and pressed-copy letterbooks in the British Library.

71. John Scott to Emma Hamilton, 8 July 1803, Pettigrew, vol. 2, p. 318.

72. Phillimore, *Parker*, vol. 1, p. 226.

73. Gatty, *Scott*, p. 124; Codrington: Bourchier, vol. 1, 32–3.

74. Vincent, *Nelson*, p. 617.

75. Phillimore, *Parker*, vol. 1, p. 122.

76. *Ibid.*, p. 229.

77. Nelson to Dalton, 13 December 1803, Nicolas, *Letters*, vol. 5, p. 310.

78. Nelson to Melville, 10 March 1805, Nicolas, *Letters*, vol. 6, p. 353. In fact, Nelson was unable to tell Melville the truth. The fault lay not with Layman but with the sloop's officer of the watch. Nelson had persuaded Layman not to produce his night orders which would have proved the man's guilt and trusted to his own influence to ensure that Layman was not censured. But the court martial found Layman guilty.

79. Layman to Nelson, 17 September 1803, BL: 34920 f. 45.

80. Nelson to Parker, Nicolas, *Letters*, vol. 5, p. 340.

81. Nelson to Pettit, BL: 35953 f. 185.

82. Nelson to Robinson, Nicolas, *Letters*, vol. 6, p. 316.

83. Nelson to Campbell, *ibid.*, p. 284. For the private letter, see White, *Letters*, pp. 65–6.

84. Richard Thomas's order book is in the private collection of Mr Ron Fiske, to whom I am indebted for allowing me to examine it. Nicolas includes selected orders from Robert Barlow's order book in the appendix to his vol. 7; Chevallier to Davison, 14 March 1805, RNM: 2002/76.

85. 'Order of Battle and Sailing' issued to Captain Sir Robert Barlow of HMS *Triumph*, 13 February 1804. Private collection.

86. The *Canopus* – formerly the *Franklin* and captured at the Nile – was a classic French 80-gunner, with a displacement of 2,257 tons (builder's measurement) as against the *Victory*'s 2,164. She also carried 36 36-pounders on her lower gun deck.

87. Nelson to Lord Mayor, 1 August 1804, Nicolas, *Letters*, vol. 6, p. 125.

88. Nelson to Clarence, 24 May 1804, BL: 46356 ff. 91–2.

89. Phillimore, *Parker*, vol. 1, p. 250.

90. Keats to Nelson, 1 August 1803, BL: 34919 f. 355.

91. Nelson's journal, Nicolas, *Letters*, vol. 5, p. 402.

92. Nelson to Donnelly, 15 February 1804, BL: 45365 f. 51b.

93. The British Consul at Barcelona.

94. Rosas. Clearly, Bolton is being sent to make contact with Nelson's agent, Edward Gayner (see p. 112).

95. Nelson to Bolton, 14 July 1804, BL: 34956 f. 252.

96. It has not been possible to establish from the available evidence whether an attack was ever seriously intended or whether this was a false alarm.

97. Nelson to Pettit, 31 January 1804, Nicolas, *Letters*, vol. 5, p. 399.

98. Gwyther, 'Turin', p. 57.

99. Viceroy to Nelson, Pettigrew, vol. 2, p. 363.

100. Nelson to Nepean, 19 March 1804, Nicolas, *Letters*, vol. 5, p. 456.

101. Nelson to Bickerton, 7 April 1804, BL: 34955 f. 267.

102. Phillimore, *Parker*, vol. 1, p. 250.

103. Nelson to Elliot, 18 June 1804, Nicolas, *Letters*, vol. 6, p. 75.

104. Nelson to Emma Hamilton, 17 June 1804, Pettigrew, vol. 2, p. 397.

105. Nelson to Melville, 1 July 1804, NAS: GD51/2/1082/7.

106. La Touche to Decres, 15 June 1804, Nicolas, *Letters*, vol. 6, p. 132.

107. Nelson to William Nelson, 8 August 1804, *ibid.*, p. 147.

108. Nelson to Emma Hamilton, 9 September 1804, Pettigrew, vol. 2, p. 420.

109. Nelson to Melville, 1 July 1804, NAS: GD51/2/1082/7.

110. Nelson to Clarence, 8 August 1804, Nicolas, *Letters*, vol. 6, p. 156.

111. Nelson to Emma Hamilton, 23 November 1804, Pettigrew, vol. 2, p. 437.

112. Nelson to the Governor, 16 November 1804, BL: 34958 ff. 47–8.

113. Scott papers RNM. These contain a large file of mail taken from the Spanish packet, mostly relating to Majorca.

114. Nelson to Malcolm, 19 December 1804, Monmouth: E160.

115. Nelson to Melville, 23 November 1804, NAS: GD51/2/1082/31.

116. Nelson to Elliot, 19 December 1805, Monmouth: E160.

117. A favourite Shakespearean quotation of Nelson's that he often used in his letters. He is misquoting slightly (as he always did) a line from *King Henry V*: 'But if it be a sin to covet honour/I am the most offending soul alive.'

118. Nelson to Melville, 1 November 1804, NAS: GD51/2/1082/21.

119. Nelson to Marsden, 26 December 1804, Nicolas, *Letters*, vol. 6, p. 300.

Chapter VI, The Trafalgar Campaign

1. These were: *Victory* (100 guns), *Royal Sovereign* (100), *Canopus* (80), *Superb* (74), *Spencer* (74), *Donegal* (74), *Tigre* (74), *Leviathan* (74), *Belleisle* (74), *Conqueror* (74), *Swiftsure* (74).

2. For a detailed explanation of this theory, see Corbett, *Trafalgar*, pp. 45–9.

3. Nelson to unknown correspondent, 16 January 1805, private collection.

4. Nelson to Louis, 18 January 1805, BL: 34958 f. 300.

5. Nelson to Elliot, 13 January 1805, Nicolas, *Letters*, vol. 6, p. 319.

6. Nelson to Camden, 16 January 1805, *ibid.*, p. 323.

7. According to Nelson's journal, the fleet was 'moored', which meant the ships had two anchors down. This of course greatly increased the task of getting under way.

8. Nelson to Boyle, 19 January 1805, private collection.

9. Nelson to Bickerton, 20 January 1805, BL: 34958 ff. 304–5.

10. It would appear from this and other brief references in his correspondence at this time that Nelson was already using an early form of Home Popham's telegraph system of signals at the beginning of 1805.

11. Nelson to Stopford, 20 January 1805, BL: 34958 f. 306.

12. Gwyther, 'Turin', p. 67.

13. Nelson to Moubray, 25 January 1805, BL: 34958 f. 316.

14. Nelson to Sotheron, 25 January 1805, BL: 34958 ff. 324–5.

15. Nelson to Leard, 30 January 1805, BL: 35958 ff. 343–4.

16. Nelson to 'The various Captains', 29 January 1805. William Clements Library, Hubert Smith Collection, vol. 1.

17. Nelson to Melville, 29 January 1805, Nicolas, *Letters*, vol. 6, p. 333.

18. Nelson to Melville, 14 February 1805, *ibid.*, p. 343.

19. Nelson to Marsden, 12 February 1805, *ibid.*, p. 341.

20. Nelson to Pacha, BL: 34958 ff. 345–6.

21. Nelson to Bickerton, 11 February 1805, BL: 34958 f. 377.

22. Nelson to Melville, 22 February 1805, NAS: GD51/2/1082/40.

23. Nelson to Emma Hamilton, Pettigrew, vol. 2, p. 462.

24. Mahan, *Life*, p. 640.

25. Schom, *Trafalgar*, p. 196.

26. Nelson to Emma Hamilton, 13 March 1805, RNM: 1973/233.

27. Nelson to William Nelson, 31 March 1805, NMM: BRP/6.

28. Nelson to Sewell, 28 March 1805, CRC/57.

29. Nelson to Curtis, 1 April 1805, Huntington: HM34073.

30. Nelson to Moira, 30 March 1805, Huntington: HA9578.

31. Nelson to Bayntun, 11 March 1805, Nicolas, *Letters*, vol. 6, p. 356.

32. Nelson to Mundy, 6 April 1805, BL: 34959 f. 215.

33. Nelson to Emma Hamilton, private collection.

34. Nelson to Melville, 5 April 1805, Nicolas, *Letters*, vol. 6, p. 397.

35. Nelson to Acton, 10 April 1805, NMM: MON/49.

36. Nelson to Elliot, 16 April 1805, Nicolas, *Letters*, vol. 6, p. 406.

37. Nelson to Ball, 10 April 1805, *ibid.*, p. 410.

38. Nelson to Otway, *ibid.*, p. 415.

39. Gatty, p. 171.

40. Nelson to Rutherfurd, 9 May 1805, BL: 35959 ff. 361–2.

41. Nelson to Seaforth, 10 May 1805, NAS: GD46/17/vol. 16; Nelson to Cochrane, 10 May 1805, Perrin, *Miscellany*, vol. 3, p. 183.

42. Nelson to Cutforth, 10 May 1805, BL: 34959 f. 385.

43. The formal letter is in Nicolas, *Letters*, vol. 6, p. 441. The private letter is in a private collection.

44. Nelson to Craig, 11 May 1805, BL: 34959 ff. 398–9.

45. Nelson to Knight, Nicolas, *Letters*, vol. 6, p. 433.

46. Nelson to Circello, 11 May 1805, BL: 34959 f. 402.

47. Gatty, p. 172.

48. Book of Common Prayer.

49. Coleman, *Nelson*, p. 509.

50. Corbett, *Trafalgar*, p. 75.

51. Nelson to Keats, 19 May 1805, Nicolas, *Letters*, vol. 6, p. 442.

52. Parker, p. 289.
53. Corbett, *Trafalgar*, p. 163.
54. Nelson to Seaforth, 29 May 1805, NAS: GD46/17/vol. 16.
55. Seaforth papers, NAS: GD/46/17/vol. 27.
56. For example, on 24 July, he told Alexander Davison, 'I resisted the opinion of General Brereton till it would have been the height of presumption to have carried my disbelief further.' Nicolas, *Letters*, vol. 6, p. 494.
57. *Ibid.*, p. 447.
58. Nelson to Henderson, 6 June 1805, BL: 34959 ff. 441–2.
59. Nelson to Emma, 4 June 1805, Monmouth: E167. Partially printed in Pettigrew, vol. 2, p. 473 but most of the passages of endearment are suppressed.
60. Nelson to Seaforth, 8 June 1805, NAS: GD46/17/vol. 16.
61. Corbett, *Trafalgar*, p. 167.
62. Nelson to Cochrane, Perrin, *Miscellany*, vol. 3, p. 189.
63. Nelson to Marsden, 12 June 1805, Nicolas, *Letters*, vol. 6, p. 452.
64. Nelson to Cochrane, 13 June 1805, Perrin, *Miscellany*, vol. 3, p. 190.
65. Nelson to senior officer, 15 June 1805, BL: 34959 f. 472.
66. Nelson to Bickerton, 17 June 1805, Monmouth: E168.
67. Nelson to Emma Hamilton, 24/25 June, private collection.
68. Hamilton, *Byam Martin*, vol. 3, p. 308.
69. Bayntun to Nelson, 21 June 1805, BL: 34930.
70. Nelson to Bayntun, 21 June 1805, private collection.
71. Nelson's Journal, Nicolas, *Letters*, vol. 6, p. 475.
72. Collingwood to Nelson, 19 July 1805, *ibid.*, p. 477.
73. Nelson to Cornwallis, *ibid.*, p. 500.
74. Nelson to Knight, 21 July 1805, *ibid.*, p. 482.
75. Nelson's Journal, *ibid.*, vol. 7, p. 4.
76. Nelson to Louis, *ibid.*, p. 4.

Chapter VII, The Battle of Trafalgar

1. Nelson to Fremantle, 16 August 1805, Nicolas, *Letters*, vol. 7, p. 5.
2. Minto, *Elliot*, vol. 3, p. 363.
3. Radstock to Nelson, 3 September 1805, BL 34931 f. 58; Angerstein to Nelson, 6 September 1805, *ibid.*, f. 101; West India merchants' address: Nicolas, *Letters*, vol. 6, p. 17. Angerstein, in common with some of Nelson's other acquaintances, addressed him as 'Your Grace' because he was Duke of Bronte.
4. Clarke and M'Arthur, *Life*, vol. 2, p. 116.
5. Nelson to Bickerton, 20 September 1805, Monmouth: E187.
6. See White, 'Nelson's Shopping Spree'.
7. Scott to Baird, August 1805, BL; Nelson to Pitt, 11 September 1805, BL: 46119 f. 145; Nelson to Barham, 13 September 1805, private collection; Nelson to Thompson, 5 September 1805, Nicolas, *Letters*, vol. 7, p. 28; Hasleham's testimonial, Pierpont Morgan Library: MA321; Nelson's notes, NMM: BRP/6.
8. Keats's memorandum, Nicolas, *Letters*, vol. 6, p. 241.
9. Nelson to Sidmouth, 8 September 1805, DRO: 152M/C1805/ON (6).
10. Nicolas, *Letters*, vol. 7, p. 15.
11. Nelson to Durham, 11 September 1805, *ibid.*, p. 32.
12. Smith to Windham, Windham, vol. 2, p. 291.
13. For a full examination of the development and trial of these secret weapons, see Pocock, *Terror before Trafalgar*.
14. Nelson to Castlereagh, 1 and 3 October 1805, BL: 34960 f. 125 and f. 130.
15. Hippisley to Nelson, BL: 34931 f. 129.
16. Louis to Nelson, 17 August 1805, William Clements, Hubert Smith, vol. 1; Malcolm to Nelson, 5 September 1805, Pettigrew, vol. 2, p. 502.
17. Hood to Nelson, 5 September 1805, BL: 34931 f. 96; Camden to Nelson, 7 September 1805, Nicolas, *Letters*, vol. 7, p. 33.
18. Nelson to Pitt, 29 August 1805, *ibid.*, p. 20. Nicolas mentions that Nelson sent Minto letterbooks with the relevant letters marked but adds, 'The letter books referred to have not come under the Editor's observation.' This indicates that the books Minto was shown were the pressed-copy ones, since we know that Nicolas did not see these.
19. Gatty, *Scott*, p. 149.
20. Nelson to Keats, 24 August 1805, Nicolas, *Letters*, vol. 7, p. 16.

21. Fraser, *Beloved Emma*, pp. 319–20.

22. Croker papers, vol. 2, p. 233.

23. Minto papers, vol. 3, p. 370.

24. Harrison, *Life*, vol. 2, p. 456.

25. Nelson to Rose, 3 September 1805, Nicolas, *Letters*, vol. 7, p. 29; Nelson to Frances Nisbet, 4 May 1786, Naish, *Letters*, p. 32.

26. It is possible that the ceremony took place at home, although the weight of the very limited evidence points to the church as the location. The rings have survived – Nelson's is in the collection of the National Maritime Museum; Emma's in the Royal Naval Museum.

27. The witness for the ceremony and Nelson's words is again Lady Bessborough. Quoted in Edgecumbe, *Diary*.

28. Emma to John Scott, 13 September, Clive Richards Collection.

29. Nelson to Emma Hamilton, 14 September 1805, Pierpont Morgan Library: MA321.

30. Nelson to Murray, 14 September 1805, Nicolas, *Letters*, vol. 7, p. 36.

31. Egremont, *Wyndham*, p. 36.

32. The tunnel, moat, and the remains of the passageway and door through which he got to the beach are still there, and the recent installation, by Portsmouth City Council, of a new bridge over the moat means that it is now possible to walk directly in Nelson's footsteps.

33. Pocock, *Nelson*, p. 316.

34. Nelson to Viceroy, Gwyther, 'Turin'; Nelson to Bickerton, Monmouth: E187; Nelson's Journal, Nicolas, *Letters*, vol. 7, p. 51.

35. Nelson to Louis, 29 September 1805, BL: 60484, ff. 101–2.

36. Fremantle's Journal, *Mariner's Mirror* 16 (1930), p. 410; Duff to his wife, 1 October 1805, Nicolas, *Letters*, vol. 7, p. 71; Codrington to his wife, 30 September 1805, Bourchier, *Codrington*, p. 52.

37. Nelson to Northesk, 3 October 1805, private collection.

38. For a detailed analysis of the Trafalgar captains, their background, previous experience and previous association with Nelson, see my introductory essay to *The Trafalgar Captains*.

39. Clayton and Craig, *Trafalgar*, p. 81.

40. Nelson to Collingwood, 7 October 1805, Nicolas, *Letters*, vol. 7, p. 83.

41. Nelson was a vice admiral of the white and Collingwood a vice admiral of the blue.

42. All these orders, with the exception of the last, are printed by Nicolas in his vol. 7. The order about night sailing is in the Clive Richards Collection: CRC/66.

43. Fremantle, Journal.

44. Nelson to Louis, 2 October 1805, BL: 34960 ff. 146–7. Nelson to Knight, 30 September 1805, Dartmouth College Library, Hanover, New Hampshire, USA: Mss 805530.1.

45. Nelson to Barham, 1 October 1805, HL: HM23623. Nelson to Barham, 13 October 1805, RNM: 1988/267 (7); Nelson to Bolton, 30 September 1805, Houghton: 196.5/47.

46. Nelson to Calder, 13 October 1805, Clive Richards Collection: CRC/67.

47. Bayntun to Nelson, 25 September 1805, BL: 34931; Nelson to Elliot, 9 October 1805, NMM: MON/54; Nelson to Emma Hamilton, 13 October 1805, Nicolas, *Letters*, vol. 7, p. 385.

48. Nelson to Blackwood, 4 October 1805, *ibid.*, p. 73; Blackwood to his wife, 19 October 1805, *ibid.*, p. 131.

49. Hardy to Thompson, 5 May 1806, Laughton, *Barham*, vol. 3, p. 398.

50. Nelson to Collingwood, 19 October 1805, Nicolas, *Letters*, vol. 7, p. 129. Nelson's Journal, 20 October 1805, *ibid.*, p. 137.

51. Hewson to his father, 2 November 1805, Houghton: ENG 196.5 f. 134.

52. It is not the purpose of this book to describe the battle in detail. A number of excellent modern accounts exist, details of which will be found in the bibliography. This account will focus on Nelson's own role, and will analyse how well his battle plan worked in practice.

53. See my essay, 'Apotheosised: The creation of the Nelson Legend, 1797–1850' in Cannandine (ed.), *Admiral Lord Nelson*.

54. The codicil is printed by Nicolas, *Letters*, vol. 7, pp. 140–1.

55. Minutes of the *Minotaur*, NMM: JOD/41.

56. Pasco's account is in Nicolas, *Letters*, vol. 7, p. 150.

57. Only ten of the ships record 'England Expects' in some way – either in the official

log or in personal accounts. On the other
hand, twenty mention 'Close Action'.

58. Minutes of the *Minotaur*, NMM: JOD/41.

59. Hewson to his father, 2 November 1805,
Houghton: ENG 196.5 f. 134.

60. Today, the signal is flown on board the
Victory on Trafalgar Day all at once.
However, on the day, the signal was sent in
six separate 'hoists', two words at a time.

61. *Minotaur*'s Minutes, NMM: JOD/41.
Collingwood's reaction: Newnham
Collingwood, p. 123.

62. Message to Fremantle: Lt Andrew Green's
Minutes, HL: STG Box 150 (1); Message to
the Captains, Clarke and M'Arthur, *Life*,
vol. 3, p. 151.

63. Both quotations: Legg, *Trafalgar*, p. 68.

64. Fremantle and the Neptune: Lt Green's
notes, HL: STG Box 150 (1).

65. Corbett, *Trafalgar*, p. 374.

66. Codrington: Nicolas, *Letters*, vol. 7, p. 154;
Signal: see Tunstall and Tracy, p. 251 and
Czisnik, *Trafalgar*; Dumanoir: *The Times*,
2 January 1806; Plan: Houghton: ENG
196.5 f. 161.

67. This version of the wording of the exchange,
which differs slightly from that usually given
in biographies, comes from Clarke and

M'Arthur, *Life*, vol. 3, p. 240. It is not usual
for the latter to be preferred over other
sources but, in this case, their source for the
words was Hardy himself.

68. There are three contemporary accounts of
Nelson's death: Surgeon Beatty's, Chaplain
Scott's and Purser Burke's (for details see
Bibliography). Beatty's is the most famous:
but it is also the most sanitised – written for
publication, it tended to play down the
appalling suffering Nelson endured. In this
account it has been balanced with material
from Scott's and Burke's private, and thus
less bowdlerised, versions.

69. Beatty's account, Nicolas, *Letters*, vol. 7,
p. 251.

70. All three of the contemporary accounts
mentioned in note 68 mention the kiss, and
all the writers were very close to Nelson at
the time he made the request.

71. Blackwood to his wife, 22 October 1805,
Nicolas, *Letters*, vol. 7, p. 224.

72. Woolnough's account, private collection;
Green's account, Houghton: STD 150 (1);
Hewson's account, HL: ENG 196.5 f. 134.

73. Mahan, *Life*, vol. 2, pp. 396–7.

74. Hamilton, *Byam Martin*, vol. 3, pp. 307–8;
Hubback and Edith, *Sailor Brothers*, p. 156.

Bibliography

For a full Nelson bibliography see:
Cowie, Leonard W. *Lord Nelson 1758–1805: A Bibliography*, Westport, Conn., Meckler, 1990

THE MAIN BIOGRAPHIES

Coleman, Terry. *Nelson*, London, Bloomsbury, 2001
A thought-provoking and often contentious biography by a brilliant investigative journalist. Based on extensive research in the archives, and so includes some of the new material. A little thin on those aspects of Nelson's naval career not concerned with combat.

Knight, Roger. *Nelson: the Pursuit of Victory*, London, Penguin, 2005
An impressive study by a respected naval historian with a lifelong knowledge of the eighteenth-century Royal Navy and of the archival resources regarding it. Particularly good at placing Nelson in his naval context and on the practical seamanship aspects of the story. Also good in its coverage of the non-combat aspects of Nelson's career. Some excellent battle plans and charts illustrating Nelson's voyages and a generous collection of appendices covering all aspects of his life and the people, and ships, associated with him.

Lambert, Andrew. *Nelson: Britannia's God of War*, London, Faber, 2004
A thorough and very readable broad-brush resumé of Nelson's life and career – including a very good section on his 'after-life' as The Hero. Incorporates some of the new material and offers some useful insights on Nelson as a tactician and strategist.

Mahan, Alfred Thayer. *The Life of Nelson, the Embodiment of the Sea Power of Great Britain*, London, Sampson Low, 1897
Still one of the best biographies on Nelson's naval career, and particularly good on aspects which many other biographers neglect – notably the Italian campaign of 1795–6 and the Mediterranean campaign of 1803–5. Less sure-footed on his personal life, with some unattractive Victorian moralising about Emma Hamilton.

Oman, Carola. *Nelson*, London, Hodder & Stoughton, 1947
One of the best studies of Nelson the man, distilled from faithful reading of thousands of his letters. Particularly good on his relationships with women, and the first of Nelson's biographers to judge Emma Hamilton fairly. Less detailed on the battles and no new insights on his ability as a commander.
Pocock, Tom. *Horatio Nelson*, London, Bodley Head, 1987

An excellent all-round biography, offering a first-rate introduction to all aspects of Nelson's story and written in a warm and accessible style. Particularly good on descriptions of places where Nelson lived and served, all of which the author has visited himself. However, it was written before all the new material emerged and so it is now a little dated.

Southey, Robert. *The Life of Nelson*, London, John Murray, 1813
Still regarded as one of the great Nelson biographies – but more because of its superb style than its content, much of which is now known to be inaccurate. It is best read in the 1922 edition, with an introduction by Geoffrey Callender, which corrects most of the mistakes.

Sugden, John. *Nelson: A Dream of Glory*, New York, Henry Holt and Co., 2004
A very detailed and thorough study of Nelson's early life that includes a large amount of the recently located new material, as well as the fruits of the author's own researches in various byways of the Nelson story. Excellent on Nelson's personal life and on his many relationships – less sure-footed on his naval career and battles.

Vincent, Edgar. *Nelson, Love and Fame*, New Haven and London, Yale University Press, 2003
A thoughtful and extremely well-written survey of Nelson's life, with some useful insights. However, since it is based mainly on Nicolas, it is fairly traditional, both in its judgements and in the evidence that it uses to support them.

White, Colin (ed.). *Nelson – The New Letters*, London, Boydell and Brewer, 2005
A collection of 500 of the most important of the 1,400 unpublished letters located and transcribed by the Nelson Letters Project between 1999 and 2004. Arranged so that Nelson tells his own story, and particularly rich in operational material.

BOOKS AND ARTICLES CONSULTED IN THE PREPARATION OF THIS BOOK

Baring, Mrs Henry. *The Diary of the Right Honourable William Windham*, London, 1866
Battesti, Michelle. *La Bataille d'Aboukir*, Paris, Economica, 1997
Beatty, William. *Authentic Narrative of the Death of Lord Nelson*, London, T. Cadell & W. Davies, 1807
Bennet, Geoffrey. *Nelson, the Commander*, London, Batsford, 1972
Beresford and Wilson, Herbert. *Nelson and his Times*, London, Eyre & Spottiswood, 1897
Berry, Edward. *An Authentic Narrative of the Proceedings of His Majesty's Squadron under the Command of Rear Admiral Sir Horatio Nelson*, London, 1798
Bethune, John Drinkwater. *A Narrative of the Battle of St Vincent with Anecdotes of Nelson before and after that Battle*, London, Saunders & Otley, 1840
Bonner-Smith, David. *Letters of Lord St Vincent*, London, Navy Records Society, 1921
Bourchier, Jane, Lady (ed.). *Memoir of the Life of Sir Edward Codrington*, 2 vols, London, Longmans, Green & Co., 1873
Buckland, Kirstie. *The Miller Papers*, Shelton, The 1805 Club, 1999
Callo, Joseph, *Nelson in the Caribbean*, Annapolis, Naval Institute Press, 2003
Cannadine, David (ed.). *Admiral Lord Nelson*, London, Palgrave Macmillan, 2005
Charnock, John. *Biographical Memoirs of Lord Nelson*, London, 1806
Clarke, J.S. and M'Arthur, J. *The Life of Admiral Lord Nelson*, London, Cadell & Davies & Miller, 1809
Clayton, Tim and Craig, Phil. *Trafalgar: the men, the battle, the storm*, London, Hodder & Stoughton, 2004
Coleman, Terry. 'Nelson, the King and his Ministers', *The Trafalgar Chronicle* 13, The 1805 Club, 2003
Collingwood, Newnham (ed.). *Correspondence and Memoirs of Vice Admiral Lord Collingwood*, London, 1829

Constantine, David. *Fields of Fire: A Life of Sir William Hamilton*, London, Phoenix Press, 2001

Corbett, Julian. *The Campaign of Trafalgar*, London, Longmans, Green & Co., 1910

—— (ed.). *The Spencer Papers*, 2 vols, London, Navy Records Society, 1913/14

Czisnik, Marianne. 'Nelson at Naples, A Review of Events and Arguments', *The Trafalgar Chronicle* 12, The 1805 Club, 2002

——. 'Nelson at Naples, The Development of the Story', *The Trafalgar Chronicle* 13, 2003

——. 'Admiral Nelson's Tactics at the Battle of Trafalgar', *History* 89, 2004

Dann, John C. (ed.). *The Nagle Journal*, New York, Weidenfeld & Nicolson, 1988

Desbrière, Edouard. *The Trafalgar Campaign*, trans. Constance Eastwick, 2 vols, Oxford, Clarendon Press, 1933

Deutsch, Otto. *Admiral Nelson and Joseph Haydn*, London, The Nelson Society, 2000

Duffy, Michael. 'British Naval Intelligence and Bonaparte's Egyptian Expedition of 1798', *The Mariner's Mirror* 84, 1998

Edgecumbe, Richard (ed.). *Diary of Frances Lady Shelley*, 1912

Egremont, Lord. *Wyndham and Children*, London, Macmillan, 1969

Faye, Claude (ed.). *Echec à Nelson*, Boulogne, Association Boulogne Culture Editions Expositions, 2001

Feldbaek, Ole. *The Battle of Copenhagen*, London, Pen & Sword Press, 2002

Fenwick, Kenneth. *HMS Victory*, London, Cassell, 1959

Foreman, Laura and Phillips, Ellen Blue. *Napoleon's Lost Fleet*, New York, Random House Press, 1999

Fraser, Flora. *Beloved Emma*, London, Weidenfeld & Nicolson, 1986

Fremantle, Anne (ed.). *The Wynne Diaries*, 3 vols, Oxford, OUP, 1940

Gardiner, Robert (ed.). *Fleet Battle and Blockade*, London, Chatham Publishing, 1996

——. *The Campaign of Trafalgar*, London, Chatham Publishing, 1997

——. *Nelson against Napoleon*, London, Chatham Publishing, 1997

——. *Warships of the Napoleonic Era*, London, Chatham Publishing, 1999

Gatty, Margaret. *Recollections of the Life of Rev A.J. Scott, DD*, London, Saunders & Otley, 1842

Goodwin, Peter. *Nelson's Ships*, London, Conway Maritime Press, 2003

Gray, Peter. 'Turning a blind eye', *The Trafalgar Chronicle* 11, The 1805 Club, 2001

Grenfell, Russell. *Nelson the Sailor*, London, Faber & Faber, 1949

Guimerá, Agustin. *Nelson and Tenerife*, Shelton, The 1805 Club, 1999

Gwyther, John. 'Nelson's Gifts to la Maddalena', *The Trafalgar Chronicle* 10, The 1805 Club, 2000

——. 'Nelson in Turin', *The Trafalgar Chronicle* 12, The 1805 Club, 2002

——. 'Nelson in Carloforte', *The Trafalgar Chronicle* 13, The 1805 Club, 2003

Harrison, James. *The Life of the Right Honourable Horatio Lord Viscount Nelson*, London, C. Chapple, 1806

Hayward, Joel. *For God and Glory: Lord Nelson and his Way of War*, Annapolis, Naval Institute Press, 2003

Hibbert, Christopher. *Nelson: a personal history*, London, Viking, 1994

Hill, Richard. *The Prizes of War*, Stroud, Sutton Publishing and the Royal Naval Museum, 1998

Hills, Ann-Mary. 'Nelson's Illnesses', *Journal of the Royal Naval Medical Service* 86, 2, 2000

——. 'Nelson's Illnesses 1780–1782', *The Trafalgar Chronicle* 12, The 1805 Club, 2002

Howarth, David. *Trafalgar. The Nelson Touch*, London, Collins, 1969

Howarth, David and Howarth, Stephen. *The Immortal Memory*, London, J.N. Dent, 1998

Howarth, Stephen (ed.). *Proceedings of the Battle of Cape St Vincent 200 Conference*, Shelton, The 1805 Club, 1998

——. *Proceedings of the Battle of Copenhagen 200 Conference*, Shelton, The 1805 Club, 2003

Hubback, J.H. and Edith, C. *Jane Austen's Sailor Brothers*, London, Bodley Head, 1906

Jennings, Louis (ed.). *The Croker Papers*, London, 1884

Kennedy, Ludovic. *The Band of Brothers*, London, Oldhams, 1951

Kerr, A.E.F. *The Sailor's Nelson*, London, Hurst & Blackett, 1932

Knight, Carlo. 'The British at Naples in 1799', *The Trafalgar Chronicle* 11, The 1805 Club, 2001

Knight, Cornelia. *Autobiography of Miss Cornelia Knight*, 2 vols, London, 1861

Laughton, J.K. *The Naval Miscellany Volume I*, London, Navy Records Society, 1902

——. *Letters of Lord Barham, Volume III*, London, Navy Records Society, 1910

Lavery, Brian. *Nelson's Navy*, London, Conway, 1989

——. *Nelson and the Nile*, London, Chatham Publishing, 1998

——. *The Battle of the Nile*, Shelton, The 1805 Club, 2000

——. *Horatio, Lord Nelson*, London, The British Library, 2003

——. *Nelson's Fleet at Trafalgar*, London, National Maritime Museum, 2004

LeFevre, Peter and Harding, Richard (eds). *The Precursors of Nelson*, London, Chatham Publishing, 2000

——. *The Contemporaries of Nelson*, London, Chatham Publishing, 2005

Legg, Stuart (ed.). *Trafalgar: An Eyewitness Account of a Great Battle*, London, Rupert Hart-Davis, 1966

Lequesne, Leslie. 'Nelson and his Surgeons', *Journal of the Royal Naval Medical Service* 86, 2, 2000

Lloyd, Christopher. *The Nile Campaign. Nelson and Napoleon in Egypt*, Newton Abbot, David & Charles, 1973

Macdonald, Janet. *Feeding Nelson's Navy*, London, Chatham Publishing, 2004

McGowan, Alan. *HMS Victory: Her Construction, Career and Restoration*, London, Chatham Publishing, 1999

Mackenzie, Robert. *The Trafalgar Roll*, London, George Allen, 1913

Maffeo, Stephen. *Most Secret and Confidential*, London, Chatham Publishing, 2000

Minto, Countess of (ed.). *Life and Letters of Sir Gilbert Elliot, First Earl of Minto*, London, 1874

Monarque, Rémi. 'Latouche-Tréville: The Admiral who Defied Nelson', *The Mariner's Mirror* 86, the Society for Nautical Research, 2000

Morris, Roger. *Nelson: The Life and Letters of a Hero*, London, Collins & Brown, 1996

Morrison, Alfred. *The Collection of Autograph Letters and Historical Documents Formed by Alfred Morrison: The Nelson and Hamilton Papers*, privately printed, 1893–4

Morriss, Roger, Lavery, Brian and Deuchar, Stephen. *Nelson: An Illustrated History*, London, Laurence King and National Maritime Museum, 1995

Naish, George, P.B. (ed.). *Nelson's Letters to His Wife and Other Documents, 1785–1831*, London, Navy Records Society with Routledge and Kegan Paul, 1958

The Naval Chronicle

The Naval Review

Nicolas, Sir Nicholas Harris. *The Dispatches and Letters of Vice Admiral Lord Viscount Nelson, with notes*, 7 vols, London, Henry Colburn, 1844–6

Padfield, Peter. *Nelson's War*, London, Hart-Davis, MacGibbon, 1976

Palmer, M.A.J. 'Sir John's Victory. The Battle of Cape St Vincent Reconsidered', *Mariner's Mirror* 77, 1991

Perrin, W.G. *The Naval Miscellany Volume III*, London, Navy Records Society, 1927

Pettigrew, Thomas. *Memoirs of the Life of Vice Admiral Lord Nelson*, 2 vols, London, 1849

Phillimore, A. *The Life of Sir William Parker*, London, 1876

Pocock, Tom. *Nelson and his World*, London, Thames & Hudson, 1968

——. *The Young Nelson in the Americas*, London, Collins, 1980

——. *Nelson in Corsica*, Shelton, The 1805 Club, 1994

——. *Nelson's Women*, London, André Deutsch, 1999

——. *The Terror before Trafalgar*, London, John Murray, 2002

Pope, Dudley. *England Expects*, London, Weidenfeld & Nicolson, 1959

——. *The Great Gamble*, London, Weidenfeld & Nicolson, 1972

Pugh, P.D. Gordon. *Nelson and his Surgeons*, Edinburgh, E. & S. Livingstone, 1968

Rawson, Geoffrey (ed.). *Letters from Lord Nelson*, London, Staples Press, 1949

Rodger, Nicholas. *The Wooden World*, London, Collins, 1986

——. *Command of the Ocean*, London, Penguin, 2005

Ross, Sir John. *Memoirs and Correspondence of Admiral Lord de Saumarez*, London, 1838

Russell, Jack. *Nelson and the Hamiltons*, London, Antony Blond, 1969

Schom, Alan. *Trafalgar: Countdown to Battle*, London, Michael Joseph, 1990

Sharman, Victor. *Nelson's Hero: Captain William Locker*, London, Pen & Sword, 2005

Sturges-Jackson, T. *Logs of the Great Sea Fights*, vols 1 and 2, London, Navy Records Society, 1899 and 1900

Syrett, David. 'Nelson's Uncle', *The Mariner's Mirror* 88, 2002

Tracy, Nicolas. *Nelson's Battles*, London, Chatham Publishing, 1996

Tunstall, Brian and Tracy, Nicolas (eds). *Naval Warfare in the Age of Sail*, London, Conway, 1990

Tushingham, Eric and Mansfield, Clifford. *Nelson's Flagship at Copenhagen: HMS Elephant*, The Nelson Society, 2001

Walker, Richard. *The Nelson Portraits*, Portsmouth, Royal Naval Museum, 1998

Warner, Oliver. *A Portrait of Lord Nelson*, London, Chatto & Windus, 1953

——. *Nelson and the Age of Fighting Sail*, New York, American Heritage, 1963

——. *Nelson's Battles*, London, Batsford, 1965

White, Colin. *The Nelson Companion*, Stroud, Sutton Publishing and the Royal Naval Museum, 1995

——. *Nelson's Last Walk*, London, The Nelson Society, 1996

——. *The Battle of Cape St Vincent*, Shelton, The 1805 Club, 1997

——. *1797: Nelson's Year of Destiny*, Stroud, Sutton Publishing and the Royal Naval Museum, 1998

——. 'Nelson and Shakespeare', *The Nelson Dispatch*, 7, 2000

——. 'Nelson's 1805 Battle Plan', *Journal of Maritime Research*, www.jmr.nmm.ac.uk, 2002

——. *The Nelson Encyclopaedia*, London, Chatham Publishing, 2003

——. 'The Wife's Tale: Frances Nelson and the breakdown of her marriage', *Journal of Maritime Research*, www.jmr.nmm.ac.uk, 2003

——. 'The Public Order Book of Vice Admiral Lord Nelson' in M. Duffy (ed.), *The Naval Miscellany*, vol. 6, London, Navy Records Society, 2003

—— (ed.). *The Trafalgar Captains*, London, Chatham Publishing, 2005

——. *Nelson – the new letters*, London, Boydell & Brewer, 2005

Willyams, Revd Cooper. *A Voyage in the Mediterranean in HMS Swiftsure*, London, 1802

The Trafalgar Chronicle (Journal of the 1805 Club) and *The Nelson Dispatch* (Journal of the Nelson Society) are rich sources of current Nelsonian research and news. For details of these societies, and their current secretaries, contact them at their websites:

The 1805 Club: www.admiralnelson.org

The Nelson Society: www.nelson-society.org

Index

Entries marked *pl* are colour plates. Page numbers in *italic* denote illustrations in the text.